MW01073533

READING PAUL *as* CHRISTIAN SCRIPTURE

• READING •
CHRISTIAN SCRIPTURE

VOLUMES AVAILABLE

Reading the New Testament as Christian Scripture
Constantine R. Campbell and Jonathan T. Pennington

Reading Wisdom and Psalms as Christian Scripture
Christopher B. Ansberry

Reading the Prophets as Christian Scripture
Eric J. Tully

Reading the Gospels as Christian Scripture
Joshua W. Jipp

Reading Paul as Christian Scripture
Constantine R. Campbell

READING PAUL *as* CHRISTIAN SCRIPTURE

A LITERARY, CANONICAL, AND THEOLOGICAL INTRODUCTION

CONSTANTINE R. CAMPBELL

B
Baker Academic
a division of Baker Publishing Group
Grand Rapids, Michigan

Published by Baker Academic
a division of Baker Publishing Group
Grand Rapids, Michigan
BakerAcademic.com

Printed in the United States of America

Library of Congress Cataloging-in-Publication Data
Names: Campbell, Constantine R., author.
Title: Reading Paul as Christian scripture : a literary, canonical, and theological introduction / Constantine R. Campbell.
Description: Grand Rapids, Michigan : Baker Academic, a division of Baker Publishing Group, [2024] | Series: Reading Christian scripture | Includes bibliographical references and index.
Identifiers: LCCN 2023049247 | ISBN 9780801098758 (cloth) | ISBN 9781493445967 (ebook) | ISBN 9781493445974 (pdf)
Subjects: LCSH: Bible. Epistles of Paul—Criticism, interpretation, etc. | Paul, the Apostle, Saint.
Classification: LCC BS2506.3 .C364 2024 | DDC 227/.061—dc23/eng/20231213
LC record available at https://lccn.loc.gov/2023049247

Unless otherwise noted, Scripture quotations are the author's own translation.

Cover art: *Saint Paul à Ephèse* by Jean-François Brémond

Baker Publishing Group publications use paper produced from sustainable forestry practices and postconsumer waste whenever possible.

24 25 26 27 28 29 30 7 6 5 4 3 2 1

For Paul Dale,
the other Paul in my life

Contents

Part 5 Paul on Trial for Christ

Part 6 Paul's Theology

Acknowledgments

The world hardly needs another book on Paul. Books about the apostle are produced faster than any human can possibly read them. And while it's exciting to see so much interest and discussion and so many new insights into Paul's life and thought, the whole state of affairs can be intimidating for some who just want to read and understand Paul. All the more so for those who want to read Paul *as Christian Scripture*. For that reason, I am glad for the series of which this book is a part, as it seeks to help the reader to navigate the tricky issues surrounding the text while also helping the reader to read the text itself—not only in light of scholarship, but in light of the entire canon of Scripture and how others have read it in the past, and for its theological contributions and implications. Few books on Paul attempt to do all that, so I believe this one has a relatively rare place and purpose.

The fist volume in the series, *Reading the New Testament as Christian Scripture*, was written by Jonathan Pennington and me, and suffice to say, I sorely missed Jonathan's collaboration as I wrote this present volume. I have come to a new appreciation of how much I relied on his wisdom, experience, knowledge, and good-natured partnership. So I suppose this is a retrospective acknowledgment of his invaluable contribution to that previous volume, which also helped to set the trajectory of the entire series—not least this book on Paul.

I offer my thanks to the delightful and highly skilled team at Baker Academic, especially Jim Kinney, Bryan Dyer, James Korsmo, and Dustyn Keepers. I'm grateful for their vision for this book and this series, both of which continue along a genre-bending trajectory intended to help a new generation of readers to grasp and interpret these historical and literary documents as transformative beacons of the knowledge of God in Christ.

Finally, I thank my dear friend and brother Paul Dale. While he did not directly contribute to this book, it would not have been possible at all without his contribution to my life.

Reading Paul as Christian Scripture

Paul's writings continue to challenge, inspire, instruct, confuse, and infuriate their readers today as they have done for two millennia. Indeed, it is probably impossible to hold a neutral position with respect to Paul—love him or hate him, Paul demands a response. This should come as no surprise, since many who heard him preach and teach wanted either to follow him or to stone him. And in that sense, Paul was no doubt happy to follow in his Lord's footsteps.

In this introduction we address some of the difficulties we face when reading Paul as Christian Scripture today. These include the seemingly unending scholarship surrounding Paul's letters, how Paul connects to the rest of the Scriptures, and the huge historical and cultural distance between us and Paul. The following discussion is necessarily oversimplified, but it includes some (hopefully helpful) tips for navigating through such issues, and also serves to set the groundwork for the chapters to follow. Any reader of Paul needs to consider his chronology, the nature of the source material, the nature of Pauline scholarship, how Paul fits with the rest of the Bible, the historical gap between Paul and ourselves, and how Paul's writings relate to the life of the church today. Finally, some orientation for reading this book is offered at the end of this chapter.

RECEPTION HISTORY

Haters Gonna Hate

While Jesus commands near-universal respect and love from Christians and non-Christians alike, poor Paul has been hated by many through the centuries. So much so that Patrick Gray authored a book entirely dedicated to discussing Paul's critics over the past two millennia, including scholars, spiritual leaders, authors, philosophers, and cultural icons. Philosopher Søren Kierkegaard said that Paul made Protestantism completely untenable. Author George Bernard Shaw claimed that Paul said and did nothing that Jesus would have said or done. Psychologist Carl Jung thought that Paul hardly ever allowed Jesus to get a word in. Author James Baldwin said that Paul was mercilessly fanatical and self-righteous. Nazi dictator Adolf Hitler claimed that Paul's doctrine mobilized the criminal underworld. Writer Nikos Kazantzakis depicted Paul telling Jesus that the church no longer needed him. And Episcopal bishop John Shelby Spong said that Paul was gay, deeply repressed, self-loathing, and rigid in denial.[1]

What about Paul's Chronology?

We will piece together the relevant elements of Paul's chronology as we go, but for now it is worth taking a bird's-eye view of the most important events and dates for Paul's life and mission. The dates below are figured out from Paul's time in Corinth in AD 50–52, since we know that the proconsul Gallio (see Acts 18:12) was in Corinth in AD 51–52. The rest of Paul's chronology is figured out from this fixed date (along with the fire of Rome in AD 64). Relevant portions of the table will be reproduced as needed throughout the book.

Bartolomeo Montagna, *Saint Paul*, 1482

Paul's Chronology

ca. 6–46	**Part 1: Paul's Birth and Rebirth**
ca. 6	Birth
ca. 33	"Conversion" and commissioning
ca. 33–35	Period in Arabia
ca. 36	First visit to Jerusalem after conversion
ca. 36–46	Ministry in Cilicia and Syria
ca. 46	Famine collection from Antioch taken to Jerusalem
ca. 46–48	**Part 2: Paul's First Mission**
ca. 46	From Antioch to Cyprus
ca. 46	From Cyprus to Perga and Pisidian Antioch
ca. 46	To Iconium, Lystra, Derbe—cities of South Galatia
ca. 47	Return to Perga, then by ship to Syrian Antioch
ca. 48	The apostolic council in Jerusalem
ca. 49	Galatians written around this time
ca. 49–52	**Part 3: Paul's Second Mission**
ca. 49	Overland from Syrian Antioch through Galatia
ca. 49	Churches in Philippi, Thessalonica, and Berea
ca. 49	The visit to Athens
50–52	Eighteen months in Corinth
50	1 and 2 Thessalonians written in Corinth
52	A quick trip to Ephesus
52	Return to Syrian Antioch

ca. 52–57	**Part 4: Paul's Third Mission**
ca. 52	From Syrian Antioch through Galatia to Ephesus
ca. 52–55	Three years in Ephesus
ca. 54	1 Corinthians written in Ephesus
ca. 55	Leaves for Macedonia
ca. 56	2 Corinthians written in Philippi
ca. 57	Three months in Corinth, where Romans was written
ca. 57	Bids farewell to the Ephesian elders in Miletus
ca. 57	Sails to Caesarea, then on to Jerusalem
ca. 57–??	**Part 5: Paul on Trial for Christ**
ca. 57–59	Imprisoned by the governor Felix in Caesarea
ca. 59–60	Sails for Rome, spends three months in Malta
ca. 60–62	House arrest in Rome
ca. 61	Philippians, Ephesians, Colossians, Philemon written
ca. 63–??	Visit to Spain?
ca. 63?	1 and 2 Timothy, Titus written
64	Great fire of Rome and persecution of Christians
ca. 65?	Paul is executed

What about the Sources?

There are five types of sources for grappling with Paul. First are his seven undisputed letters—Romans, 1 Corinthians, 2 Corinthians, Galatians, Philippians, 1 Thessalonians, and Philemon—which all scholars agree were written by Paul the apostle. Second are the six disputed letters attributed to Paul but whose authenticity is not accepted by all scholars: Ephesians, Colossians, 2 Thessalonians, 1 Timothy, 2 Timothy, and Titus. Third is Acts of the Apostles, the second half of which is largely devoted to narrating Paul's missions and ministry. Fourth are writings from prominent figures within early church history who comment on Paul, such as Eusebius, Tertullian, and Clement of Rome. Fifth are books written about Paul well after the apostolic era, such as Acts of Paul and Thecla.

Of these sources, scholars generally regard the undisputed letters as most

HISTORICAL MATTERS

Acts of Paul and Thecla

Acts of Paul and Thecla is a second-century work that portrays the novel-like story of a young woman named Thecla, who heard Paul preach in Iconium, believed his message, refused to marry her fiancé as a result, was saved from martyrdom more than once, and had a lifelong ministry in Seleucia. The work was rejected by early church fathers due to its content, though it was relatively popular in the early centuries of the church. Unlike other works about Paul, Acts of Paul and Thecla includes a physical description of Paul, who is depicted as "a man small in size, bald-headed, bandy-legged, of noble mien, with eyebrows meeting, rather hook-nosed, full of grace."[2]

Public domain / Wikimedia Commons

Greek copy of the last page of the Epistle to the Ephesians (6:20–24) and the first page of Paul's Epistle to the Galatians (1:1–8), dated to about AD 150 to 250

authoritative. Though many scholars regard some or all of the disputed epistles as authentic, they are generally less authoritative within the guild for the simple reason that not all scholars accept their authorship as Pauline. Similarly, while Acts is a major source of information about Paul, Luke's presentation is regarded by some as shaped by his own priorities. Comments about Paul from church figures must be assessed case by case, recognizing their chronological distance from the events of Paul's life. And apocryphal books about Paul are generally dismissed as unverified legend.

Since this book is primarily concerned with reading Paul—and less so *about* Paul—we will naturally focus on his letters, with equal attention given to those undisputed and disputed. Luke's account of Paul in his Acts of the Apostles is also a vital source because it is difficult, if not impossible, to understand the context of Paul's letters without an account of his narrative. And while some scholars might approach Luke's narrative with caution, it nevertheless remains by far the most detailed and authoritative narrative account of Paul's life that we have. Not only does Luke's narrative provide much-needed context, but also it supplies the historical framework in which to situate Paul's letters.

What about Pauline Scholarship?

Today there is probably more scholarly literature being produced on Paul and his writings than ever before, which is remarkable, given that Paul's writings have been around for two millennia. And it is not only the quantity of scholarly literature that is noteworthy; the nature of the discussions is also striking. On a range of issues, Paul's writings are being reassessed—being read through differing lenses—while long-held assumptions about his thought are under review. It is an exciting time to be interested in Paul, with numerous debates and fresh insights being offered through a variety of schools of thought.

The New Perspective on Paul

One of the most famous (or infamous, depending on whom you ask) debates about Paul in recent decades revolves around the so-called New Perspective on Paul (NPP). It is difficult to summarize this school of thought because each of its major contributors (e.g., E. P. Sanders, James Dunn, N. T. Wright) holds differing views about a range of issues. However, the common thread that runs through their work is the emphasis on Paul's Jewishness and how that affects our understanding of his teaching on justification by faith.

The general argument is that since the Protestant Reformation we have tended to read Paul's statements about justification by faith as primarily concerning how believers are made right with God through faith rather than through good works. Justification is therefore a "vertical" concept (about us and God), and the relationship between God and humans is not dependent on our merit through good deeds. The NPP, however, argues that justification is not primarily vertical but "horizontal" and that the works that Paul critiques are not general good deeds, but specifically Jewish observances of the law of Moses.

The horizontal aspect of justification concerns the reconciliation between Jews and gentiles, which means that it is not primarily about how humans are made right with God but about how God is no longer going to treat Jews and gentiles differently with respect to salvation. Salvation is not dependent on being Jewish or on keeping Jewish laws. It is the gift of God to Jews and gentiles and is received by faith rather than by observance of the law of Moses, circumcision, or Jewish ethnic identity. This means that there is no spiritual superiority of Jew over gentile, as the promises to Abraham are received by Jew and gentile alike on the equal footing of faith in Jesus.

While the NPP has generated much discussion and debate, many New Testament scholars have adopted a mediating position that accepts certain correctives from it while not necessarily accepting all of its claims. It is true that Paul's discussions about justification are normally in the context of Jewish-gentile relations and how Jews and gentiles are made equal and reconciled in Christ. It is also true that when Paul discusses "works," the works of the law of Moses are normally in view. However, many scholars uphold the pre-NPP view that justification is nevertheless about the vertical aspect

RECEPTION HISTORY

E. P. Sanders

A major step toward a new perspective on Paul was E. P. Sanders's perspective on Judaism in his watershed work, *Paul and Palestinian Judaism*, published in 1977.[3] Sanders deconstructed the prominent caricature of legalistic Judaism and instead portrayed a "pattern of religion" within Judaism that he called "covenantal nomism." Salvation was understood to be based on divine grace, not legalistic righteousness, along with atonement and forgiveness within the bounds of God's covenant with his people. Though Paul was a Jew of the Second Temple period, Sanders did not think that Paul's pattern of religion was in continuity with the Jewish pattern he outlined.

(humans being made right with God) even though the NPP has helpfully highlighted that there is also a horizontal aspect involved (Jew-gentile reconciliation in Christ).

Overall, the NPP has recovered the historical reality that the Judaism of Paul's day was not the same as the medieval Catholicism that Martin Luther opposed in the sixteenth century. It has also recovered the reality that Paul's doctrine of justification by faith was a major element in his understanding of how Jews and gentiles have become one in Christ.

The Apocalyptic Paul

Another area of recent debate has been Paul's apparent "apocalypticism." The "Apocalyptic Paul" school has argued that Paul shares many, if not all, of the theological characteristics typically associated with Jewish apocalypticism. Apocalypticism was a trend within the Judaism of Paul's day that affirmed that God will act in a world-shattering way to deliver his people Israel from their oppressors, restore justice to the world, and abolish evil. Apocalypticism sought to explain God's apparent silence in the face of centuries of oppression and abhorrent treatment of Jews by various nations and empires. It held that God's silence was in anticipation of dramatic action to achieve his purposes.

Jewish apocalypticism produced the writings that we now call apocalyptic literature. These works usually involve a human being given special revelation of secret heavenly realities and a sneak peek into the future dramatic works of God. The New Testament book of Revelation is a classic example of apocalyptic literature and, in keeping with the genre, is full of bizarre and otherworldly beings and images, such as weird seven-headed beasts. Such images were not supposed to be taken literally but were of symbolic value and were meant to express realities beyond our world and understanding. The Apocalyptic Paul school does not claim that his writings are apocalypses in any sense—they're letters, not apocalypses—but that his letters bear the influence of apocalyptic thought on his theology. Some of the evidence for such claims will be explored later, but suffice it to say that apocalyptic influence clearly exists.

RECEPTION HISTORY

Albert Schweitzer

An early precursor of the Apocalyptic Paul school was the French-German theologian Albert Schweitzer, whose 1931 landmark book, *The Mysticism of Paul the Apostle*,[4] consistently portrays Paul's theology through the lens of Jewish apocalypses and an apocalyptic worldview. Schweitzer argued that Paul expresses a "thoroughgoing eschatology," with a belief in the imminent end of the world. Paul's eschatology exhibits belief in angelic and demonic powers and a cosmic conception of salvation, rather than it being an individual transaction. And Paul's central theme of Christ mysticism (otherwise known as union with Christ) enables believers to participate now in the age to come and its cosmic redemption. Schweitzer's work has been massively influential on twentieth-century study of Paul. Schweitzer went on to win the Nobel Peace Prize for his humanitarian work, including the hospital he built in French Equatorial Africa (now Gabon).

Some scholars within the Apocalyptic Paul school claim that because Paul was an apocalyptic theologian, he was not really a covenantal theologian, or that he did not teach salvation history—the gradual and slow working of God through human history. A prominent proponent of this view is Douglas Campbell, who argues that apocalypticism is incompatible with salvation history because it features the dramatic vertical intervention of God rather than the slow horizontal work of God through history. Other scholars (e.g., N. T. Wright), however, have countered Campbell to argue that, for Paul at least, the vertical and the horizontal are not incompatible, since Paul clearly demonstrates *both* apocalyptic ideas and salvation-historical elements.

As with the New Perspective on Paul, the most likely solution is both-and, not either-or, and that is where many Pauline scholars have landed on the issue. The Apocalyptic Paul school has provided important insights about the influence of apocalyptic Judaism on Paul's thought and theology, which in turn helps us to interpret his writings with greater insight.

Paul's Jewishness (or Otherwise)

An ever-present element of Pauline scholarship has sought to evaluate to what degree Judaism shaped Paul's beliefs and thought compared to Greco-Roman intellectual influences. On the one hand, Paul was a Jew raised and schooled in Judaism. On the other hand, he was born outside Israel within a hub of Greco-Roman intellectual activity and demonstrated the influence of non-Jewish thinkers.

Pauline scholarship a century ago was dominated by the view that Paul was influenced primarily by the Greco-Roman intellectual tradition. Today the situation has reversed, in part thanks to the New Perspective on Paul and the Apocalyptic Paul movements, introduced above. Some scholars still insist on the primacy of Greco-Roman influence on Paul, but most scholars today affirm that Judaism is Paul's primary intellectual heritage. This does not mean that Paul was not influenced by non-Jewish thinkers; it seems clear that he was. But in keeping with other Jewish intellectuals of his day, such as Philo of Alexandria, Paul was able to engage Greco-Roman thought without abandoning his essential Jewishness.

The upshot of this discussion is to affirm what many Christians today naturally assume: Paul was a Jew who drew on the Jewish Scriptures and traditions in his understanding and preaching of Christ. The Hebrew Bible and Second Temple Judaism are our primary sources of information for understanding Paul's intellectual worldview. But we must also appreciate the reality that Paul was not limited by his Jewish intellectual heritage and was able to engage Greek intellectuals on their own terms, as Luke portrays him doing at the Athenian Areopagus (Acts 17). Indeed, Paul's astute understanding of the intellectual and spiritual heritages outside his own was a fundamental feature of his ministry as apostle to the gentiles.

Moving Forward

Such a flurry of discussion can be disorienting, confusing, and perhaps even threatening. Readers today might choose to put Paul in the "too hard" basket, thanks to the many long-winded books, complicated arguments, and perpetual state of flux that characterize Pauline scholarship. Nevertheless, it is better not to lose sight of Paul in the midst of his many interpreters. His letters are still available to be read by anyone who opens the New Testament; they are not too long to be read quickly; and the major thrusts of his writings are clear enough to be understood by most people with some Bible-reading experience. Indeed, Paul's letters remain a vital part of Christian Scripture, and they invite believers today to go in deep.

A helpful approach to Paul's letters is to read them regularly and in whole. Virtually every letter contains details that can become confusing, but it is best not to get bogged down with them. Instead, a good grasp of the whole will be the best way to unravel some of the tricky details. And more important, a good grasp of the whole of each letter will also enable the reader to take in their most important themes and ideas. Beyond their themes and ideas, it is important to remember that Paul's letters are written for the spiritual health of believing communities. They are not abstract works of theology designed solely for spiritual contemplation and theological reflection. They are intended to induce worship, to shape hearts and minds, and to encourage appropriate behavior as a result. The worst way to read Paul's letters is to abstract them from their author's original pastoral and missional intent.

What about the Rest of Scripture?

It is also important to read Paul's letters in light of the whole of Scripture. Paul can become so intriguing—and dare I say intoxicating—that it is all too easy to spend most of one's time reading his letters while ignoring the remainder of the Bible. Indeed, history is full of examples of movements, theologians, and preachers who developed a lopsided approach to Christian thought simply because they read Paul too much! Paul's letters point outside themselves, showing how his main themes and concerns resonate with wider biblical teaching. The letters simultaneously offer a way to interpret the rest of Scripture in light of Christ, while also requiring some knowledge of the whole Bible in order to understand Paul's teaching. Thus, a very fruitful approach to Paul's letters is to read them in concert with the other Scriptures in a recursive fashion: the more of the Bible one understands, the better one will understand Paul, and vice versa.

Saying that we should read Paul in light of the rest of Scripture might sound ideal, but in practice it can be rather daunting. A few tips can help the aspiring reader to get started. First, most Bibles contain cross-references that help readers to locate Paul's hundreds of scriptural quotations, citations, and allusions. It is not too difficult to flip open cross-referenced passages to get the gist of Paul's references to various Scriptures. For those reading Paul in the original Greek, the Greek New Testament produced by the United Bible Societies (referred to as UBS^5) contains a detailed index of scriptural references for each part of the New Testament. Even for those content to read Paul in English, the Scripture index at the back of UBS^5 can be very helpful.

Second, it is helpful to remember that New Testament authors, including Paul, quoted Scripture in an expansive way. Rarely do the quoted words alone convey the author's full intent. Thus, when chasing down Paul's cross-references, it is important to read them in context. Sometimes he had a whole paragraph or larger section in mind. It was conventional for authors to cite a part of a text that would indicate a wider passage, just as the words "Four score and seven years ago" immediately point contemporary Americans to Abraham Lincoln's Gettysburg Address. Thus, we need to look at the wider passages from which quotations come.

Third, alongside chasing down cross-references, it is even more beneficial to have a grasp of the whole of Scripture, as Paul did. He sometimes points to the big themes and story of the Bible in ways that cannot be captured through cross-references. For instance, a reader ideally should understand Abraham's basic narrative as outlined in Genesis in order to comprehend Paul's arguments about Abraham in Galatians. The cross-references are not enough. So, while it might seem a little grandiose, the best way to understand Paul's use of Scripture is to understand the whole of Scripture. And this again underscores the importance of reading the whole Bible, not just Paul.

Fourth, it has often been suggested that Paul's teaching differed significantly from Jesus's teaching. To be sure, there are many differences between the teachings of Jesus and Paul, since they were different teachers in different contexts addressing different people about different things. Differences are to be expected. But these differences can also be overplayed to suggest

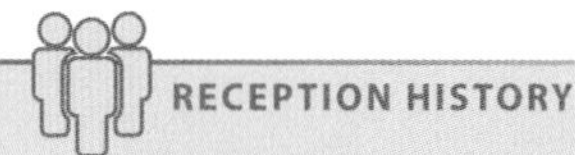

RECEPTION HISTORY

Paul as the Corrupter of Christianity

In keeping with Paul's many critics (see the sidebar "Haters Gonna Hate" above), a common and consistent criticism is that Paul reinvented Christianity and steered it away from the teaching and mission of Jesus. For example, the first prime minister of the State of Israel, David Ben-Gurion, stated that Jesus probably was a typical Jew of his day, but Paul gave Christianity its "anti-Jewish emphasis." And Mahatma Gandhi said, "I draw a great distinction between the Sermon on the Mount and the Letters of Paul," making it clear that he preferred the former over the latter. And poet Kahlil Gibran believed that while Jesus taught people to be free, Paul put them back in chains.[5]

that Paul in some ways contradicts Jesus, or that he distorts the Christianity of Jesus in a Pauline fashion. Paul has even been called the founder of Christianity!

But it is not too difficult to demonstrate that all the major claims of Jesus—and claims about Jesus by the Gospel writers—match Paul's major claims about Jesus. He is the Messiah of Israel, come in fulfillment of Scripture, who came from God, lived among us, died for our sins, rose again in defeat of death, and ascended to his Father's right hand. Both Jesus and Paul affirm that the message of Jesus is for both Jews and gentiles, who, by repentance and faith in Jesus, can join in the kingdom and family of God in fulfillment of the promises to Abraham. Both Jesus and Paul affirm the authority of the old covenant of Moses, while also acknowledging that it has been superseded by the new covenant established by Jesus's blood. Both speak of the work of the Holy Spirit, who connects Jesus to his followers during his (physical) absence. Both Jesus and Paul look ahead to a day of judgment in which God will reveal people's secret sins, destroy evil, and establish everlasting justice and peace. They also present a Father God who forgives sin and grants eternal life to those who entrust themselves to him. Jesus and Paul should be understood together in a complementary, rather than competitive, fashion, since their distinct voices sing the same song in the same choir.

What about the Historical Gap between Paul and Us?

Reading an author from two thousand years ago raises a number of other challenges that must be navigated with care. Though we need not be qualified scholars of ancient history to properly understand the major themes and intent of ancient documents, we nevertheless must recognize the major historical and cultural gap between those days and our own. No doubt some of the issues within Paul's letters are challenging and perplexing because of this gap. He writes at a time and within a culture that presupposed a number of shared beliefs and perspectives that we do not necessarily share today. Sometimes Paul challenges the shared beliefs, perspectives, and culture of his day, and at other times he happily goes along with them. It can be tricky for us, then, as we read Paul's letters today, since some understanding of these historical elements provides much-needed context. It can also be tricky to figure out how much the differences between Paul's day and ours should affect our understanding of Paul's theology and our application of it.

The "gap" between us and Paul gives rise to much Pauline scholarship today as scholars seek to locate Paul within his historical and cultural context(s) and to shed light on his intended meaning as a result. To some extent, Pauline scholarship is therefore absolutely necessary, and the average reader can access its most essential contributions through various user-friendly resources (including books like this one). A helpful one-stop resource is *The IVP Bible Background Commentary: New Testament*, by Craig Keener. Keener is a respected expert in biblical backgrounds, and this single volume provides everything that most readers need to navigate the historical and cultural gap between Paul and us. Good study Bibles also offer informed help, though they are necessarily superficial, and readers of this book probably will need more than they're able to offer. Ultimately, we need historical background information to read Paul well, but we shouldn't think that we can't read him at all unless we have a degree in history.

What about Pauline Theology?

New Testament scholarship went through a long phase in which it was not deemed "scholarly" to think much about the theological claims of the New Testament authors. This was largely an effort to keep New Testament scholarship historical, literary, and, above all, respectable within the academic guild. It was also an attempt to keep academic inquiry free from the influence of confessional (i.e., church) agendas. But even if a scholar does not believe the theological claims made by the authors of the New Testament, it should be immediately obvious that these authors *did* make theological claims. And that means that any respectable reading of their literature must seek to understand the theological claims they contain. They are not only historical and literary documents; they are also theological documents and must be read as such. Happily, New Testament scholarship has moved (or is moving) to a more sensible position that respects the theological elements of these theological texts. As such, New Testament theology has made quite the comeback, and so too has Pauline theology.

Pauline theology is a fascinating area of study that puts together Paul's collective teachings from across his letters. Many New Testament scholars have produced their own take on Paul's theology in single-volume publications (or two volumes, in the case of N. T. Wright), seeking to package up the apostle's teaching in a coherent thematic presentation. Other scholars have written lengthy volumes addressing a single theme within Paul's teaching. Pauline theology is regarded as a subset within New Testament theology, which seeks to do much the same thing, but for the whole New Testament instead of just one author.

Pauline theology relies on detailed exegesis of each of Paul's letters but seeks to relate all the disparate pieces to one another to arrive at an expression of Paul's theological mind. Of course, such attempts are naturally limited by the fact that Paul's letters are occasional, addressing specific people about specific issues. There is no reason to assume that the New Testament letters bearing Paul's name capture *everything* he thought theologically. A mind such as Paul's no doubt kept expanding and evolving, so it would be foolish to think that he managed to write down everything he ever thought about God, Jesus, and the church. Thus, Pauline theology can never claim to be exhaustive; at best it simply attempts to capture Paul's theology as expressed in his extant letters.

In keeping with the "evolving" comment above, many scholars have held that Paul's theology changed over the course of his life and ministry. This would have been natural, but it is worth considering the nature of such change. Just as the relationship between the teachings of Paul and Jesus can be understood as different but not contrary, so the changes in Paul's thought may be understood as evolving in the same direction rather than shifting away from previously held positions. The view expressed in this book is that Paul is a remarkably coherent thinker, whose thought deepens and expands over time. He focuses on different issues depending on the needs of his audience, and his theology is always presented in the context of ministry and mission, which means that no two letters are the same. It also means that he can address similar issues in different ways. This is not evidence of course correction (nor of alternate authorship) but rather reflects a creative and adaptable mind at work. In my view, most scholarly claims that see contradictions within Paul—or quickly resort to alternate authorship—simply underestimate him. Given his obvious towering intellect, it seems a little absurd to put limits on what he was and was not capable of doing from an intellectual perspective. Great minds can flex and reformulate according to need. It should come as no surprise to see Paul do just that.

What about Putting Paul into Practice?

Paul generally does not hold back from telling his readers what he thinks they should do or how he thinks they should live. But the first thing to note is that Paul is no moralist whose instructions are to be obeyed "because I said so." Paul's ethical content is always grounded in theological arguments and in his theological understanding of reality. This is clearer in some letters than others, such as Ephesians, for example. Paul dedicates the first half of that letter to developing his robust theological argument, which is then applied to the life of the church in the second half. Without the first half of the letter, the instructions in the second half would lose their power and rationale. Indeed, it is better to see them as the natural overflow from Paul's theological argumentation. Christian living flows inextricably out of Christian theology. Either one without the other would become a corrupted caricature of itself.

This means that before we ask how to apply Paul's teachings to the life of the church today, we must first understand the theological underpinnings of his instructions. Many parents instruct their children not to play in the street. Obedient children should just do what they're told, and not play in the street, right? But it is even better if children understand the reason behind the instruction: playing in the street can get you hit by a car. While a parent might rightly insist, "Just do what I say, because I know best," children will be more motivated to obey if they understand why the instruction exists—assuming they also want to avoid being hit by a car! It also means that in some situations, children might decide that it's okay to play in the street—if, for example, it's a quiet cul-de-sac, or a street for pedestrians only. This little illustration is not intended to encourage us to disregard Paul's instructions if we think we know better now. It simply raises the point that it is usually better to understand why an instruction exists rather than to follow it blindly.

Having said that, there may be instances in which Paul's specific application no longer makes sense today. If we understand the theological reasoning behind such instructions, we are able to apply his thought in ways that address contemporary needs and challenges. For example, Paul tells the Thessalonians to work with their own hands (1 Thess. 4:11). The important point here is that believers not be idle and work to support themselves rather than become a burden on others. Paul's instruction should not be applied today to mean that only manual labor (with their hands) is acceptable for Christians. There is no good reason, theological or otherwise, why Christians should engage only in manual labor and not in other kinds of work. So, if we understand Paul's theological intention—that members of the church ought to take responsibility for their own welfare as far as possible so that the church can care for those who really need help—then we can apply it in a way that makes sense today.

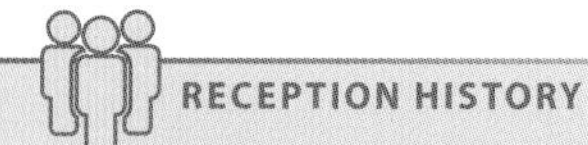

RECEPTION HISTORY

Greet One Another with a . . . Hearty Handshake?

In Romans 16:16, Paul instructs his readers, "Greet one another with a holy kiss," reflecting the Mediterranean practice of his day (and today) of greeting one another with a kiss on the cheek (regardless of gender). In an effort to communicate the intention behind this instruction to his more reserved British readers, J. B. Phillips's translation of the New Testament rendered the verse, "Give one another a hearty handshake all round."

It is also important to recognize that much of Paul's vision for Christians is about who they are, rather than what they do. If believers are captivated by a strong sense of identity as the adopted children of God and members of his family, it will affect how they live. Moreover, if believers deeply know that they are united to Christ and participate in his death, resurrection, and ascension, it will likewise impact their conduct. For Paul, believers' identity in Christ is primary and their action is secondary. They must first know *who they are* before they can figure out *how to live*.

When it comes to putting Paul's teaching into practice, these are but a few points to keep in mind. Suffice it to say, application of Paul to life today is not always direct but might require multiple steps. Neither is it always obvious; it will require careful reflection. And application will sometimes be complicated, given that life is, well, complicated.

What about This Book?

Those who seek to read Paul as Christian Scripture must tread carefully and humbly, always seeking to handle these texts well, to understand their historical contexts, to appreciate their theological depth, and to apply them in ways that benefit the church and the world today. These elements and more are addressed in the pages to follow. This book seeks to read Paul in light of the whole Bible and to address his themes, his theology, and his significance for the church today.

Something that makes a huge difference for understanding and appreciating Paul's letters is to read them in the context of his life and mission. This makes the letters resonate in a whole new way as we better appreciate what's going on for Paul as he writes and for the people he addresses. A key element of this textbook, then, is to approach each of Paul's letters in light of his life and mission. In order to read Paul this way, the book is structured around the major episodes of his life and mission. These episodes are called parts and numbered 1 through 5. Each one of Paul's letters is associated with one of these parts. Part 6 then steps back and looks at Paul's theology and at reading Paul's letters as Christian Scripture today.

This does not necessarily mean that each letter was written during the period of its associated part. For instance, Philippians likely was written during part 5 while Paul was in Rome, but here it is included with part 3 because that is when he was in Philippi. Since the letter addresses the church in Philippi, it is more important to read it in the context of Paul's ministry there rather than of wherever he happened to be when he wrote the letter (though that is not unimportant).

This means that the letters are approached in their historical order (. . . sort of, as noted above) rather than the order in which they appear in the Bible. This might be confusing at first if you are used to the biblical ordering of Paul's letters, but it is worth navigating a little bit of confusion in order to read the letters afresh according to their historical contexts.

- Part 1 addresses Paul's birth, early life, and rebirth.
- Part 2 addresses Paul's first mission and the letter associated with it (Galatians).
- Part 3 addresses Paul's second mission and the letters associated with it (Philippians, 1 and 2 Thessalonians, 1 and 2 Corinthians).
- Part 4 addresses Paul's third mission and the letters associated with it (Ephesians, Colossians, Philemon).
- Part 5 addresses Paul's Roman imprisonment through to the end of his life, and the letters associated with it (Romans, 1 and 2 Timothy, Titus).
- Part 6 addresses Paul's theology and how we read his letters today.

Some readers may already be familiar with *Reading the New Testament as Christian Scripture: A Literary, Canonical, and Theological Survey*, by Jonathan Pennington and me, which belongs to the same series, Reading Christian Scripture. The present volume is intended to complement that book, going deeper into Paul's contribution to the New Testament and tackling his history and theology in more detail. However, this book also stands alone as an introduction to Paul and his writings.

As with *Reading the New Testament as Christian Scripture*, there is an emphasis here on reading the biblical texts themselves, rather than just what others have to say about them. As we move through Paul's life and letters, there are a number of prompts to read specific short passages, which will help you to remember key points or highlights of Paul's material. But even better is to read each letter in whole as we move through—they're not very long!

In keeping with the approach of *Reading the New Testament as Christian Scripture*, each chapter includes sidebars organized into various categories: Historical Matters, Literary Notes, Theological Issues, Canonical Connections, and Reception History. And this book adds one more: Postcards from the Mediterranean.

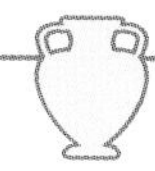

HISTORICAL MATTERS

Historical Matters sidebars offer information about issues going on behind the text. They include information about the historical settings of Paul's letters. They might also include cultural, political, or geographical information that sheds light on certain events, customs, places, and practices reflected in the text.

LITERARY NOTES

Literary Notes sidebars focus on issues related to how Paul's letters are written, authorship, audience, and other questions related to the literary composition of each letter.

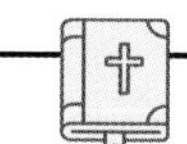

THEOLOGICAL ISSUES

Theological Issues sidebars discuss theological questions, problems, or insights raised by Paul's letters. They help to make connections between specific texts and wider theological reflections and to dig deeper into Paul's theological mind.

CANONICAL CONNECTIONS

Canonical Connections sidebars reveal some of the ways in which the whole Bible can be read as one story. The canon is beautifully diverse, but it also shares a unified voice. Canonical Connections sidebars highlight how a particular Pauline text can be read in dialogue with other passages in the Old and New Testaments.

RECEPTION HISTORY

Reception History sidebars offer examples of how portions of Paul's letters have been received, understood, and applied in the history of the church. Reception History sidebars help us to read Paul's texts with fresh eyes as we come to appreciate how others have interpreted these texts over millennia.

POSTCARDS FROM THE MEDITERRANEAN

Postcards from the Mediterranean sidebars comment on various locations related to Paul that can be visited today and what it is like to do so. Though most such locations have dramatically changed since Paul's day, they can still offer a fresh perspective for understanding his life and mission. And they are often beautiful places that stimulate imagination and adventure.

A Note to Professors

Dear Professor, I respect what you do and offer thanks for assigning this book to your class. While it will work well for individual readers doing their own thing, the book is designed for classroom use, and I hope it will make your life as an educator a bit easier. More than that, I hope you will really enjoy teaching with this book! The number of chapters allows it to fit into a standard teaching semester; it comes complete with discussion questions;

and the core material is balanced by a variety of historical anecdotes, interesting tangents, and points to inspire further study.

As explained above, the book does not present Paul's letters in their canonical order (the order in which they are presented in the New Testament). I think that this is the best way to approach the letters, since it anchors each one in Paul's biographical narrative, giving them the necessary historical scaffolding to be read well. But some professors may prefer to stick with the canonical order—or a different order altogether—for a variety of reasons. The good news is that the main chapters of the book can be read in any order (though it makes best sense to keep the introductory and concluding chapters where they are). But I would suggest that for each chapter that addresses a letter (or letters), students should first read the introduction to the part to which the chapter belongs. For example, chapter 8, "Philippians," is found within part 3, "Paul's Second Mission," so students should read the introduction to part 3 before they read chapter 8. This will help them to grasp the backstory of Paul's visit to Philippi, his ministry there, and the historical context preceding his writing from Rome to the church in Philippi.

PART 1

Paul's Birth and Rebirth

CHAPTER TWO

Introduction to Paul's Birth and Rebirth

Chronology of Part 1: Paul's Birth and Rebirth (ca. 6–46)

ca. 6	Birth
ca. 33	"Conversion" and commissioning
ca. 33–35	Period in Arabia
ca. 36	First visit to Jerusalem after conversion
ca. 36–46	Ministry in Cilicia and Syria
ca. 46	Famine collection from Antioch taken to Jerusalem

Birth

Around AD 6, Saul was born a Jew in the Roman city of Tarsus, on the southeastern coast of modern-day Türkiye (formerly Turkey). He was born into the tribe of Benjamin (Phil. 3:5), and likely was named after King Saul, the most prominent Benjaminite. Although Saul's ancestry and religious heritage were Jewish (Phil. 3:5), his citizenship was Roman, which was a privilege beyond the reach of most inhabitants of the Roman Empire. As a Jew and a Roman citizen, he had a Hebrew name, Saul, and a Roman name, Paul. He was fluent in Aramaic (Acts 21:40; 22:2) and Greek (21:37 [and all his letters are written in Greek]). He likely knew Hebrew too, given his extensive study of the law of Moses (Phil. 3:5) and the traditions of his ancestors (Gal. 1:14).

HISTORICAL MATTERS

Born in Tarsus

Tarsus was an important city, as the capital of the Roman province of Cilicia, and was known for its university. Tarsus became part of the Roman Empire in 64 BC and was a center of culture and learning. One of its other famous sons was Athenadorus, the Stoic philosopher who rose to the position of teacher of the Roman emperor Octavian. It's possible that Saul's parents or grandparents had been taken from Gischala in Judea to Tarsus as prisoners of war after Pompey's invasion of Jerusalem in 63 BC.

HISTORICAL MATTERS

The Jewish Diaspora

The Jewish diaspora refers to the dispersion of Israelites or Jews outside their ancestral homeland of Israel and their settlement in other locations. Jews were expelled from Israel through enforced exile in the eighth and sixth centuries BC by the Assyrians and Babylonians. But there were also several voluntary Jewish settlements outside Israel, such as in the Aegean Islands, Greece, Asia Minor, Cyrenaica, Italy, and Egypt. By the time of the first century, there were approximately five million Jews living outside Palestine and one million within it.

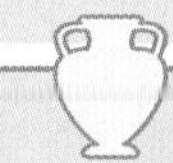

HISTORICAL MATTERS

Born a Roman Citizen

Saul likely inherited his Roman citizenship from his father or grandfather, who probably was given the status of freedman through emancipation from slavery or distinguished service and then became a Roman citizen. Citizenship was a privileged political and legal status that gave the right to vote (for men) and certain protections throughout the empire. Roman citizens had the right to a legal trial, as well as the right to appeal the decisions of magistrates. They could not be tortured or whipped. If found guilty of treason and sentenced to death, Roman citizens could not be crucified.

The Mediterranean in Paul's time

Baker Publishing Group

Saul left Tarsus for Jerusalem as a teenager, possibly accompanied by his family (Acts 23:16), in order to study under the renowned instructor Gamaliel (22:3). He became a Pharisee and advanced quickly for his age (Gal. 1:14). When confronted with the new movement known as "the Way"—consisting of the followers of Jesus—Saul differed sharply from his teacher. Gamaliel advocated for peace (Acts 5:34–39), while Saul was consumed by a zealous rage against the new movement (8:3; 9:1; 26:11). It's likely that the stoning and death of Stephen, the first Christian martyr, set off Saul's violent fury (7:57–8:3).

Immediately after Stephen's death, Saul became the spearhead of a severe persecution against the church in Jerusalem, causing many believers to scatter to surrounding regions. He wasted no time in trying to destroy the church, going from house to house, dragging the followers of Jesus into prison (Acts 8:1–3; 11:19; Gal. 1:13, 23). Saul approved of the use of violence to destroy the church, as he endorsed killing (Acts 8:1; 26:10), and breathed threats and murder against the disciples of Jesus (9:1). But he also engaged other methods, such as gaining the high priest's support. Knowing that the followers of Jesus were already scattering beyond Jerusalem, Saul requested letters from the high priest to the synagogues in Damascus, Syria, so that he could bring disciples back to Jerusalem as his prisoners (9:1–2). Saul's intense persecution of the church was powered by his zeal and devotion to the traditions of his ancestors (Acts 22:3; Gal. 1:14; Phil. 3:6).

Public domain / Wikimedia Commons

Michael Damaskin, *Stoning of Stephen*, 1590

Rebirth

Saul had quickly established himself as Christian enemy number one, as his violent zeal was set against a movement that he sincerely believed to be idolatrous and evil. Given that reality, what happened next was truly mind-blowing. On his way to Damascus, Saul was surrounded by a dazzling light, which caused him to fall to the ground. A voice addressed him, "Saul, Saul, why are you persecuting me?" When Saul asked who was speaking to him, the voice replied, "I am Jesus, the one you are persecuting." Jesus told Saul that he has appointed him "as a servant and a witness of what you have seen and will see of me." Jesus said he would rescue Saul from opposition and send him to Jews and gentiles so that they may turn to God, receive forgiveness of sins, and join those set apart by faith in Jesus. But for now, Saul was to get up and go into the city. There he would be told what to do. Following the vision of light, Saul discovered he had been blinded, so the men traveling with him led him by the hand into Damascus, where he did not eat or drink for three days (Acts 9:3–8; 22:6–11; 26:13–18).

Meanwhile, a disciple in Damascus named Ananias received a vision in which the Lord instructed him to go find Saul. Ananias resisted because he was well aware of Saul's persecution of the church, but the Lord insisted that Saul "is my chosen instrument to take my name to gentiles, kings, and Israelites." So, Ananias went and found Saul. He laid his hands on him and

HISTORICAL MATTERS

Zeal and Violence

Zealous animosity was respected by many Jews of the Second Temple period, with characters such as Phinehas, Elijah, and Mattathias celebrated for their devotion to God and the law of Moses. Phinehas, one of Aaron's grandsons, killed an Israelite man who was committing adultery with a Midianite woman—who was regarded as idolatrous—in full knowledge of the whole community. Phinehas was commended by God for his zeal, and his action ended a plague caused by idolatry (Num. 25:6–13). The prophet Elijah's zeal likewise inspired violence against the worshipers of the false god Baal in order to restore God's honor (1 Kings 18–19). In 167 BC, Mattathias ben Johanan's zeal for the law led him to kill a Seleucid official who had ordered him to worship Greek gods. This act instigated the Maccabean Revolt, which won the temporary freedom of Judea from Seleucid rule. Phinehas, Elijah, and Mattathias exemplified the connection between religious zeal and violence that likely inspired Saul's wrath against the church.

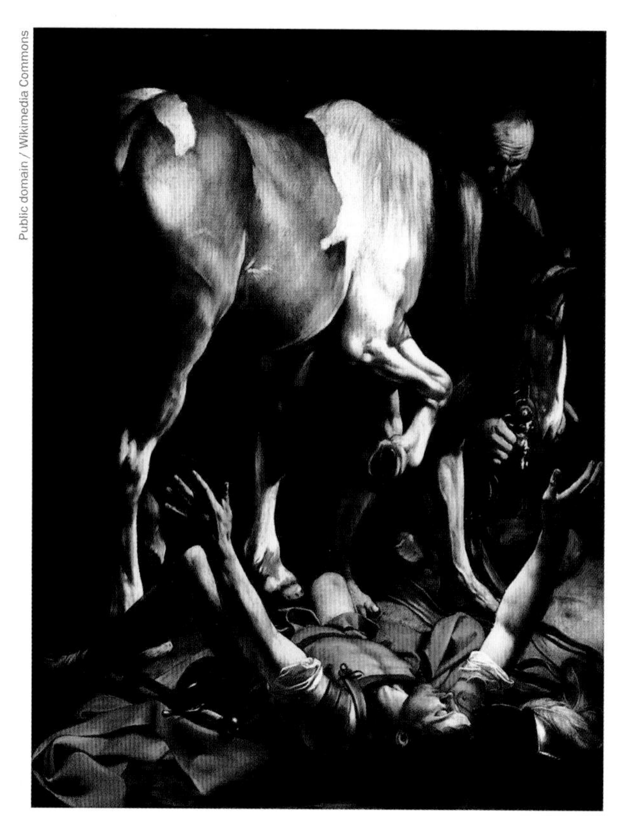

Caravaggio, *Conversion on the Way to Damascus*, 1600

addressed him as "Brother Saul." He told him that the Lord had sent him so that Saul would regain his sight and receive the Holy Spirit. Ananias told Saul that God had appointed him to see and hear Jesus, the Righteous One, and to be his witness to all people. At that moment, scales fell from Saul's eyes and he could see again. He got up and was baptized and began to regain his strength (9:10–19; 22:12–16).

Saul remained in Damascus "for some time" (we don't know how long), and immediately he began preaching in the synagogues that Jesus is the Son of God. He had originally planned to visit the synagogues in Damascus in order to hunt down and imprison the followers of Jesus, but instead he visited them *as* a follower of Jesus. The turnaround must have been staggering. Indeed, everyone who heard Saul was astounded as he grew in his ability to demonstrate that Jesus is the Messiah. As a result, Saul became the target of a Jewish conspiracy to kill him, but he escaped Damascus through a hole in the city wall (9:19b–25; 2 Cor. 11:33).

Formation

The writing of history is always selective, and what happened next has been omitted from Luke's account in Acts, which jumps straight from Damascus to Jerusalem (Acts 9:26; 22:17; 26:20). But Paul himself reveals an episode wedged between the two. In Galatians 1:17–18, he reports that after Jesus had been revealed to him, he "went to Arabia and came back to Damascus. Then after three years I did go up to Jerusalem." This is the first of two pieces of evidence that Paul went to Arabia. The second is found in 2 Corinthians 11:32, where he mentions that "a ruler under King Aretas guarded the city of Damascus in order to arrest me." King Aretas was ruler of the Nabatean kingdom, which was known also as Arabia. So, it seems that during his time in Arabia he managed to offend the king somehow (probably through preaching), who therefore was trying to capture him.

We have no knowledge of Saul's activities during this three-year period, but we're left with a couple of clues. First, as mentioned above, Saul was in trouble with the Nabatean king, and, if the rest of his story is any indication, this happened probably because of his preaching. Second, we know that he began preaching in Damascus immediately after he recovered from his encounter with Christ. Given such immediacy, it is reasonable to conclude that he continued to preach during his time in Arabia. Putting those two clues together, we can surmise that it's very likely that Saul spent his time in Arabia preaching Christ.

HISTORICAL MATTERS

Who Were the Nabateans?

The Nabateans were an ancient Arab people who inhabited northern Arabia and the southern Levant. They were nomadic Bedouin tribes who traveled throughout the Arabian Desert. The Nabatean kingdom emerged between the fourth and second centuries BC, with Petra as its capital. The Nabatean kingdom was annexed into the Roman Empire in AD 106, and it later converted to Christianity, centuries after Saul preached among them.

POSTCARDS FROM THE MEDITERRANEAN

Petra

Petra was the capital of the Nabatean kingdom and is now part of Jordan, directly south from Damascus in Syria. It is an absolutely spectacular place to visit, with the whole city carved into stone. The most famous site is known as the Treasury, and is recognizable from the film *Indiana Jones and the Last Crusade.* But it is actually a tomb. And who's buried there? Why, it's none other than King Aretas IV—the very king who pursued Paul.

After Arabia, Saul returned to Damascus in Syria, but he had to flee King Aretas, who wanted him arrested (2 Cor. 11:32–33), and the Jews, who wanted him dead (Acts 9:23–25). Three years after encountering the

Petra

risen Christ on the road to Damascus, Saul finally made his way back to Jerusalem a very changed man. But believers in Jerusalem were skeptical about Saul being a genuine follower of Jesus and were afraid of him. Nevertheless, Barnabas took Saul to the apostles and explained what had happened to him. The apostles accepted him, and they spent time together. He preached boldly in the name of Christ in Jerusalem, which again angered the Jews, as it had in Damascus. So they conspired to kill him, just as they had in Damascus. While Saul was praying in the temple, the Lord spoke to him in a vision, telling him to leave Jerusalem quickly because of the threat to him and that he would be sent far away to the gentiles. When some believers learned of the plot to kill Saul, they took him to Caesarea on the coast, where he sailed off to his birthplace, Tarsus (9:26–30; 22:17–21).

Ten years passed. After significant growth of the church in Syrian Antioch, the church in Jerusalem sent Barnabas there to assist. In need of help, Barnabas went to Tarsus to find Saul and brought him back to Antioch. For a year, Barnabas and Saul served together in Antioch as its church continued to expand (11:19–26).

Although Acts gives relatively little space to it, the period between Saul's encounter with Christ and his ministry in Antioch represents about fourteen years. We know that much of that time was spent preaching, since that's what Saul does almost immediately in Damascus. And nearly all of that time was outside Jerusalem. So it seems that Saul had quite an extensive "incubation" period, in which he figured out how to preach Christ to Jews and gentiles. It no doubt took time to process the implications of the truth that Jesus is the Christ, risen from the dead. Saul's extensive knowledge of the Scriptures as a well-trained Pharisee needed to be reconsidered in light of Christ. He had to reconsider his eschatological framework and learn what it means to be "in Christ." None of these things happened automatically, and this incubation period was no doubt important for Paul's theological and ministry formation.

CHAPTER THREE

Paul's World

A Jew in the Roman Empire

Born in Tarsus, on the southeastern coast of what is now Türkiye, Paul was born and raised a Jew within the Jewish diaspora. The "diaspora," or "dispersion," refers to Jewish populations scattered throughout the world, outside Palestine. Jews were first scattered out from Israel and Judah during the deportations in 722 and 586 BC. According to ancient sources, most of the Jewish diaspora population was found in Cyrenaica (northern Libya), Alexandria (Egypt), Phoenicia (Lebanon), Syria, Babylonia (Iraq), the Parthian kingdom (northern Iran), Cyprus, Asia Minor (Türkiye), Greece, Macedonia, and Rome. By the end of the first century BC, the Roman historian Strabo claimed that the Jewish people had made their way into every city and it was difficult to find anywhere in the known world that had not hosted the Jews (cited in Josephus, *Jewish Antiquities* 14.115).

Roman religion formed the backdrop for all Christian mission and ministry. Rome was committed to polytheism and the acceptance and integration of additional gods into the Roman pantheon. As the Roman Empire expanded, it absorbed the deities of their conquered peoples and cities. Religious inclusivity was a cultural value as well as an explicit imperial policy, since it was believed that local worship was good for the well-being of the people and economies that Rome governed. Roman gods even merged with local gods, such as in the cases of Mars Alator and Sulis Minerva. The city of Rome was personified as the main deity, with several impressive temples that functioned as centers of public social life with their entertainment, celebrations, concerts, and meetings. The state ruled over civil religion through its network of priestly pontiffs, augurs, and flamens.

HISTORICAL MATTERS

The Imperial Cult

The imperial cult, beginning with the posthumous deification of Julius Caesar after his assassination in 44 BC, involved the direct worship of the emperor through sacrifice and prayer in temples and religious festivals. Thus, at the center of Roman religion was emperor worship, which was embedded throughout Roman religious, economic, social, and political systems.

Head of the goddess Sulis Minerva

Greek influence was prominent within Roman religious experience as well, with its philosophies of Neoplatonism and Stoicism being practiced as religions within the empire. Mystery religions were secret cults with intricate initiation practices. Some Romans participated in foreign cults such as Mithraism, the Eleusinian mysteries, and the cult of Isis. New religions often found their way to Rome through its military, which imported gods from far-flung corners of the empire. The military was also responsible for spreading Roman religion across the known world. But there were exceptions to the Roman embrace of foreign gods, with Egyptian cults, mystery religions, and Judaism receiving official criticism and opposition. A particularly noteworthy example was Emperor Claudius's expulsion of all Jews from the city of Rome in AD 49.

Religion permeated all aspects of Roman culture, both public and private—including ethics, politics, economics, mathematics, and philosophy. The piety of individuals and families was believed to affect the welfare of a city and even the whole Roman Empire. Failure to conform to religious expectations could be regarded as a threat to society's well-being. Religion received attention in every element of Roman life. Certain cultural values and social institutions were deemed religious in nature—including honor, patronage, and masculinity.

Paul's writings demonstrate Jewish, Greek, and Roman influences—various overlapping cultural influences. Sometimes he relies on these influences, and other times he pushes against them. Scholars debate the extent of Jewish influence on Paul's thought, even though he was Jewish and identified with the people of Israel (Rom. 9:1–5). The influence on Paul of Greco-Roman culture, language, and customs is seen especially in the form of his letters and his awareness of Greco-Roman thought and philosophy.

Paul appeals to foundational beliefs of Judaism, most significantly the assumption of monotheism in the context of polytheistic cultures within the Roman Empire. In 1 Corinthians 8:6, Paul states, "There is one God, the Father, from whom are all things, and we exist for him; and one Lord, Jesus Christ, by whom are all things, and we exist through him." He appeals to the foundation of Jewish monotheism to argue for the divinity of Christ—a highly controversial claim for most first-century Jews. By appealing to Deuteronomy 6:4 (the Shema), Paul establishes his claim of Jesus's deity on the central foundation of Judaism.

Many Jews of the first century linked salvation to ethnicity, so that one's identity as either Jew or gentile was the key issue. Paul rejected this notion and argued that believers were justified by faith—as was the case for the patriarch Abraham—regardless of ethnicity. Indeed, Abraham's faith set the precedent for believing gentiles to receive the blessings of God's covenantal promises.

There is debate as to whether Paul intended to subvert the rule of the Roman Empire through his writings (and, if he did, to what extent). Some see Paul implicitly (and sometimes overtly) pitting the gospel of Jesus against the Roman imperial religion and the imperial authority of Rome in general. Others believe that Paul showed very little interest in the political realm and simply did not give Rome any prominence within his theology.

An Educated Pharisee

According to Paul's self-description in Philippians 3, he had a distinguished Jewish pedigree: he was circumcised on the eighth day; he belonged to the people of Israel and to the tribe of Benjamin; he was a Hebrew of Hebrews. With respect to the law of Moses, he was a devoted Pharisee. As for religious zeal, he was a persecutor of the church. As for righteousness under the law, he was blameless (Phil. 3:5–6). In Acts 22, Paul adds that he was born in Tarsus in Cilicia, was brought up in Jerusalem, and received an education from the teacher Gamaliel according to the strict manner of the law (Acts 22:3).

Tarsus was among the most prestigious locations for education, but Jerusalem was the greatest center for the study of the Hebrew Bible. Though born in Tarsus, Paul seems to have moved to Jerusalem at an early age and studied to become a teacher of the law under the famous Gamaliel I, the successor of Rabbi Hillel. This suggests that Paul came from a wealthy family who could fund such a privileged education. Though born elsewhere, Paul could claim that he was a Jerusalemite by upbringing and an orthodox Pharisee by training.

Paul likely began learning the law at the age of five and other Pharisaic teachings at around the age of ten. He likely was qualified to teach the law

Josephus Flavius, unknown artist, 18th century

after turning thirteen and would have completed his discipleship before the age of twenty. Besides the Jewish historian Josephus, Paul is the only person whose personal claim to be a Pharisee has been preserved by history (Phil. 3:5), and he is the only diaspora Jew known to be a Pharisee.

The major sources for our understanding of the Pharisees are the New Testament Gospels and the ancient Jewish historian Josephus. The Pharisees are generally depicted as key antagonists in Gospel accounts of Jesus's ministry. While some Pharisees simply questioned and challenged Jesus, others became outrightly opposed to him and sought to catch him out in his responses to their challenges. And while Jesus often criticized or rebuked certain Pharisees, he also acknowledged their reputation for piety and righteousness—though he suggested that this often was only an outward show rather than an inner reality. A notable exception in John's Gospel is the Pharisee Nicodemus, whose questions of Jesus seem to reflect a genuine desire to learn (John 3:1–10); he appears sympathetic toward Jesus (7:50–51), and he even attended to Jesus's body after his crucifixion (19:39–40). It may be that John used

HISTORICAL MATTERS

The Pharisees

The Pharisees were a sect within early Judaism beginning around 150 BC before merging into the rabbinic movement at around AD 135. The sect was known for its strict adherence to the law of Moses and for its elaborate system of extensions of the law that served to protect Jewish identity and purity. In fact, the term "Pharisee" comes from an Aramaic word that means "to separate, divide, distinguish." The Pharisees became the dominant voice within Judaism after the destruction of the Jerusalem temple in AD 70, but the function of the group varied over time, making its nature difficult to generalize.

HISTORICAL MATTERS

Josephus the Pharisee

The first-century Jewish historian Josephus identified himself as a Pharisee, which he regarded as one of three main sects within Judaism alongside the Sadducees and Essenes (Josephus, *Life* 10; *Jewish Antiquities* 13.171; 18.11; *Jewish War* 2.119). According to Josephus, the Pharisees were influential within the Sanhedrin (the council responsible for Jewish matters in Roman Palestine) and among general Jewish society. He states that at one point the Pharisees numbered six thousand and that they were focused on their strict devotion to and knowledge of the law (*Jewish Antiquities* 17.41–42; *Jewish War* 2.162; *Life* 191). They were rational; they honored their elders; they held the tension between divine sovereignty and human agency; they believed in the immortality of the soul; and they believed in rewards and punishment in the afterlife (*Jewish Antiquities* 18.12–14). Josephus also described the Pharisees as peaceable, brotherly, and civic-minded (*Jewish War* 2.166).

Nicodemus as a counterexample of Pharisaism to demonstrate that not all were opposed to Jesus or malicious in intent.

Scholars continue to wrestle with the historical, theological, and cultural nature of Pharisaism, and it is important to recognize that not all Pharisees were the same. Christians have tended to demonize the Pharisees because the Gospels generally depict them negatively, but this may not be a fair understanding of the movement as a whole. Having said that, our first encounter with the Pharisee Saul in Acts 8 is far from positive as he breathes murderous threats against the followers of Jesus.

A Letter Writer

Scholars debate whether Paul used standard types of rhetoric in his letters. Some claim that Paul reflects certain Greco-Roman literary conventions, while others see little explicit reliance on such forms, though acknowledging characteristics that resemble Greco-Roman letters.

Paul's letters generally have three to four sections.

1. **Salutation.** Letters typically opened with a greeting that identified the author and recipient(s). New Testament letters tended to substitute the word "grace" for "greetings," which likely was a play on words and an indication of the letter's Christian content. Paul may have invented this practice, since his are the earliest known letters to include this feature. Paul's greetings also include the word "peace," which was a feature of Jewish letters from the period. Thus, the combination of "grace" and "peace" combined the traditional Jewish greeting with a transformed version of the Roman greeting. Paul does not normally identify himself simply as "Paul" (cf. 1 Thess. 1:1) but usually as "Paul, an apostle of Christ Jesus by the will of God" (2 Cor. 1:1) or something similar. Nor does he address his readers simply as "the church of God in Corinth" but typically elaborates with something like "those who are sanctified in Christ Jesus, called to be saints" (1 Cor. 1:2).
2. **Thanksgiving.** Paul retains the Greco-Roman feature of including a brief word of thanksgiving for his recipients. But rather than thanking the gods for good health, or rescue from danger, or some such thing, Paul offers thanks to God

LITERARY NOTES

Ancient Letters

Greco-Roman handbooks provide instructions for how to write specific types of letters to achieve certain goals. These include letters of friendship, prayer, congratulations, consolation, recommendation, inquiry, response, report, supplication, thanks, excuse, instruction, advice, encouragement, exhortation, accusation, threat, defense, and praise. Paul's letters are longer than typical examples of such letters and generally represent a mix of types. But all of Paul's letters incorporate aspects of these various letter types as they seek to achieve their differing functions.

Valentin de Boulogne, *Saint Paul Writing His Epistles*, 1618

in Christian terms (e.g., "through Jesus Christ" [Rom. 1:8]), and he thanks God for his readers' faithfulness and for God's good work among them. Paul sometimes includes hints of the letter's forthcoming content in his thanksgivings, which sometimes are very long—the thanksgiving in 1 Thessalonians arguably continues to 3:13, spanning more than half the letter. And it is painfully notable that his letter to the Galatians contains no thanksgiving at all, for reasons that become immediately clear in the body of the letter.

3. **Body.** The main body of Greco-Roman letters was open to be shaped in whatever way suited the author's intent and content, allowing for great variety among letters at this point. While Galatians, for instance, is an angry letter of rebuke, Philippians is a letter of warm friendship and thanksgiving. This part of a letter could also contain a variety of styles and subgenres, such as hymns (Phil. 2:6–11), liturgical formulas (1 Cor. 6:11), church traditions (1 Cor. 11:23–25), creeds (1 Tim. 3:16), virtue and vice lists (Gal. 5:19–23), household codes (Eph. 5:22–6:9), autobiography (Gal. 1:10–2:21), travelogues (Rom. 15:14–33), topical discussions (Rom. 13:1–7), and prayers (1 Thess. 3:11–13).

LITERARY NOTES

Greco-Roman Terms

On occasion Paul used certain terminology and language that reflect the influence of Greco-Roman culture, including geographical, scientific, and literary parallels: "guardian" (Gal. 3:24–25); "judgment seat" (2 Cor. 5:10); legal language (Col. 2:14); athletic imagery (1 Cor. 9:24–27); slogans such as "all things are permitted for me" (1 Cor. 6:12); adoption terminology (Gal. 4:5); references to boasting (2 Cor. 10:17); language related to the Greco-Roman concept of patronage (Rom. 16:1–2); and statements that challenge or modify Greco-Roman views on leadership (1 Cor. 4:9).

4. **Closing.** Greco-Roman letters often closed with a wish for good health and an expression of farewell. Paul's letters sometime close haphazardly, with mention of travel plans (1 Cor. 16:5–9), greetings to specific individuals (Rom. 16:3–16), exhortations (1 Thess. 5:12–28), a recap of an important point (Gal. 6:15–16), a doxology (Rom. 16:25–27), a benediction (Philem. 25), or a prayer (2 Cor. 13:13).

The average length of a personal letter in the Greco-Roman period was around 90 words, while Paul's letters average 1,300 words, and Romans is 7,101 words. These statistics demonstrate the considerable trouble, time, and planning that Paul must have put into his letter writing. Each letter was a significant investment. They were certainly nothing like our hastily produced and sent emails!

Christian Reading Questions

1. Read Acts 22:30–23:8. Notice that Paul describes himself as *still* being a Pharisee as he speaks to the chief priests and the Sanhedrin (23:6). Do you find this surprising? Why or why not?
2. Take a look at 1 Thessalonians and think about its structure in light of the typical letter sections outlined above. Where do the sections begin and end? Do you notice anything else about its structure?

CHAPTER FOUR

Paul the Jew and the Risen Jesus

According to Paul—and everyone who knew him—his life dramatically changed when he encountered Jesus Christ risen from the dead. While it is common to refer to this event as Paul's "conversion" experience, in an important sense he did not convert from one religion to another. He understood the resurrected Jesus to be the promised king of Israel, the Messiah, so that what we call "Christianity" was simply a type of Judaism. But in another sense, "conversion" seems an appropriate term to use of Paul's experience because it so dramatically changed him, his message, and his mission. In this chapter we explore the ways in which Paul's Christ experience changed his Jewish theology and practice—and also the ways that his theology and practice did *not* change. After all, Paul remained a Jew whose faith in Jesus as the Messiah of Israel was consistent with his beliefs prior to encountering the risen Jesus.

RECEPTION HISTORY

Krister Stendahl

Dean of Harvard Divinity School and bishop of Stockholm, Krister Stendahl was a prominent twentieth-century voice to challenge the common view that Paul was converted to become a Christian by underscoring how much Paul's theological undergirding as a Pharisee remained after his experience on the Damascus road.[1] By challenging prevailing views about Judaism, he was also an early precursor of the New Perspective on Paul, along with E. P. Sanders, James Dunn, and N. T. Wright.

Still a Jew

In Second Temple Judaism there were many different ways of being a Jew. The question is not whether or not Paul was a real Jew but what sort of Jew he was. At the center of Paul's Jewishness was a firm belief in the covenants and promises of God. God would keep his promises to restore Israel by sending a Messiah descended from King David and in fulfillment of the promises to Abraham. And as we know, Paul identified himself as a Pharisee—before *and* after encountering the risen Jesus (Acts 23:6). Rather than saying that Paul converted from Judaism to Christianity, it may be more accurate to say that he "converted" from one type of Judaism to another—one that acknowledged Jesus as their long-awaited Messiah.

HISTORICAL MATTERS

What Was Second Temple Judaism?

Second Temple Judaism refers to the Judaism of the period 515 BC–AD 70, after the Hebrew people returned from exile in Babylon and set about rebuilding the temple in Jerusalem, as depicted in the books of Ezra and Nehemiah. The Jews of this period experienced several significant events, and they produced influential historical and theological writings. The era was decisively ended when the second temple was destroyed by the Romans in AD 70. Second Temple Judaism provides an important part of the complex background for understanding Paul's writings, and much contemporary scholarship is focused on its varied historical, literary, and theological elements.

Affirming the Jewishness of Paul does not assume that he was a Jew like everyone else or that he was not an original thinker. If Paul thought outside the box and arrived at "original" ideas, this does not mean he was betraying his Judaism, just as Philo or Josephus or Hillel were not betraying Judaism when they too formulated "original" answers to the questions of their age. It is better to regard Paul as Jewish in his inherited ideas and beliefs as well as in his "original" or Christ-inspired ideas and beliefs. There is no hint in Paul's writings that he ever disavowed being a Jew—even though he no longer put confidence in his Jewish credentials in order to enjoy right standing with God. While Paul was thoroughly Jewish, he was nonetheless incredibly controversial within Judaism. But Paul's criticisms of other Jews—especially those who rejected Jesus as their Messiah—did not undermine his Jewishness. Even if a Jew expressed radical self-criticism

Model of the second temple in the Israel Museum

toward their own religious tradition, or against other forms of Judaism, this did not undermine their own Jewishness. Instead, it would constitute an insider's critique.

Within Second Temple Judaism there was a range of Jewish messianic hopes, and Paul's belief about Jesus as the Messiah reflects a particular Jewish messianism of his time. Although Paul frequently used the term "Christ" (or "Messiah"), it was not as a name applied to Jesus but as an honorific title, in keeping with Jewish use of the term in that period. The Christ was expected to act as God's agent of redemption, which is consistent with how Paul uses the term. In fact, the key passages in which Paul discusses Christ fit the expectations of a first-century Jewish Messiah text. Nevertheless, there were certain features of Paul's messianism that were noteworthy, as discussed below.

In keeping with some forms of Judaism, Paul shared an "apocalyptic" worldview in which God has done something radically new in continuity

HISTORICAL MATTERS

1 Enoch

The book of Enoch, also known as 1 Enoch, is a prominent example of a Jewish apocalyptic text. It was pseudonymously attributed to the patriarch Enoch, with parts dating to 300–200 BC and later parts dating to around 100 BC. It depicts Enoch receiving a vision from the heavens in which God will come from his dwelling and march upon Mount Sinai with mighty power; mountains will fall down and judgment will fall upon all humanity (1 Enoch 1:2–7). The book discusses why certain angels fell from heaven (chap. 6), the coming of the Son of Man (chap. 48), and the resurrection of the dead (chap. 51), among many other themes. Several parts of 1 Enoch are found within the Dead Sea Scrolls, and the book was known to early Christians who cited it in the first and second centuries. It is even briefly cited in the New Testament, with Jude 1:14–15 quoting 1 Enoch 1:9.

Greek manuscript of the book of Enoch, 4th century AD

Public domain / Wikimedia Commons

with his gradual work throughout history. An "apocalypse" was a piece of literature in which an otherworldly being mediates a revelation to a human being, disclosing a transcendent reality including eschatological salvation.

Apocalyptic literature was produced in the Jewish social setting that can be described as apocalyptic in outlook. Though the Jews had been subdued by Persians, Greeks, and Romans—creating the impression that God was no longer working through history—apocalypticism held that God had withdrawn to appear at the end time, when God will bring all evil to an end and reward the righteous and faithful Jews. According to apocalyptic eschatology, the end time will return humans to the situation of being with God and being at peace with others in a paradise—as it was in the garden of Eden. A first-century Jew who read an apocalypse was transported from this horrid world by imagining the heavenly world above, beyond time. Their hope was transferred to another realm where peace and harmony were found. The poor were revealed to be rich, the conquered became the conquerors, and the lost were found.

Though Paul wrote letters and not apocalypses, there is plenty of evidence in his writings of an apocalyptic worldview. For instance, in 1 Thessalonians 4:14–18 Paul articulates apocalyptic thought:

> For if we believe that Jesus died and rose again, in the same way, through Jesus, God will bring with him those who have fallen asleep. For we say this to you by a word from the Lord: We who are still alive at the Lord's coming will certainly not precede those who have fallen asleep. For the Lord himself will descend from heaven with a shout, with the archangel's voice, and with the trumpet of God, and the dead in Christ will rise first. Then we who are still alive, who are left, will be caught up together with them in the clouds to meet the Lord in the air, and so we will always be with the Lord. Therefore encourage one another with these words.

Though some believers in Thessalonica were concerned that other believers had died before Christ had returned, Paul comforts them with the assurance that God will send Jesus from heaven to call all to be with the Lord Jesus for eternity. The whole passage would have been recognizably apocalyptic to any Jew of the first century.

In 2 Corinthians 12:2–4, Paul describes "revelations of the Lord" that he has experienced:

> I know a man in Christ who was caught up to the third heaven fourteen years ago. Whether he was in the body or out of the body, I don't know; God knows. I know that this man—whether in the body or out of the body I don't

know; God knows—was caught up into paradise and heard inexpressible words, which a human being is not allowed to speak.

Paul—the "man in Christ," as many interpreters understand the phrase—was taken up into the "third heaven," saw paradise, and heard things that can never be revealed. Such concepts were developed within the Jewish apocalypses and apocalyptic writing. From this example and others, it is clear that Paul's worldview was indebted to Jewish apocalypticism, which relates to his thought on justification, salvation, reconciliation, redemption, freedom, sanctification, transformation, new creation, and glorification. The key difference for Paul's apocalypticism compared to that of other Jews of his day was the centrality of Jesus Christ within it.

The Jesus Difference

Before becoming the apostle to the gentiles, Paul became a member of the Jesus movement. As such, he fully embraced the claim that Jesus the Messiah had already come and that he would return at the end of the age. For the first Jesus followers, the Messiah had come before the end so that there would be forgiveness of sins in his name—an idea that was a logical extension of ideas found in certain Jewish texts such as 1 Enoch. For Paul, the problems of the origin of evil, the freedom of human will, and

St. Paul statue in front of St. Peter's Basilica (Vatican) sculpted by Adamo Tadolini

the forgiveness of sin were at the center of his thought. But these were not uniquely Pauline problems; they were Second Temple Jewish problems. Paul's contribution was to answer these problems in light of Christ. As a Jew and a follower of Jesus, Paul claimed that forgiveness of sins was the major accomplishment of Jesus the Messiah for Jews and gentiles alike in the cosmic battle that Jesus fought against demonic forces.

Paul did not think that his belief in Jesus as the Messiah contradicted traditional Jewish messianism, but it formed a distinct development as Paul saw Jesus's death, resurrection, and ascension as God's declaration that Jesus is "the Son of God"—his chosen Lord and ruler (Rom. 1:3–4). Indeed, the most distinctive feature of Paul's messianism is that the Messiah had been crucified and that God had raised him from the dead. And part of the reason why other Jews rejected Paul's message was that, according to him, the Messiah had been crucified and was, therefore, a failed Messiah. While many Jews came to accept that Jesus is the Messiah, many did not, and such claims were later regarded as a Jewish heresy.

Another distinct feature of Paul's messianism was the belief that believers would become incorporated into Christ. By faith, they share in his death, resurrection, and ascension. They are united to Christ and become members of his body. In this sense, Paul's Messiah was not simply a ruler who redeems his people, and his death and resurrection were not embarrassing oddities in the context of Jewish messianic expectation. Instead, Paul's Messiah shares himself with his people, including them in his blessings, and they even participate in those central events of Christ's narrative—his death, burial, resurrection, and ascension. Even more striking is the fact that Paul and the early church engaged in devotion and worship of Jesus in a way that had been reserved only for God within Judaism, demonstrating that they identified the Messiah of God with the Lord of the Heavens.

Paul's firmly Jewish understanding of covenantal election and final judgment was altered by his interpretation of the death and resurrection of Jesus Christ. The resurrection of Christ ushered in a new era of salvation history in which sin and death had been conquered. His previous view, inherited from Judaism, was that the new era of the general resurrection of the dead would occur at the end of the previous era, but the resurrection of Jesus "in the middle of time" (rather than at the end) forced an alternate understanding. The new era has come, but not yet in all its fullness, so that Paul is living in overlapping eras: resurrection and justification are a reality now, but sin and death still exist. Believers are to participate in the new reality by sharing in Jesus's death and resurrection through faith, and by sharing in the promised Holy Spirit. Jesus's resurrection is the beginning of

CANONICAL CONNECTIONS

Biblical Anticipation of the Messianic Rule over Gentiles

The Hebrew Bible anticipates that the Messiah will rule over gentile nations with peace and justice, and such anticipation finds early roots. Genesis 49:8–12 tells of a coming ruler from the tribe of Judah who is described as "the expectation of the nations," and Numbers 24:7 (LXX) speaks of one "who will rule over many nations." The psalms include several royal hymns that foretell the righteous reign of a Davidic king over the earth. The gentile nations will come and worship God's anointed ruler (e.g., Pss. 72:1–18; 89:1–28). God makes promises to his anointed king—addressed as the Son of God—that the nations will be his inheritance (Ps. 2:6–8). And Isaiah 11:1–15 looks ahead to the rule of the Davidic king over the nations with justice.

the general resurrection of the dead and is the "firstfruits" of the harvest to come in the future.

Like the other early Jesus followers, Paul shared the belief that Jesus the Messiah had come to earth as the Son of Man to bring forgiveness to sinners and to reconcile the created cosmos to himself. He believed that Jesus would soon return to carry out judgment, and that gentiles were able to receive forgiveness of their sins ahead of judgment day. Contrary to some, Paul rejected the idea that believing gentiles were in any way inferior to believing Jews, since both were saved by faith, even though Jews remained Jews and gentiles remained gentiles.

Paul came to believe that Jews who did not worship Jesus were failing to accept the true trajectory of their own religion. Paul's Christ experience also changed his attitude toward non-Jews, the gentiles of the nations. Instead of the typical Jewish view that the gentiles were excluded from the promises and covenants of God, the "Christian" Paul now believed that Jesus had opened a way for people of all nations—Jews and gentiles alike—to become the children of God, to share in his blessings and inheritance, as the spiritual descendants of Abraham. But this did not mean that Paul thought that any differences between Jews and gentiles were obliterated. Though he says, "There is no longer Jew or Greek," he also says, "There is no longer slave or free, there is no longer male and female; for all are one in Christ Jesus" (Gal. 3:28). But Paul clearly still regards slaves as slaves, not free (see Philemon), and women and men as distinct (1 Cor. 11:3). To be sure, these categories have altered because of Christ, they are no longer reasons for division or inequality. And yet none of these categories has been abolished. Jews are still Jews, and gentiles are still gentiles. But now they share a common equality and freedom in Christ.

Christian Reading Questions

1. In your own words, try to describe what "apocalypticism" is. Besides the examples mentioned above, can you think of other instances in which Paul seems to be expressing his apparent apocalypticism?
2. How did Paul's belief that Jesus is the Messiah alter his other beliefs? What major areas of his Jewish belief remained the same?

PART 2

Paul's First Mission

CHAPTER FIVE

Introduction to Paul's First Mission

Chronology of Part 2: Paul's First Mission (ca. 46–48)

ca. 46	From Antioch to Cyprus
ca. 46	From Cyprus to Perga and Pisidian Antioch
ca. 46	To Iconium, Lystra, Derbe—cities of South Galatia
ca. 47	Return to Perga, then by ship to Syrian Antioch
ca. 48	The apostolic council in Jerusalem
ca. 49	Galatians written around this time

After a long period of relative silence, in which we know little about Paul's activities (for what we do know, see "Formation" in chap. 2), Saul's story resumes in Acts 13. He is in Antioch along with Barnabas and some other prophets and teachers (13:1). By this stage, Antioch had become the major center for gentile Christians outside Jerusalem. Located north of Jerusalem in Syria (therefore known as Syrian Antioch to distinguish it from Pisidian Antioch, which will feature later), it was relatively close to the Jewish heart of the church, but far enough away to have its own orbit, with better access to other parts of the Roman Empire.

During a time of worship, the Holy Spirit said, "Set apart for me Barnabas and Saul for the work to which I have called them." After prayer and fasting, the group commissioned Barnabas and Saul through the laying on of hands and sent them on to their first great adventure together (13:2–3).

POSTCARDS FROM THE MEDITERRANEAN

Antioch Today

Today, Antioch is called Antakya, and it has been part of Türkiye rather than Syria since 1939. This means that it can still be visited, since Türkiye is safe for travel. (Sadly, at the time of this writing, Syria cannot be visited due to civil war.) I enjoyed my visit to the city, though I was surprised to see that the once thriving Orontes River, which runs through Antioch/Antakya, has been reduced to a trickle. I especially enjoyed my sampling of the cheesy local dessert, *kunefe.*

Antioch (Antakya)

THEOLOGICAL ISSUES

How Did the Spirit Speak?

We don't know how the Holy Spirit "spoke" to Saul, Barnabas, and their group—whether through an audible "voice" or by some other means, such as bringing everyone to a consensus on the same point of view. But the way Luke reports the event, using a quotation, implies that direct speech was involved.

Cyprus

Around AD 46, Barnabas and Saul went south from Antioch to Seleucia, and then set sail for Cyprus (Acts 13:4). Given that their first mission would focus on the interior of mainland Türkiye, they could have traveled there by foot from Syrian Antioch—as Paul does for his second and third missions. So they went out of their way to visit the island of Cyprus first. The most likely reason for going there first was that Barnabas was from Cyprus. Not only would that give the missionaries the opportunity to preach to Barnabas's compatriots, but also they may have thought that it would offer a gentle start to their mission, being among family and friends.

Barnabas and Saul arrived in Salamis, on the northeastern coast of Cyprus, having sailed into the beach that remains virtually unchanged today. Their first act of ministry was to proclaim "the word of God in the Jewish synagogues" (13:5). And with this they established the pattern that would characterize all of Paul's missions: preaching first in the synagogues before going to the gentiles. Preaching in the synagogues first reflects Paul's theology as well as his pragmatism. Theologically, he believed that the gospel message of Jesus as Messiah belongs first to the Jew and then to the gentile (Rom. 1:16). Pragmatically, Jews who embrace Jesus as their Messiah would become excellent leaders of new churches, given their knowledge of the Scriptures, their messianic expectation, and their understanding of God's covenants and promises.

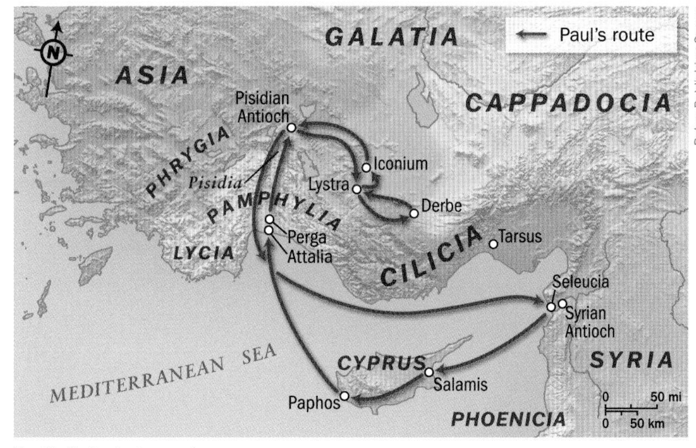

Paul's first missionary journey

Along with John (aka John Mark), who was a Cypriot and the cousin of Barnabas, the missionaries made their way around the whole island, arriving in the capital, Paphos, on the southwestern coast. There they encountered their first recorded opponent—the first of many—a Jewish sorcerer and false prophet by the names of Bar-Jesus and Elymas. Elymas

Salamis

HISTORICAL MATTERS

"Saul" vs. "Paul"

It is sometimes assumed that "Saul" was Paul's preconversion Jewish name, and "Paul" his Christian name. But this is mistaken. First, the narrative of Acts clearly calls him Saul long after his encounter with Jesus in chapter 9. Second, it was not unusual for Jews born outside Judea to be given a Hebrew name *and* a Roman name at birth. Since Saul was born in the Roman province of Tarsus to Jewish parents, he was given two names. It is notable that Acts switches from "Saul" to "Paul" during his first mission to the gentiles. His Roman name came in handy in this mission, especially as he evangelized the Roman consul Sergius *Paulus*. Acts never switches back to "Saul" after this point, because he is now Paul, "the apostle to the gentiles."

interfered with the missionaries' audience with the Roman proconsul of Cyprus, Sergius Paulus. Though Sergius wanted to hear from Barnabas and Saul, the sorcerer tried to turn him against them. But Saul—here introduced for the first time in the narrative as Paul—rebuked Elymas and performed his first recorded miracle, causing the sorcerer to become blind, which in turn led the proconsul to believe the missionaries' teaching (Acts 13:6–12).

Pisidian Antioch

The missionaries sailed up from Paphos in Cyprus to Perga on the southern coast of mainland Türkiye, where John parted company with the team. We're not told why John left, but it may have had something to do with the grueling journey ahead of them through the Taurus mountain range. That trek involved dangerous terrain and potential treachery from bandits, as the Jewish community in Perga would have warned. But relying on supplies and hospitality from local Jewish communities along the way, Barnabas and Saul completed the 120-mile trek through the mountains to Pisidian Antioch in lower central Türkiye. As in Cyprus, their first ministry activity was to

Baker Publishing Group

Temple at Pisidian Antioch

visit the synagogue on the Sabbath, where Paul gave his first recorded sermon (Acts 13:13–41).

READ ACTS 13:16–41

Paul's sermon at Pisidian Antioch gives a quick historical sketch from the Israelites' captivity in Egypt through to the ascendency of King David. Paul refers to God's promise to David (2 Sam. 7:1–17) that a savior of Israel would come from among his descendants. He then gives a sketch of Jesus's ministry beginning with John the Baptist's anticipation of Jesus through to his crucifixion, resurrection, and resurrection appearances (Acts 13:16–31). After this brief rundown from the Egyptian exodus to the resurrection of Jesus, Paul proclaims the good news of God's fulfilled promises to David. Unlike David, who is dead and buried, God's Holy One will not see decay, since he has been raised from the dead—in fulfillment of the Scriptures. Through him comes forgiveness of sins and justification through faith, which the law of Moses could not offer. But Paul's proclamation also issues a warning that his hearers should not fall into disbelief, as the prophets forecast (13:32–39).

Paul's sermon was positively received, resulting in the whole town coming to hear him and Barnabas the following Sabbath. But their popularity incited jealousy among some Jews, who began to oppose them. This became the trigger for Paul and Barnabas (notice that it's no longer "Barnabas and Saul") to turn to the gentiles, in fulfillment of prophecy. Many gentiles believed, and the word of the Lord spread throughout the region. But Jewish opposition increased, leading to the expulsion of Paul and Barnabas from the city (13:42–52).

CANONICAL CONNECTIONS

Proclamation through Biblical Theology

Paul's sermon in Pisidian Antioch is perfectly tailored for his Jewish audience through its appeal to salvation history. He looks to God's workings through the history of Israel as well as his promises recorded in Scripture. By showing the big picture of God's plans, Paul provides the scriptural context for the Jews to understand who Jesus is and the significance of his ministry. It is worth comparing how different Paul's sermon is to the Greeks in Athens, who did not know this scriptural context, in Acts 17.

POSTCARDS FROM THE MEDITERRANEAN

Perga and Pisidian Antioch

The trip up from Perga to Pisidian Antioch is a beautiful drive into the Turkish interior. Both sites are excavated and are well worth a visit. Perga especially is highly developed and fascinating. At the site of the ancient synagogue in Pisidian Antioch stands a sign indicating the location of Paul's "first sermon." This is not technically correct, since Paul preached (likely many times) before his first mission, but it is the site of his first *recorded* sermon.

Iconium and Lystra

A similar thing happened in the next town, Iconium. After some initial success among Jews and gentiles, Paul and Barnabas's ministry provoked opposition from other Jews. The city became divided over them, and the missionaries fled upon learning about a plot to stone them (Acts 14:1–7).

HISTORICAL MATTERS

Roman Roads

It has been estimated that Paul may have traveled some 20,000 km, or 12,400 miles, on his mission journeys. By land, the easiest way to visit cities was to follow the roads of the time, and a considerable part of the distance that Paul covered was on Roman roads, which tended to follow even more-ancient routes. These roads were built to carry the Roman armies along the straightest route as swiftly as possible, and Paul and his traveling companions were able to walk them with relative ease and safety because of the Roman presence. Under the Pax Romana, the Roman peace, instituted by Emperor Augustus, the roads were generally kept free from thieves and in good condition. There were no maps available to travelers, so they moved from one place to the next by asking directions, but milestones were placed along the main roads, showing the distance in Roman miles—about four thousand milestones have survived. Inns or hostels were known to be dirty and dangerous or frequented by prostitutes, so no doubt Paul would have sought Jewish (or later, Christian) accommodation where possible.

A Roman road

In the next town, Lystra, Paul miraculously healed a paralytic man, which caused the crowds to believe that Barnabas and Paul were gods—Zeus and Hermes, respectively. They were even prepared to sacrifice bulls to these "gods." But the missionaries tore their robes and declared that they were just ordinary people, no different from them, and had come to proclaim the good news so that the crowds would turn and worship the true and living God (14:8–18).

Some of the Jews who opposed Paul and Barnabas in Antioch and Iconium came to Lystra, and after winning over the crowd, they stoned Paul, dragged him out of the city, and left him for dead. But Paul got up and went back into town; he then left with Barnabas for Derbe (14:19–20).

Heading Home

After preaching in Derbe, Paul and Barnabas retraced their steps, going back through Lystra, Iconium, and Antioch, in order to encourage the new believers in those places. They also appointed elders for the church in each town. Paul and Barnabas preached in Perga, on the southern coast of Türkiye, where they had begun their mainland mission, and they sailed from its port back to Syrian Antioch, where it had all begun a year or so earlier. They reported to the church in Antioch all that God had done through them to reach out to the gentiles (Acts 14:21–28). Paul and Barnabas also had the opportunity to report about their gentile ministry to the apostles in Jerusalem in AD 48 (15:1–4, 12).

Paul's first mission achieved several things. First, a great number of gentiles turned from their gods to worship the God of Jesus. Second, as a result, many new churches popped up in central Türkiye along with appointed leaders. Third,

Saul embraced his identity as Paul, the apostle to the gentiles. Fourth, Paul emerged as a bold leader with great preaching skills and miraculous abilities. Fifth, the mission helped the other apostles to understand God's intention to include the gentiles in the people of God. Sixth, this mission became a template for Paul's next two missions, which would become much more expansive, daring, and adventurous. The region where all this took place was known as Galatia. That's why we call the letter that Paul wrote to these churches his Letter to the *Galatians*.

CHAPTER SIX

Galatians

Orientation

Paul's Letter to the Galatians was written shortly after his first mission to Cyprus and the region known as Galatia, in lower central Türkiye. That mission took place around AD 46–47 and was followed by Paul's participation in the apostolic council in Jerusalem in AD 48 or 49. If Galatians was written after the Jerusalem council (which arguably is mentioned in 2:1–10), it must have been written in or shortly after AD 49, mostly likely once Paul was back in Syrian Antioch. This would make Galatians Paul's earliest extant letter (though some scholars think that 1 Thessalonians might be earlier), and if so, it is also the earliest document in the New Testament.

HISTORICAL MATTERS

The Jerusalem Council

Paul's account of going to Jerusalem and talking with the apostles James, Peter, and John (Gal. 2:1–10) refers either to the Jerusalem council recorded in Acts 15 or to a prior visit recorded in Acts 11:30. There is evidence to support both possibilities, but especially for the parallel to Acts 15. Both Galatians 2:1–10 and Acts 15 record Paul and Barnabas meeting with the apostles, discussing ministry to the gentiles, and all agreeing that Paul and Barnabas had a special calling to preach to the gentiles. Since the Jerusalem council occurred in AD 49, Galatians was written that year (or slightly after). But if Galatians 2:1–10 is parallel to Acts 11:30 rather than Acts 15, then the letter likely was written sometime before AD 49.

Paul must have been perplexed and discouraged to discover that, so soon after his first mission, the brand-new churches he planted throughout Galatia had already gone awry. He says, "I am amazed that you are so quickly turning away from him who called you by the grace of Christ and are turning to a different gospel" (Gal. 1:6). This is the reason behind Paul's Letter to the Galatians: they have turned to a different gospel and so have turned away from God, who called them to himself. Paul's shock at this negative development is clear from his sharp and exasperated tone throughout the letter, as he rebukes them and pleads with them to make a course correction.

The "different gospel" that enticed the Galatians was the belief that it was necessary for these gentile believers effectively to become Jews, by submitting to the law of Moses, getting circumcised, and observing

various Jewish rituals and cultural markers. The complex argument of Galatians is Paul's theological counterattack against this erroneous way of thinking. In short, faith in Christ is sufficient for Jew and gentile; nothing else is required to be justified before God. By faith in Christ, all people, regardless of their ethnic or cultural heritage, are regarded as the children of Abraham and are therefore his inheritors.

An Abrupt Greeting

In all of his other letters, Paul thanks God for the churches he addresses (with the exception of 2 Corinthians, where we find praise offered to God instead), but he does not thank God for the Galatians. Instead of a thanksgiving, Paul begins with a blunt rebuke. The Galatians have turned to a different gospel from the one Paul preached to them (Gal. 1:6–7), and this is disastrous. The letter's abrupt beginning and striking omission reveal the tone of the letter as a whole and the gravity of the situation it addresses.

Paul's Letter to the Galatians is dramatic, bold, and fiery. Its incendiary tone conveys Paul's seriousness as he issues a clear call for the preservation of the true gospel. Faith in Christ alone is how people are reconciled to God. It does not come through membership in a particular people group, observing certain customs, or obeying demanding rules. Christ became the curse of the law so that believers would not be condemned for their failure to keep God's standards. Moreover, those who trust in Christ are the inheritors of the promises to Abraham and have become the children of God. And as God's children, they are free and should not submit again to slavery. But such freedom is to be used for love, not for self-gratification, as believers walk by the Spirit rather than by the flesh.

Overview of Galatians

The structure of the letter falls neatly into two halves. Chapters 1–3 address the key polemical issue of justification by faith, while chapters 4–6 address the themes of sonship and spiritual freedom in Christ.

Galatians 1–3

- Paul accuses his readers of turning from the one true gospel, which he had taught them. He asserts that there is no other gospel than the one he preached to them, and he knows this because it was revealed to him directly by Christ (1:6–12).
- In support of this claim, Paul recounts his own story, beginning with his persecution of the church and his advancement within Judaism and continuing through to the calling of God to preach Christ among the gentiles (1:13–16a).
- Paul stresses that he was not dependent on the other apostles to learn the gospel, but when he went to Jerusalem after fourteen

years, they agreed that Paul would preach to the gentiles, who were not required to be circumcised in order to belong to the church (1:16b–2:10).

- But Paul opposed Cephas (Peter) when he came to Antioch, because Peter had come under the influence of "the circumcision party" and distanced himself from gentile believers. Paul told Peter that both Jews and gentiles are justified by faith in Christ, not by keeping the Jewish law (2:11–21).
- Paul argues that the Galatians received the Spirit by faith, not by works. Those with the faith of Abraham are Abraham's sons and daughters, having been justified by faith like he was (3:1–9).
- Those who rely on the works of the law are under a curse, but Christ redeemed us from the curse of the law by becoming a curse for us (3:10–13).
- The inheritance belonging to Abraham's descendants comes by faith, not by the law, which was given 430 years after the promises God made to Abraham. The function of the law was to highlight sin, but it does not undo God's promise, which comes by faith in Christ (3:14–26).
- In Christ there is no Jew or Greek, slave or free, male or female—all are one in Christ Jesus (3:27–28).

Galatians 4–6

- Paul argues that God sent his Son to redeem those under the law so that they would be adopted as sons and daughters and know God as Father (4:1–7).
- Rather than enslaving themselves all over again, the Galatians ought to be like Paul, though the false teachers have tried to drive a wedge between him and them (4:8–20).
- Paul then engages in an extended allegory based on Abraham's two sons—one born of a slave, the other of a free woman. Hagar represents the Mosaic covenant, which creates slaves to the law, while Sarah represents the new covenant, which brings freedom (4:21–27).
- Believers are children of the promise and the Spirit, but they will be persecuted by those born of the flesh (4:28–31).
- Paul exclaims that it is for freedom that Christ set us free. But the Galatians will become slaves if they try to keep the law of Moses, while the false teachers leading them astray will pay the penalty (5:1–12).

- The Galatians should embrace their freedom but only use it for love. If they walk by the Spirit, they will not carry out the desires of the flesh (5:13–26).
- Believers will fulfill the "law of Christ" if they love one another and will reap what they sow, so they should not tire of doing good (6:1–10).
- Paul concludes by reflecting on the cross and circumcision. He will boast only in the cross of Christ, and circumcision is nothing. What matters is a new creation (6:11–18).

RECEPTION HISTORY

Galatians and the Protestant Reformation

Martin Luther depended heavily on Galatians in shaping the theology of the Protestant Reformation. First published in 1519, his lectures on Galatians showed him gravitating toward what would become known as Protestantism. His second commentary on Galatians (published in 1535) is a defense of his settled theological position. From Galatians Luther learned that adding anything to faith in Christ is a distortion of the gospel. The medieval Roman Catholic Church required many things added on to Christ for salvation. But to add to the gospel was to detract from it and would lead people into slavery instead of freedom. The issues differed from those of Paul's day, but the principle remained the same.

Exploration

The major themes of Galatians can be addressed through several dichotomies, as laid out below. The adversarial lens (e.g., "faith versus works") is fitting, given the nature of the letter as a whole. Paul mounts a case against a false gospel, and his argument proceeds by pitting a series of truths against a series of falsehoods.

Public domain / Cranach Digital Archive / Wikimedia Commons

Lucas Cranach, *Martin Luther*, 1529

True Gospel vs. False Gospel

READ GALATIANS 1:6–9

The argument of the letter begins with Paul's amazement that the Galatians are so quickly turning to "a different gospel" (1:6). The issue of the true gospel is the overarching concern of the letter as Paul's various arguments unfold in order to reaffirm it and to counter the false gospel.

This "different gospel," Paul quickly adds, is actually *no* gospel at all but a distortion of the true "gospel of Christ" (1:7). The fact that someone else could come along after Paul and preach a different gospel from the one he preached raises this question: Whom should we trust? Is Paul right, or are these other teachers right? Paul anticipates this question and immediately undercuts it by claiming that *anyone*—an angel from heaven or even Paul and his associates—who preaches a different gospel is mistaken. In fact, they are more than mistaken: they will be damned (1:8–9)!

So, the issue is not *who* but *what*. Before anyone gets into a debate about Paul's legitimacy as an apostle, or whether he has more or less authority than his opponents, Paul claims that the gospel he preaches has come *straight from Jesus himself*. It is not of human origin. It was not passed on to him by another human being. Rather, "it came by a revelation of Jesus Christ" (1:11–12). This is a tremendously bold claim that, if true, ought to resolve any debate about the gospel. If Paul is simply a vehicle for the gospel that Jesus revealed to him, any distortion of it must be rejected.

In order to support his bold claim, Paul launches into a personal narrative that demonstrates God's intervention in his life (1:13–2:10). God called him by his grace and revealed his Son to him, so that he could preach Christ among the gentiles (1:15–16a). Since his commission to preach Christ came directly from God, Paul stresses the fact that he "did not immediately consult with anyone." He didn't go to Jerusalem to see the other apostles until three years later (1:16b–18). Even then he got to know only Cephas (Peter) and James, not the other apostles (1:18–19). The point again is that Paul's commission to preach the gospel came directly from God.

After fourteen years, Paul went again to Jerusalem and presented to the church leaders the gospel he had been preaching to the gentiles. The leadership acknowledged his legitimacy as an apostle to the gentiles and did not require him to alter his gospel. They recognized the grace of God given to Paul and affirmed their fellowship (2:1–10). Though Paul did not depend on human verification of the divinely revealed gospel he preached, it was given to him nonetheless, demonstrating that he was in harmony with the other leaders of the church.

The relative insignificance of human authority is further underscored as Paul recounts his opposition to the apostle Peter in 2:11–14. He claims that when Peter visited Paul's home of Antioch, he effectively undermined both Paul's gospel and the consensus reached among the apostles in Jerusalem. This account achieves two things for Paul's argument. First, it shows that human apostles can make mistakes, which again (implicitly) asserts the authority of Paul's gospel—since it came directly from Christ, not from human apostolic authority. Second, it introduces the presenting issue at the heart of the false gospel that Paul counteracts in the letter: the supposed need for gentile believers to become Jews.

Peter's preference for table fellowship with Jewish believers, to the neglect of gentiles, was, for Paul, a deviation from the truth of the gospel (2:14). The privileging of Jews over gentiles revealed a faulty understanding of the implications of the gospel. Instead of recognizing that all are of equal standing before God in Christ, Peter had unwittingly undermined gentile status. The true gospel, however, affirms that justification comes not through keeping the law of Moses but by faith in Jesus Christ (2:16). This was foretold by Scripture when it "proclaimed the gospel ahead of time to Abraham, saying, 'All the nations will be blessed through you.'" All who have faith like Abraham are blessed (3:8–9).

According to Galatians, Paul's gospel announces that all people are justified—declared right with God—through faith in Jesus. Justification is not granted on the basis of becoming a Jew, keeping the law of Moses, or getting circumcised. It was the alteration of this gospel that prompted Paul to write the letter, calling the Galatians to return to the one true gospel—not because Paul says so, but because his gospel comes directly from God.

Faith vs. Works

READ GALATIANS 2:15–16

At the heart of Paul's discussion of the gospel is the issue of faith versus works. After his account of rebuking Peter in 2:11–14, Paul acknowledges their common Judaism—"We are Jews by birth and not 'gentile sinners'"—but then states that even "*we*" are "justified by faith in Christ and not by the works of the law." Indeed, no one can be justified by works of the law (2:15–16).

Paul thus frames the "faith versus works" discussion in terms of Jew-gentile relations. The modern tendency to interpret "works" as any good deed is not so much wrong as missing the immediate point. Paul is primarily interested in showing that Jews and gentiles are justified the same way, and it's not by keeping the law of Moses—a central marker of Jewish identity. In other words, gentile believers do not need to become Jews in order to be right with God.

Paul states somewhat cryptically, "For through the law I died to the law, so that I might live for God" (2:19). It is not yet clear what the phrase "I died to

THEOLOGICAL ISSUES 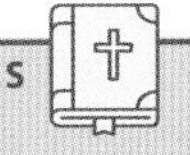

Works of the Law

There is some debate as to what "works" or "works of the law" refer to in Paul's argument. While traditional Protestant interpretation has understood works of the law to refer to obedience to the law of Moses, some scholars associated with the New Perspective on Paul have argued that Paul primarily has in mind those elements that demonstrate membership in the people of Israel and participation in the covenant that God established between himself and Israel. An issue such as circumcision would then be regarded as a "badge" of covenant membership. This distinction raises the question of whether Paul is countering the view that believers must perform good deeds to be right with God or the view that they must become Jews to be right with God. A mediating position is best, so that works of the law demand obedience, while also signaling Jewish identity and membership in the covenant of Israel. Paul's argument, therefore, is that believers are justified solely through their faith in Christ and that no human credentials can achieve justification—whether they include good deeds or a certain identification.

the law" means, or how that happened "through the law." It will, however, become clearer as the argument progresses, beginning with the next statement, "I have been crucified with Christ, and I no longer live, but Christ lives in me" (2:20a). The notion of crucifixion will become important in the following chapter, especially in relation to the law. For now, it is clear that Paul lives by faith in Jesus, who died for him. But if righteousness comes through the law, "then Christ died for nothing" (2:20b–21).

Since Abraham was credited with righteousness by believing God, those who have faith are Abraham's sons and daughters and are blessed as he was (3:7–9). But those who rely on the works of the law are under a curse, because "everyone who does not do everything written in the book of the law is cursed" (3:10; cf. Deut. 27:26). In other words, if you are going to try to keep the law, you have to keep *all* of it, and since no one can do that, you will find yourself under the curse of the law. No one can be justified before God by the law, since righteousness comes by faith (3:11).

Now crucifixion reenters the argument, as Paul states that "Christ redeemed us from the curse of the law by becoming a curse for us, because it is written, 'Cursed is everyone who is hung on a tree'" (3:13; Deut. 21:23). This pregnant statement is full of significance for Paul's argument, so it is important to unpack it. If we take it in reverse order, Paul regards crucifixion as being "hung on a tree," which means that Jesus was "cursed," in accordance with Deuteronomy 21:23. By being crucified, Jesus therefore became "a curse for us," indicating that his crucifixion was in some sense on our behalf. By becoming a curse for us, "Christ redeemed us from the curse of the law."

This now sheds light on the cryptic statements introduced above, that through the law Paul has died to the law and that he has been crucified with Christ (2:19–20). The logic is that the law condemned him, since no one can keep it and therefore he was under its curse (3:10). But being "crucified with Christ" means that the curse upon him has been borne by Christ, and since Paul regards himself as cocrucified with Christ, he has died, meaning that the law no longer has any claim on him. Its curse has been fulfilled and taken away, so Paul has "died to the law."

It is a knotty and complex argument, but being crucified with Christ, and therefore no longer being under the curse of the law, goes deep into Paul's theology of the gospel. It also explains why works of the law are now irrelevant

THEOLOGICAL ISSUES

Crucified with Christ

Paul relies heavily on the notion of being "crucified with Christ" (2:20) for his argument concerning his relationship to the law of Moses. This notion expresses Paul's theology of participation with Christ, in which believers share in the crucial events of Christ's narrative, such as his death, burial, resurrection, and ascension. Participation in Christ's crucifixion means that Paul has spiritually died with Christ and therefore has been released from the law's sentence of death. Paul no longer lives, but Christ lives in him (2:19–20). Participation with Christ thus enables Paul's death to the law and his subsequent life in the Spirit of Christ.

for justification, and why relying on them is dangerous. It can only be by faith in Christ—the one who suffered the law's curse through crucifixion—that believers can avoid the curse that comes with failing to keep the law and maintain a right standing with God.

While this is enough to resolve the issue of faith versus works, Paul does not leave it there. He then goes into apologetics mode and explains the role of the law in the plan of God. Why was the law given? "It was added for the sake of transgressions" until the coming of Christ (3:19). It functioned to point out human sin and failure, effectively imprisoning God's people "until the coming faith was revealed" (3:22–23). In this sense, the law was a placeholder that pointed to the need for rescue, so that when the time was right, "we could be justified by faith" (3:24). But now, those "trying to be justified by the law are alienated from Christ" (5:4).

New Covenant vs. Mosaic Covenant

READ GALATIANS 3:17–18

The distinction between faith and works leads directly into the distinction between the old and new covenants. Paul states that the law belongs to the Mosaic covenant, which has been fulfilled in Christ. While works of the law indicated participation in the Mosaic covenant, faith in Christ indicates participation in the new covenant.

Paul argues for the legitimacy of the new covenant by demonstrating its continuity with God's covenant with Abraham, which precedes the giving of the law. God promised Abraham, "All the nations will be blessed through you" (3:8; cf. Gen. 12:3; 18:18), and Paul concludes that those who share the faith of Abraham will share in his blessing (3:7–9). The law, however, "came 430 years later," and it "does not invalidate a covenant previously established by God and thus cancel the promise" (3:17). In other words, God's promise that the nations would be blessed through Abraham, by having the faith of Abraham, is not undermined by the later coming of the law. The inheritance promised to Abraham's descendants, therefore, relies not on the law but on God's promise (3:18).

By this stage of the argument, the "law" has become shorthand for the Mosaic covenant, while

CANONICAL CONNECTIONS

Abrahamic vs. Mosaic Covenants

Moses—and the covenant he mediated between God and Israel after their redemption from slavery in Egypt—dominated the Judaism of Paul's day. While the earlier patriarch Abraham remained important—since Jews were regarded as the children of Abraham—his significance tended to be overshadowed by the covenant of Moses and its 613 laws. Paul's argument, however, is that *Abraham*, rather than Moses, is the more important figure. This is because God's covenant with Abraham is prior to the Mosaic covenant and extends beyond it. While the new covenant established by Christ brings the old (Mosaic) covenant to an end, it renews the Abrahamic covenant. Christ's death fulfilled the curse of the law of Moses, bringing its requirements to completion. But it also opened up the way of justification by faith to Jews and gentiles, thus fulfilling God's promise to Abraham that all the nations would be blessed through him. And since the Abrahamic covenant remains in effect—while the Mosaic covenant has become obsolete—its requirement of faith remains, while the law of Moses is no longer in effect.

Benjamin West, *Hagar and Ishmael*, 1776

"promise" refers to the Abrahamic covenant and, by extension, the new covenant. Paul now explains the point of the law, which was to imprison everything under sin's power, "so that the promise might be given on the basis of faith in Jesus Christ to those who believe" (3:22). Beforehand, the law (and the Mosaic covenant to which it belonged) functioned as a guardian, or babysitter, until Christ came. But once he came, the guardian is no longer necessary (3:24–25). The law and the old Mosaic covenant were not, therefore, opposed to the plan and promises of God but played a vital role. It is important to understand that role, however, so that believers do not put themselves under a guardian they no longer need.

In perhaps the most challenging section of the letter, Paul engages in an extended allegory to contrast the old and new covenants (4:21–31). The allegory begins by comparing the two sons of Abraham—one born to a slave woman (Hagar) and the other to a free woman (Sarah). The first son (Ishmael) was born "as a result of the flesh" because Abraham took it upon himself to fulfill God's promise to him. The second son (Isaac) was born according to the promise because he was miraculously conceived (4:22–23). Paul then focuses on the two mothers as representatives of the two covenants. Hagar represents Mount Sinai—where the Mosaic covenant was established with Israel through Moses—which also corresponds to the present Jerusalem. Sarah represents the new covenant and "the Jerusalem above" (4:24–26). The result of the allegory is to claim that true believers are like Isaac, born as children of promise, as the fruit of God's promise and action rather than the fruit of human effort to keep the law (4:28).

Sons vs. Slaves

READ GALATIANS 4:1–7

The two covenants lead to very different outcomes for those under them. Those under the Mosaic covenant are slaves, while those under the new covenant are God's sons and daughters. To begin, Paul asserts that "those who have faith are Abraham's sons" (3:7), and those who belong to Christ "are Abraham's seed, heirs according to the promise" (3:29). The notion of being the children of Abraham becomes important for the argument in chapter 4, as Paul likens a child to a slave in that both are under authority—the difference being that the child is the heir and "is the owner of everything" (4:1). There was a time when the people of God were "children," under slavery to the law, but now that God's Son has redeemed those under the law, they have received adoption as sons and daughters (4:3–5). There is a distinction here between a "child" and a "son" or "daughter," since the former implies someone underage, while sons and daughters are of mature age. Since they are now adopted sons and daughters, God sent the Spirit of his Son into believers' hearts, so they would call on God as Father. Believers are no longer slaves, but sons and daughters, and therefore heirs of God (4:6–7).

The allegory of 4:21–31 is also important for this theme, as it contrasts the two sons of Abraham: one "was born as a result of the flesh," while the other "was born through promise" (4:22–23). As noted above, their respective mothers represent the two covenants (4:24). Like Isaac—Abraham's son by promise—believers are children of promise and will be persecuted by those born of the flesh (4:28–29). Since believers are children of the free woman (4:31) and have been set free by Christ, they are not to submit to a yoke of slavery (5:1).

Spirit vs. Flesh

READ GALATIANS 5:16–18

With a slightly mocking tone, Paul asks the Galatians if they received the Spirit "by the works of the law or by believing" the gospel they heard (3:2). Since in fact they began with the latter—belief—he asks if they are going to try to finish "by the flesh." Does God give the Spirit because of their works of the law (3:3–5)? While these questions serve Paul's argument about faith versus works (see above), they also introduce the theme of the Spirit, which is picked up again later in the letter.

God put the Spirit of his Son into the hearts of believers (4:6), who have been born by the Spirit (4:29). As such, believers are to "walk by the Spirit" rather than carry out the desire of the flesh (5:16). The flesh is in conflict with the Spirit; they are "opposed to each other, so that you don't do what you want" (5:17). Being led by the Spirit, however, means that believers do not rely on the law to know what to do (5:18).

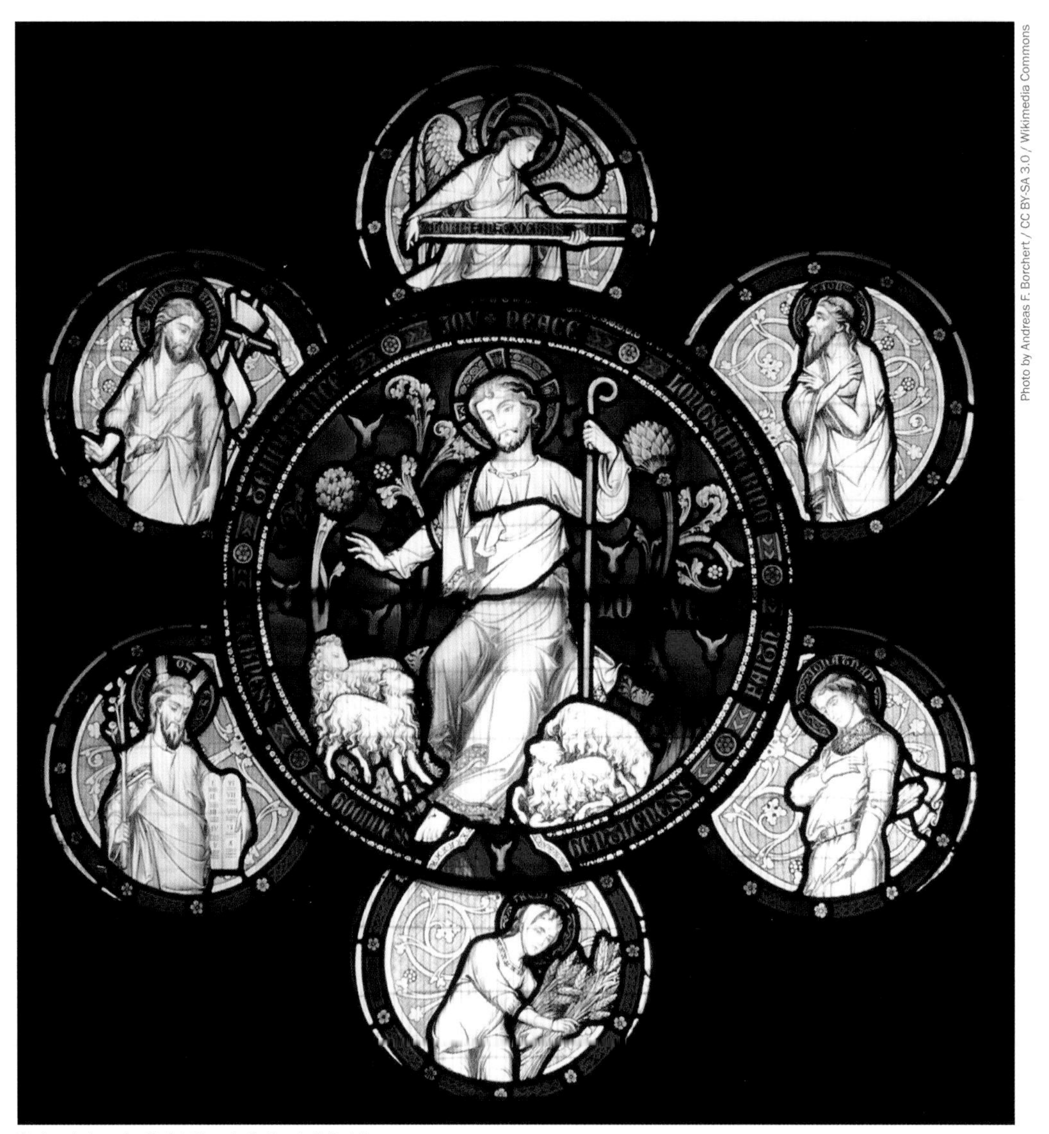

Stained glass in Christ Church Cathedral, Dublin

Paul recounts some of the works of the flesh in a vice list that includes sexual immorality, idolatry, and envy (5:19–21a). He warns that those living by such works "will not inherit the kingdom of God" (5:21b), which, given the inheritance theme already seen in the letter, likely means that such living reveals that a person is not a genuine son or daughter of God.

The fruit of the Spirit, however, includes love, peace, and gentleness (5:22–23a). Paul adds that "the law is not against such things," revealing that the Spirit takes the place of the law as the guide for the sons and daughters of God to live by. Living by the Spirit will prevent believers from falling into fleshly vices (5:25–26). Indeed, the one who sows according to the flesh will reap destruction, but the one who sows according to the Spirit will reap eternal life (6:8).

Putting It Together

The themes of Galatians work together in a (sometimes confusing) interlocking fashion. At the heart of it, Paul affirms that those in Christ live under a new covenant, which is the fulfillment of God's promises to Abraham. The Mosaic covenant, which came after Abraham, does not supplant Abraham but is supplanted by Christ. In this way, the new covenant is not entirely new, but reaches back to Abraham and therefore is more enduring than the Mosaic covenant, which played a role for a time—but that time is now over.

The law belongs to the Mosaic covenant, which is why it is no longer appropriate for God's people. The era of the Mosaic covenant is over and so, therefore, is the era of the law. The era of the new covenant is defined by the promise of God, both to Abraham and in Christ.

Those who put themselves under the law seek to be justified by the works of the law. But since the new covenant is defined by promise, not by works, the proper response is to believe God's promise and rely on him rather than human deeds. Those who do so are justified by faith, not works. Those who seek to be justified by works of the law are powered by human flesh, but those who have faith in the promise of God are powered by the Spirit of God.

This can be summarized by the following schematic:

Mosaic covenant/law/works/flesh
versus
new covenant/promise/faith/Spirit

Living by the Spirit empowers believers to live according to love, and they thus fulfill the intent of the law without being governed by it (6:2). But anyone getting circumcised in order to obey the law misunderstands the whole situation. That is why the whole Letter to the Galatians rails against the false gospel that requires gentiles to become Jews. They are justified by faith in Christ by the power of the Spirit, not by trying to obey the law, which leads to death.

Implementation

Paul's Letter to the Galatians has several implications for life today. Though the issue of gentiles wanting to become Jews through circumcision is not prevalent today (I presume), there are parallel traps that believers might fall into.

One type of trap might be characterized as "gospel plus." This occurs when it is claimed that being a genuine Christian requires faith in Christ *plus* other things. Perhaps it is denominational membership, or belonging to the "correct" theological tribe, or abstaining from alcohol. Perhaps it is the expectation that you'll maintain regular private devotions, or that you're a member of a small-group Bible study. Perhaps it is the requirement to tithe a certain amount each week. While none of these requirements seem as dramatic as circumcision (!), they nevertheless could pose a similar threat. If believers are hoodwinked into thinking that their standing with God depends on *anything* alongside their genuine faith in Christ, they will in effect turn to a false gospel such as the one that Paul denounces in this letter.

On the other hand, an equal and opposite mistake is to think that God does not expect his people to live a certain way. After all, it might be claimed, since "gospel plus" is a false gospel, all I need to do is believe in Jesus—it doesn't matter what else I do. If I put too much stock in good deeds, I might fall into a "gospel plus" way of thinking. But Paul makes it clear that believers are to keep in step with the Spirit and not gratify the desires of the flesh. Sowing according to the Spirit leads to life, while sowing according to the flesh reaps death. The expectation to keep in step with the Spirit is not a "gospel plus" type of issue, because it is not a requirement for justification. On the contrary, it is possible only if a person has already *been* justified. As the letter articulates, God gives his Spirit to those who have been justified through faith in Christ. The Spirit then empowers believers to live according to the family likeness. Keeping in step with the Spirit is possible only once a person *has* the Spirit, and this happens only once a person is justified by faith in Christ. So that obviously means that keeping in step with the Spirit cannot be a requirement for justification, or a "gospel plus" issue. It is an expectation of those who have the Spirit, who has come subsequent to justification.

In light of these issues, it is apparent that knowledge of the Old Testament, the history of Israel, and God's covenants with his people is essential for understanding the argument of Galatians. Most of Paul's argument simply draws on these themes and shows how they relate to Christ. But it is not understanding Galatians alone that is at stake; it is understanding the gospel itself. Without some appreciation of everything that happened *before* Christ entered the world, it would be impossible to understand his significance for believers today. Suffice to say, Galatians underscores the serious need for believers to study their *whole* Bibles as Christian Scripture.

Christian Reading Questions

1. Christians today are sometimes confused about how to relate to the Old Testament law, summarized by the Ten Commandments. Drawing on the argument of Galatians, how would you address the issue?
2. Try to put into your own words the point of the allegory in Galatians 4:21–31.
3. What insights does the New Perspective on Paul offer our reading of Galatians?

PART 3

Paul's Second Mission

CHAPTER SEVEN

Introduction to Paul's Second Mission

Chronology of Part 3: Paul's Second Mission (ca. 49–52)

ca. 49	Overland from Syrian Antioch through Galatia
ca. 49	Churches in Philippi, Thessalonica, and Berea
ca. 49	The visit to Athens
50–52	Eighteen months in Corinth
50	1 and 2 Thessalonians written in Corinth
52	A quick trip to Ephesus
52	Return to Syrian Antioch

Setting Out Again

Paul's second mission began with a dispute. He suggested to Barnabas that they go back to Galatia and check in on the believers who had turned to Christ during their first mission to the area. But Barnabas wanted to bring his cousin John Mark, who had abandoned them during the first mission. Paul refused, causing a sharp dispute and split with Barnabas. Barnabas and John Mark went back to Cyprus, while Paul teamed up with a new partner, Silas, and off they went (Acts 15:36–41).

This time, rather than sailing to the south of Türkiye and trekking into the interior like last time, Paul and Silas walked north from their home base in Syrian Antioch, then west into lower central Türkiye. They revisited Derbe and Lystra from the first mission, and met Timothy in Lystra. Timothy would become a very important partner in Paul's ministry and a close

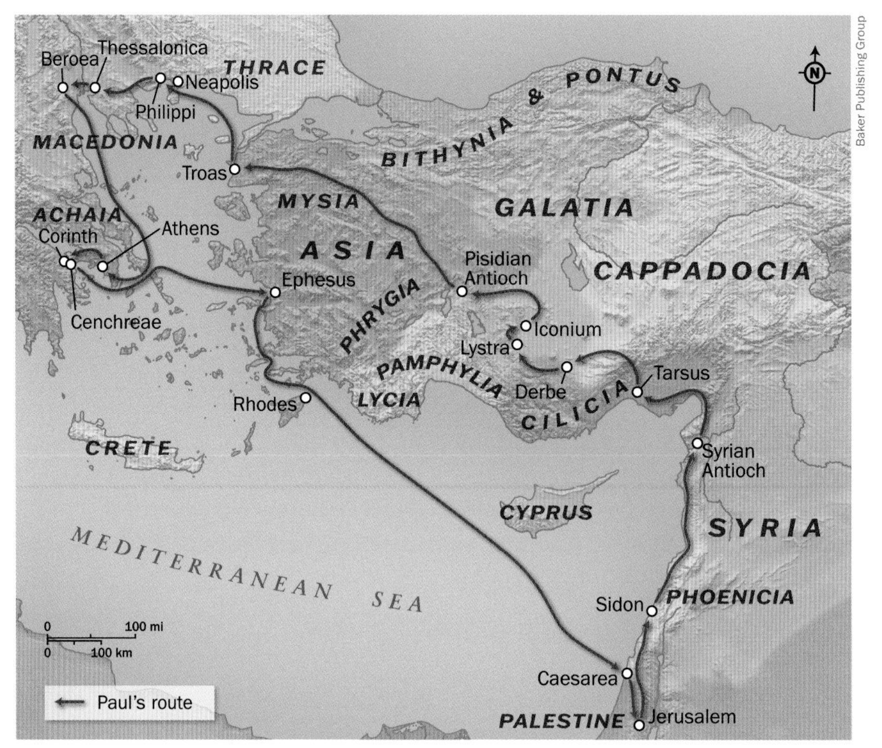

Paul's second missionary journey

friend, and he tagged along with Paul and Silas as they continued their mission (16:1–5). After trekking through various towns in Phrygia and Galatia, they headed north and farther west, arriving at Troas, the very edge of Türkiye and of the East (16:6–8). This was just the first time Paul walked from one end of Türkiye to the other.

Philippi

In Troas, Paul had a vision of a Macedonian man beckoning him, "Cross over to Macedonia and help us!" This prompted the missionaries to go there, which represented a major threshold for the gentile mission, since Macedonia was in Europe. While much of Paul's future ministry would take place within Europe, he had never set foot there until now. They sailed a short distance across to Macedonia and ended up in the Roman colony of Philippi. On the Sabbath, by a river, the missionaries led their first European resident to faith in Jesus, as Lydia and her household were baptized (Acts 16:9–15).

After expelling a spirit from a slave girl that had enabled her to predict the future and earn money for her owners, Paul and Silas were dragged into the marketplace of Philippi to be judged by the magistrates. Though the slave girl's owners were motivated by anger over their lost income, they claimed that Paul and Silas were upsetting the city by promoting customs illegal for Romans to engage in. The crowd turned on the missionaries, who were stripped, beaten, flogged, and thrown in jail (16:16–24). But at midnight an earthquake shook the foundations of the jail, loosening the prisoners' chains and flinging the doors open. The jailer was about to kill himself because he thought he'd lost his prisoners when Paul called out to let him know that they were all still there. The jailer was so relieved and affected by this that he asked how he might be saved. He and his whole family believed in the Lord Jesus and were baptized (16:25–34).

HISTORICAL MATTERS

Ancient Philippi

In 356 BC, Philip II of Macedonia formally established the city of Philippi, which bears his name, out of interest in the nearby gold and silver mines at Mount Pangaeus. The city came under Roman rule in 168–167 BC, and it became a major hub for travelers along the Via Egnatia—the new Roman road connecting Byzantium with the ports of the Adriatic Sea that led to Italy. After a nearby battle in 42 BC, Mark Antony settled many of his army veterans at Philippi and refounded Philippi as a Roman colony. After the Battle of Actium in 31 BC, Philippi received more Italian settlers and was founded anew, receiving its formal name, Colonia Julia Augusta Philippensis. The city was conferred with the possession of "Italic right," which meant that its colonists enjoyed the same rights and privileges as if their land were part of Italian soil.

Philippi

POSTCARDS FROM THE MEDITERRANEAN

Lydia's Philippi

The ancient city of Philippi is now part of Greece, not Macedonia, and is well worth a visit. The city center has been excavated, along with the marketplace, theater, and prison (possibly where Paul spent a night). Outside the city area, the location by the river where Paul met Lydia is marked and commemorated with a tribute to her. Nearby is a beautiful small church that records Paul's missionary journeys in a mosaic floor in the entry of the church. And inside the walls are frescoes that record the major points of Paul's life and ministry.

Lydia's shrine

HISTORICAL MATTERS

Roman Citizenship

Not all who lived in the Roman Empire were Roman citizens. It was a privileged political and legal status afforded to free individuals. Among several other rights, such as the right to vote (for men), Roman citizens enjoyed certain protections throughout the empire. They had the right to a legal trial if required, as well as the right to appeal the decisions of magistrates. They could not be tortured or whipped. If found guilty of treason and sentenced to death, Roman citizens could not be crucified. In Philippi, Paul and Silas were beaten and imprisoned without a trial, which was a serious breach of their rights as citizens.

Possible site where Paul was imprisoned

The next morning the situation changed when Paul revealed that he and Silas were Roman citizens. They had been beaten and thrown in jail without a trial, which was wholly inappropriate treatment for citizens. The magistrates were alarmed by this news and escorted Paul and Silas out of prison, urging them to leave town. After a final visit to Lydia's house, the missionaries moved on (16:35–40).

Thessalonica and Berea

The next stop was Thessalonica, on the northeastern coast of today's Greece. Paul preached in the synagogue on three Sabbaths, and a number of Jews and Greeks believed, including a number of leading women. But other Jews became jealous and started a riot in the city. They dragged Jason—the missionaries' host—before the city officials, accusing him of welcoming those who have "turned the world upside down" by claiming a rival to Caesar, King Jesus. This upset the crowd and officials, but they let Jason and the others go (Acts 17:1–9).

After Thessalonica, the missionaries visited Berea, farther to the west, where Paul preached in the synagogue. Luke describes the Bereans as

Roman ruins in Thessalonica

being "of more noble character than those in Thessalonica, since they received the word with eagerness and examined the Scriptures daily" to check Paul's message against the Scriptures. But some Jews from Thessalonica came down to Berea to cause a stir there as they had done in their own city. Paul was hurried away with escorts who took him to Athens, while Silas and Timothy stayed put for the time being (17:10–15).

Athens

In Athens, Paul encountered a city full of idols. He spoke with the Jews in the synagogue as well as with Greeks in the marketplace. This led some Epicurean and Stoic philosophers to invite Paul to address the council of the Areopagus, where Athenians and others listened to speakers and debated new ideas (Acts 17:16–21).

READ ACTS 17:22–31

Paul began his address to the Areopagus council by appealing to their interest in religion, objects of worship, and altars, including one dedicated "to an unknown god." He exploited this admission of ignorance (there is clearly at least one god whom the Athenians do not know about) in order to proclaim to them the God who created all things and transcends human-made shrines. Rather than needing anything from us, this God gives us everything we need and is sovereign over our lives. His intention is that people might seek and find him, "for we are also his offspring," as the Athenians' own poets had said. This God has overlooked previous ignorance of him and now calls all people to turn to him before the appointed day when he will judge the world through the man he has appointed to the task by his resurrection from the dead. Mention of the resurrection of the dead

HISTORICAL MATTERS

The Areopagus

The Areopagus, or "Mars Hill" for Romans, is a rock outcrop that sits below the Acropolis in Athens. The council of the Areopagus met on the rock in order to govern Athens and to discuss various ideas, especially philosophical and religious. It held influence over a variety of aspects of Athenian life, such as philosophy, education, morality, and foreign religions. Given the council's curiosity about new ideas, Paul's strange foreign religion would have offered much interest.

On the Areopagus with the Acropolis of Athens in the background

THEOLOGICAL ISSUES

Areopagus vs. Pisidian Antioch

When Paul preaches at the Areopagus, his approach and content are strikingly different from his first recorded sermon, given at the synagogue in Pisidian Antioch during his first mission (Acts 13). The latter is perfectly tailored for his Jewish audience through its appeal to salvation history, as Paul points to God's workings through the history of Israel as well as his promises recorded in Scripture. But for his Greek audience, which does not share Paul's conceptual universe, he begins at a starting point they understand, employs a text they know, and creates a bridge to explain what they don't know. Both sermons arrive at Jesus's resurrection from the dead.

Raphael, *St. Paul Preaching in Athens*, 1516

prompted some ridicule but also further interest. And some believed, including Dionysius, a member of the council of the Areopagus (17:22–34).

Corinth

Paul next went west to Corinth, where he would spend more time than anywhere else on his second mission. He met a Jewish couple, Aquila and Priscilla, who had left Rome due to Emperor Claudius's expulsion of all Jews from the city around AD 49. Paul lived and worked with his new friends, who, like him, were tentmakers by trade, and he spoke in the synagogue every Sabbath (Acts 18:1–4).

When Paul's support crew—Silas and Timothy—arrived in Corinth, he devoted himself to preaching. After being rejected by the Jews—though Crispus, the leader of the synagogue, believed—Paul turned to preaching to the gentiles in a house next to the synagogue, and many believed.

HISTORICAL MATTERS

Ancient Corinth

The city of Corinth was virtually destroyed in 146 BC. Its male population was exterminated and its women and children were sold into slavery. This devastating event was executed by the Roman consul Lucius Mummius as payback for the city's revolt against Rome. Julius Caesar rebuilt Corinth in 44 BC and resettled it as a Roman colony with army veterans and freedmen (former slaves) from poorer elements of society. At its height, Corinth numbered around 500,000 slaves and 200,000 nonslaves with a population made up of local Greeks, Easterners (including many Jews), and Italians. The renewed Corinth became a thriving city of new wealth and might be compared to "hip" cities like San Francisco, Chicago, or Boston.

HISTORICAL MATTERS

Jews Expelled from Rome

Three early sources refer to Emperor Claudius's expulsion of the Jews from Rome: Acts 18:2 and the Roman historians Suetonius (ca. AD 69–122) and Cassius Dio (ca. AD 150–235). Jews had been expelled from Rome twice before, in 139 BC and AD 19. This time, the expulsion appears to have been related to Jesus. Suetonius wrote, "Since the Jews constantly made disturbance at the instigation of Chrestus, he expelled them from Rome" (*Life of Claudius* 25.4). Many scholars agree that "Chrestus" likely refers to "Christus." It's not clear whether the disruption was from Jewish Christians or Jews who were objecting to Christianity. It's likely that Rome did not yet distinguish between Jews and the Jewish Jesus movement at this time, so it's difficult to have clarity around the reasons for the expulsion.

POSTCARDS FROM THE MEDITERRANEAN

Corinth

The archaeological site at Corinth is one of the best Greco-Roman cities to visit today. Much of the city has been excavated, and the scenery is spectacular, with the Temple of Apollo sitting at the foot of the Acrocorinth ("Upper Corinth"), an ancient acropolis built on a gray limestone monolithic rock that towers above the city. A trek to the top of the Acrocorinth offers stunning views of the region, including the Corinth Canal (built in 1882–93), which cuts across the Isthmus of Corinth, connecting the Corinthian Gulf to the Aegean Sea.

Constantine R. Campbell

Corinth, with the Acrocorinth in the background

HISTORICAL MATTERS

The Importance of Gallio

Gallio was the proconsul of the Roman province of Achaia—or governor of the southern part of what is Greece today. He was the elder brother of the Stoic philosopher Seneca the Younger and was known for his anti-Semitism, which resonates with his depiction in Acts 18:12–17. Gallio's mention here helps to establish the dating of Paul's life and travels. As a proconsul, his term would have been limited to one year, most likely July 1 AD 51 to July 1 AD 52—though illness cut his term short. Since Paul's appearance before Gallio seems to have come toward the end of his eighteen months in Corinth, this provides the most reliable date to anchor Paul's whole chronology.

Paul was encouraged by the Lord in a vision to keep speaking in Corinth, where he remained for a year and a half (18:5–11).

Toward the end of his time in Corinth, the Jews opposed Paul by appealing to the authorities, as others had done in Thessalonica (recall 17:5–8). In Corinth, they brought Paul to Gallio, the proconsul of Achaia, claiming that he was persuading people to worship God in ways contrary to the law. Gallio dismissed the Jews' complaints about Paul, refusing to get involved in internal disputes about their religion (18:12–17).

On the Way Home

Paul, Priscilla, and Aquila left Corinth and sailed across the Aegean Sea to Ephesus, on the western coast of modern-day Türkiye. It seems that Silas and Timothy did not go with them—at least, they're not mentioned. After speaking in the synagogue and raising some interest there, Paul departed but promised to return (Acts 18:18–21a), while Priscilla and Aquila apparently stayed in Ephesus (18:24–26). The visit prompted Paul's third mission, during which he spent more time in Ephesus than any other location in any of his missions. But a visit to Jerusalem and home was on the agenda first. Paul sailed from Ephesus across the Mediterranean Sea to Caesarea, on the western coast of Judea (now Israel), and went up to Jerusalem to greet the church there. Then he traveled north to his home base of Syrian Antioch (18:21b–22).

Paul's second mission enabled him to encourage existing churches in Türkiye and brought him for the first time into Europe, as he established churches up and down modern-day Greece. He reasoned with the Athenian intelligentsia—the heart of European thought and philosophy—and spent considerable time in the strategic port city of Corinth. Paul would return to most of these places on his third mission, though his priority would be elsewhere.

CHAPTER EIGHT

Philippians

Orientation

Paul first visited Philippi during his second mission around AD 49, after seeing a vision of a Macedonian man who bid him to leave Troas in Asia to come and help in Europe (Acts 16:6–10). He visited Philippi at least once more on his third mission (ca. AD 56), during a tour of the churches that were planted as a result of his previous time in Europe. The Letter to the Philippians was written considerably later than these visits, however, while Paul was under house arrest in Rome, around AD 62 (Phil. 1:7, 13–14, 17; 4:22).

While the tone of Philippians could not be more different from that of Galatians, there is a similar central concern: the gospel. While Galatians addresses a distortion of the gospel—a false gospel, in fact—Philippians calls its readers to live lives "worthy of the gospel of Christ" (Phil. 1:27). Paul hopes that the Philippians will contend together "for the faith of the gospel," without fear of their opponents (1:27–28). While he warns them to avoid theological error (3:2, 18–19), Paul clearly regards the Philippians as his partners in the gospel (1:5, 7; 4:3) and takes great joy in their partnership (1:4–5; 4:10).

A Friendship Letter

Philippians contains language that resonates with ancient expectations of a letter of friendship. In his ancient handbook on letters, Demetrius describes the friendship letter as one of twenty-one types of letters, and its essential elements include the following: (1) two people are separated; (2) one person attempts to converse with the other; (3) a relationship of friendship forms between the two; and (4) the writer attempts to maintain that relationship with the recipient. While Philippians cannot be limited to one type of ancient letter, it displays these essential elements as well as ten expressions of friendship language that parallel Hellenistic letters and essays on friendship. These are expressions of affection, partnership, unity of soul and spirit, like-mindedness, companionship, mutual exchange, common struggles and joys, absence and presence, virtuous friendship, and a shared moral framework.

While Paul presents his coworkers Timothy and Epaphroditus as models of living worthy of the gospel (Phil. 2:19–30), his own life is an even more stellar example in this letter. In Philippians we witness a joyful apostle—though he is in chains (1:3–20)—who expects death to be gain because he will be with Christ

(1:21–23), who counts his achievements in Judaism as nothing compared to knowing Christ (3:1–14), and who has learned to be content in any and all circumstances (4:11). Expecting an imminent (and no doubt violent) death, Paul is nevertheless full of joy, eager for his fellow believers to shine like stars in the world, and above all focused on the glory of Christ.

Overview of Philippians

The first half of the letter focuses on the gospel of Christ and living in a manner worthy of it (chaps. 1–2). The second half of the letter addresses the differences between Paul and false teachers and makes final exhortations to the Philippians (chaps. 3–4).

Philippians 1–2

- Paul gives thanks for the Philippians and their partnership in the gospel, and prays that their love would continue to grow in knowledge (1:1–11).
- He reassures the Philippians that his imprisonment actually serves to advance the gospel and that his only concern is that Christ is preached—regardless of whether he lives or dies (1:12–26).
- As for the Philippians, Paul charges them to live lives worthy of the gospel, contending together for the gospel, without fear of opposition (1:27–30).
- They are to be united in spirit and follow Christ's example of humility, who gave up his exalted position in order to submit himself to death on a cross and was consequently exalted by God to the highest place (2:1–11).
- Paul hopes that, by following the example of Christ, the Philippians will be blameless and pure children of God who will shine like stars in the world, as Timothy and Epaphroditus exemplify (2:12–30).

Philippians 3–4

- Paul warns his readers about false teachers, who put their confidence in the flesh (through circumcision). Paul, on the other hand, puts no confidence in the flesh—including his impeccable credentials within Judaism, which are nothing compared to knowing Christ (3:1–11).
- Though he has not attained the goal, Paul continues to strive toward the prize promised in Christ. Contrary to the enemies of the cross

of Christ, Paul and the Philippians' citizenship is in heaven, and they wait for Christ to come from there (3:12–21).

- Paul urges two women within the congregation to end their dispute, and he urges all to rejoice in the Lord as they focus their attention on praiseworthy things (4:1–9).
- He again rejoices in the Philippians' partnership with him in the gospel and in their care for him, while also reflecting on his contentment in all circumstances (4:10–20).

Exploration

The Gospel of Christ

READ PHILIPPIANS 1:27–30

The gospel is the first prominent theme in the letter, as Paul thanks God for the Philippians' partnership in the gospel (1:5, 7; cf. 4:15) and focuses on how his own imprisonment has served to advance the gospel. It has become known to the whole imperial guard that Paul is imprisoned for the sake of Christ, which has spurred others on to speak more boldly (1:12–14). Accordingly, Paul exhorts his readers to live lives worthy of the gospel of Christ, which will involve their standing firm together to contend for the faith of the gospel in the face of opposition (1:27–28), just as Timothy has served with Paul in gospel ministry (2:22).

While the gospel is clearly a significant theme in the letter, Paul does not define what is meant by it. He does, however, leave some clues. As part of his affirmation that his imprisonment has served to advance the gospel, Paul comments that others have gained confidence from his experience and "dare even more to speak the word fearlessly" (1:14). Since this outcome is regarded as part of the advancement of the gospel, it seems that Paul equates speaking "the word" with the gospel. The same can be said for his discussion about preaching Christ in 1:15–18. Thus, it seems that the gospel = the word = preaching Christ.

The Humility and Exaltation of Christ

READ PHILIPPIANS 2:5–11

The most famous element of the Letter to the Philippians is the so-called Christ hymn in 2:6–11. Though there is no extant evidence that 2:6–11 once existed prior to, and independent of, Philippians, its somewhat poetic form has led scholars to identify this part of the letter as a hymn of sorts.

Whether or not this hymn was composed by Paul—either prior to writing the letter or as part of writing the letter—no one knows. All we do know is that the hymn has come to us only through this letter. And even if Paul did not originally compose it, he has of course approved and made use of it.

The Christ hymn expresses some of the highest Christology in Paul's writings, with its claim that Christ preexisted before his birth, "existing in the form of God" and sharing "equality with God" (2:6). Though there is debate about what the phrase "form of God" means (e.g., the NIV has "in very nature God"), the meaning of "equality with God" is not in doubt.

Such divine credentials are not offered simply for their own sake as an intentional christological statement but are mentioned in order to depict Christ's self-humiliation. Christ did not allow his equality with God to prevent him from lowering himself to death on a cross (2:6–8). Rather, "he emptied himself by assuming the form of a servant, taking on the likeness of humanity" and became a man (2:7). Christ's self-humiliation was, therefore, more profound than anyone else's, since he lowered himself from a higher place than any other human being. No one else can claim equality with God, so it is not possible for anyone to match the depth of his condescension.

Historically, there has been debate about what is meant by the phrases "he emptied himself" and "taking on the likeness of humanity." While some have taken the first phrase to mean that Christ somehow "gave up" his deity,

RECEPTION HISTORY

John Chrysostom on Jesus's Human Likeness

Reflecting on Philippians 2:7, the major fourth-century preacher John Chrysostom asked,

> What does it mean to be in a human likeness? Does it mean that [Jesus's] appearance was merely a fantasy? This would be something merely similar to a human and not made "in the likeness of a man." For to be made "in the likeness of a man" is to be a man. . . . So what does it mean, "in human likeness"? With few exceptions he had all our common human properties. The exceptions: He was not born from sexual intercourse. He committed no sin. These properties he had which no human being has. He was not only human, which is what he appeared to be, but also God. . . . We are soul and body, but he is God, soul and body. For this reason Paul says "in the form"—and so that when you hear of his emptying you may not suppose that he underwent change, degradation and some sort of annihilation of his divinity. Rather remaining what he was he assumed what he was not. Becoming flesh, he remained the Word of God. So it is in this respect that he is in the likeness of men, and for this reason he says "and in form." His nature was not degraded, nor was there any confusion [of the two natures], but he entered *a form.* (*Homily on Philippians* 8.2.5–11)[1]

St. John Chrysostom at Chora

this is not only theologically impossible but also textually unlikely. Its most likely meaning in this context is that Christ divested himself of his position and prestige in order to become a servant. The second phrase, "taking on the likeness of humanity," does not mean that Christ only *appeared* to be human but was not—contrary to the early christological heresy known as docetism. Rather, the following phrase clarifies that Christ "had come as a human." Thus, the context—with its inclusion of certain clarifying phrases—prevents misreading those phrases that could be taken in less-than-orthodox (or heterodox) ways.

The high Christology of the Christ hymn serves to underscore the depth of Christ's humility as he left the Father's side; became a servant, a human; and "humbled himself by becoming obedient to the point of death" (2:7–8). The hymn adds an even lower point of humiliation—"even to death on a cross"—since crucifixion was shameful both to Romans and to Jews. Thus, not only did Christ humble himself in order to serve humanity by becoming a man and dying; he went to the lowest place reserved for the most shameful criminals, murderers, and rebels.

Having established the extreme humiliation of Christ—to the point of shameful crucifixion—the hymn abruptly turns to his exaltation. God "highly exalted" Christ "for this reason"—no doubt referring to his self-humiliation. Because Christ lowered himself to death on a cross, God lifted him to the highest place, giving him the name above every name (2:9). We are told that at the name of Jesus every knee will bow "in heaven and on earth and under the earth" and "every tongue will confess that Jesus Christ is Lord" (2:10–11). This language is reminiscent of enthronement passages such as Psalm 2 and Psalm 110, in which God's Messiah is exalted above all competing powers in order to rule the nations. In this sense, the Christ hymn is similar to many psalms in which the subject of the psalm experiences grief and suffering until God intervenes with salvation and blessing. Indeed, Jesus is frequently depicted in the New Testament as the "new David"—Israel's most famous and prolific psalmist. Just as King David relied on the Lord for deliverance and salvation, so David's "son" is delivered from death and exalted above all others.

CANONICAL CONNECTIONS

Isaiah's Servant of the Lord

The Servant Song of Isaiah 52:13–53:12 bears striking connections to the Christ hymn of Philippians 2:5–11. Isaiah's servant was humbled (52:14; Phil. 2:7), and he "willingly submitted to death" (53:12; Phil. 2:8), but he is exalted by God (52:13; 53:12; Phil. 2:9–11). Paul's phrase in Philippians 2:10–11—"every knee will bow . . . and every tongue will confess"—finds an echo in Isaiah 45:23. These striking parallels demonstrate that Paul views Jesus as the fulfillment of the Isaianic expectation of a great servant of the Lord who will accomplish God's redeeming work.

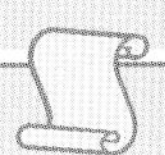

CANONICAL CONNECTIONS

The Messianic Psalms

Several of the psalms speak of the Davidic king's deliverance, exaltation, and subsequent rule under God. This king is sheltered by God (Pss. 17:8; 61:3–4), receives his victories from the strength of the Lord (21:1; 144:1–2, 10), is established by God's right hand (63:8), and participates in God's royal glory (3:3). Israelite royal ideology viewed the Lord's Messiah as invested with God's authority and power to rule (2:6–9; 89:27–29; 110:1–4). These prophetic expectations all resonate powerfully with God's exaltation of Christ, whose name is above every name and at whose feet every knee will bow as he shares the glory of God (Phil. 2:9–10).

One of the most striking things about the Christ hymn is that it is offered by way of illustration. Paul uses Christ's example to underscore his instruction, "Do nothing out of selfish ambition or conceit, but in humility consider others as more important than yourselves" (2:3). Believers' humility is to come by adopting "the same attitude as that of Christ Jesus" (2:5). Of course, the hymn takes on its own significance as an extremely important piece of Christology, but it is important to remember its primary exhortatory purpose.

Living for Christ

READ PHILIPPIANS 2:1–4

The Philippians are to look to Christ not only as an example of service and humility but as the Lord for whom they are to live. Paul begins by reflecting on his own desire to live for Christ, hoping that "Christ will be highly honored in my body, whether by life or by death" (1:20). In a compressed turn of phrase, he adds, "For me, to live is Christ and to die is gain" (1:21). This means that if he goes on living, he will engage in fruitful work in service of Jesus—*to live is Christ*. And if he dies, he will be with Christ, which is far better (1:23), and so it would be his gain.

Likewise, Paul charges the Philippians to live their lives in a manner worthy of the gospel of Christ (1:27). Such "worthy" living includes "standing firm in one spirit, in one accord, contending together for the faith of the gospel, not being frightened in any way by your opponents" (1:27–28). Thus, we see that living in a manner worthy of the gospel includes an internal focus (being united in spirit and accord) and an external focus (contending for the gospel among those who would oppose it). Contending for the gospel may invite suffering, but Paul regards it as a gift to suffer for Christ (1:29).

Next, Paul appeals to the Philippians on the grounds of the encouragement they have experienced in Christ, the consolation of his love, their fellowship with the Spirit, and the affection and mercy they have received to share the same love, being united in spirit with singular purpose (2:1–2). They are to resist acting out of selfish ambition or conceit and instead are to exercise humility in service of others, following the example of Christ (2:3–5). In light of his example, the Philippians are to do everything without grumbling and arguing and are to be blameless, pure, and faultless, shining like stars in the world as they hold firm to the word of life (2:12–16).

Besides his own example of living for Christ, Paul presents Timothy and Epaphroditus as models of other-person-centered servants of Christ.

Timothy genuinely cares about the Philippians and has the interests of Jesus at heart (2:19–21). Epaphroditus was so sick that he nearly died, but he was distressed to think that the Philippians might have been worried about him (2:25–27). These two brothers demonstrate what it means to live with the same attitude as that of Christ Jesus (cf. 2:5), as Paul hopes the Philippians will.

An important element of living for Christ is to watch out for those who would distort the gospel by putting their confidence in the flesh. The genuine followers of Jesus do not do so, even if they might have impressive grounds for such confidence, as Paul does (3:2–6). Instead, Paul regards all human impressiveness, and everything else, as a loss compared to "the surpassing value of knowing Christ Jesus my Lord" (3:7–8). Paul's righteousness comes from God through faith in Christ; it does not come from any humanly derived credentials or achievements (3:9). Rather than strive for human accomplishments, Paul makes it his goal to know Christ, the power of his resurrection, and the fellowship of his sufferings. He seeks to be conformed to Christ's death, which will entail his resurrection from the dead (3:10–11).

Paul does not think that he has "arrived" or is already perfect, but he seeks "to take hold of" the prize because he has "been taken hold of by Christ Jesus." He pursues the prize that has already been promised by God in Christ (3:12–14). In other words, Paul lives for what God has already promised will be his in Christ. His desire to live for Christ is not for any self-actualized goal but is in accord with what he is certain to receive because it is dependent on the promise of God, not on human achievement. And he expects that "all of us who are mature should think this way" (3:15). The Philippians ought to imitate Paul and pay attention to those who set a similar example, because the reality is that "many live as enemies of the cross of Christ" (3:17–18). While such people are focused on earthly things and will meet destruction as their end, the Philippians' citizenship is in heaven, and Christ will transform them into the likeness of his glorious body by his divine power (3:19–21).

The big picture of living for Jesus has implications for daily life, as we see with Paul's exhortation to Euodia and Syntyche. He urges these two women "to agree in the Lord," and he hopes that the

HISTORICAL MATTERS

Paul's Jewish Credentials

In 3:4–5, Paul recounts his impeccable credentials within Judaism. He was circumcised on the prescribed day according to the law of Moses (cf. Gen. 17:12; Lev. 12:3). He belonged to the tribe of Benjamin, which was the tribe of his namesake, King Saul. While many Jews grew up with Greek customs and language, Paul describes himself as a Hebrew born of Hebrews, and he would have grown up speaking Aramaic and immersed in Jewish culture. As a Pharisee, Saul belonged to the most zealous Jewish sect regarding obedience to the law. Paul notes his Jewish credentials to demonstrate that he is highly qualified to have "confidence in the flesh" (3:4), but he does not endorse such confidence (3:3), because righteousness comes by faith in Christ (3:9). It is important to realize that Paul does not denigrate or disown his Jewish heritage per se. He does, however, regard his confidence in his Jewish credentials as misplaced and a loss compared to knowing Christ (3:7–8).

congregation will help them to do so (4:2–3). We don't know what their disagreement or dispute was about, but clearly Paul hoped that their gospel partnership would bring forth peace. Moreover, the Philippians are to be characterized in general by rejoicing, graciousness, prayer, thanksgiving, and lack of worry (4:4–7). They are to give their attention and focus to whatever is true, honorable, just, pure, lovely, commendable, excellent, and praiseworthy (4:8).

Partnership in Christ

READ PHILIPPIANS 4:14–19

A delightful characteristic of Paul's Letter to the Philippians is the evident joy he takes in their partnership with him in the work of the gospel. The letter begins with acknowledgment of this partnership, for which Paul joyfully gives thanks to God (1:3–4). The Philippians have been Paul's partners in the gospel "from the first day until now" and are his partners in grace during his imprisonment and in his defense of the gospel (1:5, 7). Paul feels genuine affection for these brothers and sisters in Christ, holding them in his heart and missing them deeply (1:7–8).

We catch a glimpse of the Philippians' partnership with Paul when he discusses Epaphroditus—his brother, coworker, and fellow soldier, and the Philippians' messenger and minister to Paul's need (2:25–26). Apparently, the Philippians had sent Epaphroditus out from them in order to serve alongside Paul. And given how much Paul treasured this coworker, it is little surprise that he is so grateful for the Philippians' partnership. They did not merely pray for Paul or send material support; they sent him a beloved brother.

But the Philippians also partnered with Paul through gift giving. This occurred from the beginning of their relationship, as they sent gifts for Paul's benefit on several occasions (4:15–16). As Paul writes, he is fully supplied via Epaphroditus, and he considers the Philippians' generosity a fragrant offering and acceptable sacrifice, pleasing to God. He is confident that they will lack for nothing, as God will supply their needs (4:18–19).

For Paul, the Philippians' partnership demonstrates their genuine love for him and their faithful commitment to the gospel. It is also a genuine partnership, in the sense that the Philippians really do participate in Paul's mission and service. They are not merely "supporters" of someone out there doing their own thing. They are actual participants in the work by virtue of their prayers, encouragement, and tangible gifts of material goods and human resources. And the Philippians' partnership is met with God's provision of their needs and Paul's joyful love.

Implementation

A huge concern of Paul's Letter to the Philippians is the importance of living in a manner worthy of the gospel of Christ. Paul presents himself as a model of this as he seeks to live out his motto, "To live is Christ and to die is gain" (1:21). Timothy and Epaphroditus are likewise worthy models. The Philippians are to emulate such models, but most importantly they are to embody the example of Christ, who humbled himself, suffered and died for the sake of others, before God exalted him to the highest place. Believers today are to do the same, knowing that service comes before exaltation, suffering before glory, and death before resurrection.

The Christocentrism of the letter undergirds its affirmation of righteousness by faith rather than righteousness through external, human factors. Paul does not rely on his exemplary Jewish heritage, nor anything else, to be right with God. Instead, he is found in Christ and enjoys the righteousness that comes from God through faith in Christ. The implications of this for us today are the same as for the Philippians: nothing derived from our own performance, heritage, or culture can establish our standing with God. Instead, we rely on the promise of God in Christ alone.

Philippians offers a beautiful picture of what genuine gospel partnership can look like. The Philippians are not disinterested donors who reluctantly respond to Paul's guilt-tripping. Their material gifts, prayers, and sharing of human resources—namely, Ephaphroditus—are expressions of their love for Paul and for Christ. Paul receives their gifts with joy because it reveals their well-natured intent and their proper grasp of the gospel of Christ. This picture of gospel partnership can shape our expectations regarding the matter of giving and receiving. In an age when some preachers and churches put the hard word on congregants, who respond begrudgingly in turn, Paul and the Philippians demonstrate a better way. Gospel partnership ought to come from the heart, inspired by love and service, not out of guilt accompanied by disinterest.

Christian Reading Questions

1. What implications follow if the so-called Christ hymn of Philippians 2:6–11 was a preexisting poem or hymn that Paul appropriated?

2. In Philippians 3:13, Paul says that he forgets what is behind and reaches forward to what is ahead. What do you think this means, and how can it be applied by the church today?
3. What are some contemporary ways that believers today might be putting "confidence in the flesh" (Phil. 3:4)? What is alluring about these things, and how can believers resist them?

CHAPTER NINE

1 and 2 Thessalonians

Orientation

Paul visited Thessalonica on his second mission, shortly after his first visit to Philippi around AD 49 (Acts 17:1–9). Though his letter to the Philippians was written several years later, his two letters to the church in Thessalonica were written soon after his first visit, in AD 50, while Paul was based in Corinth. That makes these two letters among Paul's earliest, and some scholars regard 1 Thessalonians as *the* earliest Pauline letter, predating Galatians.

Named for the half sister of Alexander the Great, Thessalonica was a major port city in ancient Macedonia and is now known as Thessaloniki—the second-most populous city in modern Greece, after Athens. Paul's first visit to Thessalonica (accompanied by Silas and Timothy) was met with severe opposition, leading to their prompt exit. While Paul traveled south to Athens and Corinth, he had sent Timothy back to Thessalonica to help the new fledgling church there (1 Thess. 3:2–3). Afterward, Timothy's reconnection with Paul in Corinth prompted him to write the first of his two letters to the church in Thessalonica.

Both letters show a strong interest in the coming of Christ, which is mentioned at the end of each chapter of 1 Thessalonians—as well as being the focus of its fourth and fifth chapters—and occupies the whole first half of 2 Thessalonians. A problem arising from the church's relative infancy is that, for the first time, they had to think through what happens to believers who die before Jesus comes again. Moreover, the Thessalonians have faced fierce persecution, causing them to anticipate

HISTORICAL MATTERS

The Crossroads of Thessalonica

Starting in AD 44, Thessalonica was the capital of Macedonia. It was a well-populated city built on a crossroads and sat near the Via Egnatia, the Roman road that spanned from Byzantium (now Istanbul in Türkiye) in the east to Dyrrachium (now Durrës in Albania) in the west, from which travelers could sail to Italy and Rome. Thessalonica also sat on the via from Philippi and various trade routes. It was, and still is, a port city with a view of Mount Olympus across the bay.

LITERARY NOTES

The Authorship of 1 and 2 Thessalonians

There is no current debate about Paul's authorship of 1 Thessalonians. Second Thessalonians, however, has come under scrutiny in recent decades, though its authenticity was not previously doubted from the early church onward. The main arguments against the Pauline authorship of 2 Thessalonians are (1) its authoritarian tone; (2) the comment in 3:17, which sounds like the author is trying too hard to assert that he is Paul; (3) supposed eschatological differences between the two letters; and (4) its apparent dependence on 1 Thessalonians. Several recent scholars have demonstrated, however, that these arguments are less persuasive than is often asserted.

the Lord's coming with eager expectation. He will bring peace and hope to the afflicted, and judgment upon their persecutors. The hope of Christ's coming enables these new believers to stand firm in the midst of suffering and confusion.

Overview of 1 and 2 Thessalonians

Paul's First Letter to the Thessalonians contains the longest thanksgiving in Paul's extant letters, occupying more than half the letter (chaps. 1–3). The remaining two chapters are concerned with eschatologically shaped living, as Paul encourages believers to conduct themselves in light of the coming of Christ.

1 Thessalonians 1–3

- Paul expresses his thankfulness for the Thessalonians' faith, love, and hope as the gospel has had its effect among them (1:2–6).
- He acknowledges how his readers have become an example to other believers in their turning away from idols to serve the living God, as they await the coming of God's Son from heaven (1:7–10).
- Paul then recalls his time with the Thessalonians, and how he treated them as his own children and encouraged them to walk worthily of God (2:1–12).
- The Thessalonians received the word of God for what it is, even in the face of persecution, which was severe enough to force Paul to leave them (2:13–20).
- From Athens, Paul sent Timothy to the Thessalonians, and he reported back of their faith and love, which in turn caused Paul to give thanks for them (3:1–13).

1 Thessalonians 4–5

- Paul encourages the Thessalonians to flee sexual immorality and exploitation—things that will incur the anger of God—and to pursue holiness, love, and a quiet life (4:1–12).
- He comforts them regarding those who have died, assuring them that God will resurrect them when Jesus comes again (4:13–18).

- The timing of Jesus's coming cannot be predicted, but believers should be ready for it and should live in the interim as children of the light characterized by faith, hope, and love (5:1–10).
- The letter concludes with a variety of exhortations, as the Thessalonians are to rejoice, pray, give thanks, and avoid evil. Paul offers a final prayer for them (5:12–24).

2 Thessalonians

Paul's Second Letter to the Thessalonians is divided into three chapters, of which the first two focus on the glorious coming of Christ, while the third addresses life in light of the end.

- Paul promises that God will relieve the Thessalonians' afflictions when the Lord Jesus, who will judge the perpetrators, is revealed in glory (1:5–10).
- He encourages the Thessalonians to not be distressed by false claims that the day of the Lord has already come. First will come "the apostasy" and the "man of lawlessness" (2:1–7).
- He assures them that the Lord Jesus will destroy the lawless one, who deceives people in cahoots with Satan, while those chosen by God will be saved (2:8–17).
- Finally, Paul exhorts his readers not to be idle but to work to provide for themselves (3:6–15).

Exploration

The Coming of Christ

READ 1 THESSALONIANS 4:16–17

The dominant theme of both letters that Paul wrote to the Thessalonians is the coming of Christ. Mentioned at the end of every chapter in 1 Thessalonians, it also features in that letter's final two chapters and the first two chapters of the second letter.

Waiting for God's Son to come from heaven is a central characteristic of the Thessalonians' behavior upon their conversion (1 Thess. 1:9–10), and Paul anticipates that they will be his joy and crown when the Lord Jesus comes (2:19). He prays that the Lord would make the Thessalonians' hearts blameless before God at the coming of Jesus (3:13).

Icon of the second coming exhibited at the Museum of Byzantine Culture, Thessaloniki, Greece

Public domain / Wikimedia Commons

In the last section of 1 Thessalonians 4, Paul reassures the Thessalonians that those brothers and sisters who have died (or are "asleep") will be raised from the dead, just as Jesus was. When the Lord comes, God will bring with him those "who have fallen asleep" (4:14), and those who are still alive at that time will "be caught up together with them in the clouds to meet the Lord in the air" (4:17). The pastoral significance of this reassurance is that believers need not "grieve like the rest, who have no hope" (4:13). Though believers will grieve over deceased loved ones, their hope of the resurrection of the dead will enable them to grieve with hope. They will be reunited when the Lord comes.

The nature of the Lord's coming is described as nowhere else in the New Testament, as Christ will descend from heaven "with a shout, with the archangel's voice, and with the trumpet of God" (4:16). These are apocalyptic descriptions, which may or may not be taken literally, but either way they underscore the dramatic and momentous nature of the occasion in view. Several Old Testament texts describe the use of the trumpet to announce the appearances of God (Exod. 19:13, 16, 19; 20:18) and the coming day of the Lord, when God will judge the wicked and save the righteous (Isa. 27:13; Joel 2:1; Zeph. 1:14–16; Zech. 9:14). The coming of Christ will announce judgment and salvation, and it will occur in a clear, public, and undeniable fashion.

In that moment, the dead in Christ will be raised, and those alive will somehow meet with them and the Lord "in the clouds . . . in the air" (4:17). Again, it is not clear whether being "in the clouds . . . in the air" is to be taken literally or whether it simply evokes the imagery of Daniel 7:13, in which "one like a son of man" approached the Ancient of Days "with the clouds of heaven." If Daniel 7:14 is understood to foretell the ascension of Jesus (who went to be with God, "the Ancient of Days"), then

1 Thessalonians 4:17 might be using similar imagery to depict his coming again from there. This imagery of meeting him in the air may also recall that of a Roman emperor being met by a welcoming party from the city into which he is about to enter. The welcoming party would accompany the emperor into their city, just as those in Christ would accompany him back to this world.

While the Lord's coming will be accompanied by the sound of the trumpet, in 1 Thessalonians 5 Paul adds that it will come "like a thief in the night" (5:2). This does not mean it will happen secretly. Rather, as with Jesus's teaching in Matthew 24:42–44, it means that the day of the Lord will come at an unexpected time. And though the Thessalonians therefore do not know when the Lord will come, they ought not to be surprised when he does come, because they are "children of light and children of the day," not belonging to the night or the darkness (5:4–5). Thus, believers are to expect the unexpected, to be ready for the coming of the Lord whenever he comes. And Paul prays that God would keep the Thessalonians sound and blameless until then (5:23).

In the Second Letter to the Thessalonians, Paul comforts them with the hope that God will give relief to the afflicted "at the revelation of the Lord Jesus from heaven with his powerful angels" (2 Thess. 1:7). The "revelation" of Jesus is another way of speaking of his coming, which will also signal his vengeance against those who don't know God or the gospel, as they face eternal destruction from his presence (1:8–9). On that day, the Lord will also be glorified and marveled at (1:10).

The issue of when Jesus will come is addressed again as Paul asks the Thessalonians not to become troubled by prophecies or messages alleging that the day of the Lord has already come (2:1–2). Somewhat cryptically, Paul states that first "the apostasy" comes and "the man of lawlessness" is revealed. This figure sets himself in opposition to God as an object of worship, sitting in God's temple and proclaiming that he is God (2:3–4). Though we do not know who Paul intended to point to with this description—his original readers might have had a better understanding—he used familiar imagery from the Old Testament (e.g., Isa. 14:12–14; Ezek. 28:2;

CANONICAL CONNECTIONS

Clouds and the Coming of Christ

In the Old Testament, clouds are often connected to a theophany—the appearance of God (e.g., Exod. 13:21–22; 14:19–20, 24; Num. 9:15–22; 10:11–12; 1 Kings 8:10–12; 2 Chron. 5:13–14; 6:1; Neh. 9:12; Ps. 97:2; Isa. 19:1; Ezek. 1:4–28). The theophanic significance of clouds is also seen in the New Testament (Matt. 17:5; Mark 9:7; Luke 9:34–35; 1 Cor. 10:1–2). Clouds are connected not only with the ascension of Christ (Acts 1:9) but also with his return (Matt. 24:30; 26:64; Mark 13:26; 14:62; Luke 21:27; Rev. 1:7; 14:14–16). This traces back to Daniel's vision of "one like a son of man coming with the clouds of heaven" (Dan. 7:13).

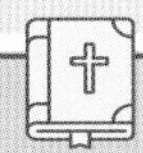

THEOLOGICAL ISSUES

Why So Serious?

This passage in 2 Thessalonians 1:6–9 is one of the fieriest depictions of God's judgment in Paul's writings. It can be difficult for modern readers to accept or understand, but it is important to remember that God's salvation always involves judgment. In the Old Testament, the day of the Lord was an expectation of God's future intervention into human history for judgment and salvation (e.g., Isa. 2:1–4:6; Jer. 46:10; Ezek. 30:2–3). And in Paul's context, relief for afflicted believers involves stopping and repaying those who perpetrate their affliction (2 Thess. 1:6–7). In other words, in order to save people from evil, it is necessary to judge and vanquish evil.

Dan. 6:7) and from the history of Israel. The Seleucid ruler Antiochus IV Epiphanes desecrated the Jerusalem temple in 167 BC, and the Roman emperor Caligula set up a statue of himself inside the temple in AD 40. Whoever this figure is, the Lord Jesus will destroy him with the breath of his mouth (2:8; cf. Isa. 11:4) and will bring him to nothing at his coming.

The prevalent theme of the Lord's coming has three main concerns in 1 and 2 Thessalonians. First, his coming will inaugurate the promised day of the Lord. Second, the day of the Lord will bring judgment alongside salvation. Third, his coming will occur as an expected surprise. In light of these elements, believers are to live in hope while keeping themselves ready for that great day.

Bust of Antiochus IV Epiphanes

Living in Light of the End

READ 1 THESSALONIANS 5:8–11

Discussion about the coming of the Lord is offered not solely for the sake of knowledge and understanding but also for its significance for Christian living. In the first instance, the hope that Jesus will come again from heaven means that believers must *wait* for him (1 Thess. 1:10). Waiting implies living with anticipation and hope as believers endure persecution and hardship, as well as the regular trials of this life. For Paul, such hope includes the anticipated glory and joy of seeing the Thessalonians on the right side of the Lord Jesus when he comes (2:19–20). For all believers, waiting means seeking to have blameless and holy hearts in preparation for the coming of the Lord Jesus (3:13). They are to don the spiritual armor of faith, love, and hope in the prospect of one day living with the Lord Jesus Christ (5:8–10).

Waiting will include seasons of grief as loved ones die, but the coming of the Lord offers comfort amid grief. The certain hope of resurrection from the dead means that believers are able to endure their grief with the knowledge that they will be reunited with those who have died in Christ (4:13–17). Paul explicitly mentions that they are to use his words as an encouragement to one another (4:18).

After depicting the fiery revelation of the Lord Jesus from heaven in 2 Thessalonians 1:7–10, Paul prays "in view of this" that God would make the Thessalonians worthy of his calling and empower them to do good

RECEPTION HISTORY

"Asleep in Jesus, Blessed Sleep"

First Thessalonians has had a strong influence in the composition of hymns. After being struck by the words "sleeping in Jesus" carved on a tombstone in Devonshire, England, Margaret Mackay wrote the hymn "Asleep in Jesus, Blessed Sleep" in 1832, drawing on 1 Thessalonians 4:13–15.

> Asleep, in Jesus! Blessed sleep,
> From which none ever wakes to weep;
> A calm and undisturbed repose,
> Unbroken by the last of foes.
>
> Asleep in Jesus! Oh, how sweet
> To be for such a slumber meet,
> With holy confidence to sing
> That death has lost his venomed sting!
>
> Asleep in Jesus! Peaceful rest,
> Whose waking is supremely blest;
> No fear, no woe, shall dim that hour
> That manifests the Savior's power.
>
> Asleep in Jesus! Oh, for me
> May such a blissful refuge be!
> Securely shall my ashes lie
> And wait the summons from on high.[1]

works produced by faith (1:11). This will lead to the glorification of the Lord Jesus Christ, who, strikingly, will also glorify them (1:12). But believers are not to be led astray by those who would manipulate their expectant anticipation of Jesus from heaven (2:1–3).

The Importance of Work

READ 2 THESSALONIANS 3:11–13

Under the theme of "brotherly love," Paul says that believers should seek "to lead a quiet life, to mind your own business, and to work with your own hands" so as not to be dependent on anyone (1 Thess. 4:11–12). The Thessalonians are to do their own work to provide for themselves and not be a burden on others. If this were an isolated statement, we might think that it was simply a general instruction that Paul could have written to anyone. But in his second letter to them, it is revealed that some of the Thessalonians seem to have had an issue with idleness.

First, Paul points to his own example: "We were not idle among you; we did not eat anyone's food free of charge; instead, we labored and toiled, working night and day, so that we would not be a burden to any of you" (2 Thess. 3:7b–8). In this, Paul and his companions set an example for the Thessalonians to imitate, and they even commanded that anyone unwilling to work should not eat (3:10)! Indeed, Paul identifies the problem explicitly: some among the Thessalonians are idle, and instead of being busy with work, they are busybodies (3:11). This reveals the nature of the problem: it's not that these idle people are unable to work due to problems of health, age, disability, or opportunity; rather, they are preoccupied with other people's personal business. Instead, they should mind their own business, do their own work, and provide for themselves (3:12).

Some have speculated that the problem of idleness among the Thessalonian believers had something to do with their expectant anticipation of the coming of the Lord Jesus Christ. The theory is that since the Thessalonians believed that Jesus was coming soon, some of them saw little point in engaging in hard work. After all, it would all be over soon! But there is no evidence in either letter to suggest that these Thessalonians were idle due to their anticipation of the coming of Jesus. It's not that they were "too heavenly minded for any earthly good." They just weren't much earthly good. In any case, the coming of Jesus should, on the contrary, inspire earnest work born of faith. This is part of what it means to wait patiently for the Lord as children of the light: they are to do honest work and pull their weight.

Heartfelt Ministry

READ 1 THESSALONIANS 2:7–12

Paul's First Letter to the Thessalonians reveals a pastor who loved his people in word, deed, and affection. Paul and his coworkers ministered to the Thessalonians with integrity, having been entrusted with the gospel, and therefore aimed to please God rather than people (1 Thess. 2:3–4). They did not engage in flattery, nor were they motivated by greed or self-glorification (2:5–6). Instead of being a burden on them, Paul and his coworkers were gentle with the Thessalonians, nurturing them like a nursing mother (2:7) and encouraging them like a loving father (2:11–12). They shared with them not only the gospel but their very lives (2:8). Along with God, the Thessalonians were witnesses of how devoutly, righteously, and blamelessly Paul's group conducted themselves among them (2:10).

Paul's ministry among the Thessalonians was holistic and from the heart. He was motivated by a genuine love for people and devotion to the Lord Jesus Christ. This pure motivation inspired integrity and eschewed selfish gain. Paul set an example for believers to follow and adopted the role of mother *and* father in the faith as he nurtured and encouraged these young devotees of Jesus.

Implementation

There is much that the Thessalonian correspondence offers to the contemporary church. Most significant is its strong, uncompromising affirmation of the imminent coming of Christ and its huge implications. In an age when the modern Western church tends to put its focus elsewhere, the Thessalonian letters offer a salient and urgent corrective to those who have lost sight of this vital event that Jesus promised and Paul anticipated. Believers are to set their hope and firm expectation on the coming of Christ, which marks the end of persecution and suffering, the judgment and vanquishing of evil in all its forms, and the reunion of loved ones in the resurrection of the dead, centered on Christ.

These two letters also offer a powerful corrective to a church culture that often celebrates flashy speakers, big preaching platforms, and self-indulgent forms of worship and ministry. In stark contrast to the modern preoccupation with worldly measures of success in ministry, Paul reveals the intimacy of his pastoral relationships, having tended to his people with love and care. He presents a picture of a pastor who is relationally bonded to his people and who rebuffs ungodly forms of influence, such as flattery, deception, and manipulation. Paul's example ought to shape those who serve in church leadership, while also helping the church to calibrate its expectations of what godly leadership in ministry looks like.

While the Thessalonians set a good example for believers today by their turning away from their previous lives of devotion to idols, it seems that some among them were nevertheless devoted to being idle. As Paul makes clear, there is no room for laziness or for creating an unnecessary burden on others. Waiting for the Lord's coming includes diligent work performed in earnest, so that the community of believers is free to provide and care for those who need it for reasons beyond their control.

Christian Reading Questions

1. New Testament scholarship has often assumed that the Thessalonian correspondence expresses Paul's belief that Jesus would return during his lifetime but that this belief shifted in Paul's later letters. What evidence can you find to support this view from the two Thessalonian letters, and are there any arguments to the contrary?
2. In 1 Thessalonians 1:9–10, Paul describes how the Thessalonians turned from idols to serve the true God as they await his Son from heaven. To what extent could this description apply to the Western church today? What about the church in other parts of the world?
3. Drawing on 2 Thessalonians 1–2, put into your own words why it is important that God's salvation comes with his judgment.

CHAPTER TEN

1 Corinthians

Orientation

Paul first visited Corinth during his second mission in AD 50, after entering Europe for the first time. After brief visits to Philippi, Thessalonica, Berea, and Athens, Paul arrived in Corinth and stayed there for a year and a half (Acts 18). Having established the church in Corinth, Paul wrote this letter during his third mission while located in Ephesus in AD 53 or 54. As the letter reveals, however, this is not the first letter that Paul wrote to the Corinthian church. He had already written to address various problems within the church, and they had written to him in response. This letter, known as

Acrocorinth and the Corinthian Gulf

"First Corinthians" or "1 Corinthians," is therefore the *second* of Paul's letters to the Corinthians, but since the previous letter has not survived, this is the first of his extant letters to the church.

Corinth was an important shipping hub, located near a short stretch of land that connects the Peloponnese to mainland Greece, with the Ionian and Aegean Seas on either side. As such, Corinth saw much commercial, military, and transportation activity, which gave rise to its reputation for vice, sexual corruption, and religious temples. The city became infamous for its debauched immorality and worldliness. Aristophanes (ca. 450–385 BC) said that "to act like a Corinthian" meant "to commit fornication," and Plato (428–348 BC) revealed that the description "Corinthian girl" was a euphemism for a prostitute. Strabo's account of the city (7 BC) indicated that the temple of Aphrodite, situated on the Acrocorinth ("upper" Corinth, on top of a large rock), housed one thousand temple prostitutes.

HISTORICAL MATTERS

A Wealthy and Diverse City

After Julius Caesar refounded Corinth as a Roman colony in 44 BC, Emperor Augustus made the city the capital of the Roman province of Achaea in 27 BC. After AD 44, Achaea was governed by a proconsul sent annually from Rome who would rule the region from Corinth. As a maritime city with two harbors, Corinth was made wealthy through trade, travel, banking, bronze making, and the Isthmian Games held every two years. The city was religiously diverse, with worship of various gods such as Apollo, Athena, Poseidon, Hera, Aphrodite, Heracles, Jupiter, Isis, and Serapis. Corinth was also home to Greek philosophers and a Jewish settlement.

It is clear that the church in Corinth was not impervious to its surrounding culture. In fact, it was beset with divisive factionalism, sexual immorality, arrogance, idolatry, worldliness, and a host of other vices. It seems that the Corinthian believers had uncritically retained the wisdom and values of their unbelieving neighbors. But most serious of all was their lack of Christian *love* and their disregard for the well-being of the body of Christ, the church.

Given the significant problems in Corinth, Paul's letter to the church offers precious insights into his ministry, as he addresses one problem after another. But rather than simply stringing together a collection of encouragements and rebukes—as the letter is sometimes understood to do—the letter offers a profoundly theological account of how the Corinthians must be reformed. The message of Christ crucified turns upside down the wisdom and values of the world. The nature of the body of Christ, the church, challenges Corinthian individualism and factionalism. And the resurrected Christ reshapes Corinthian eschatology and attitudes toward life today—in light of the future.

Overview of 1 Corinthians

- Paul begins by acknowledging the giftedness of the Corinthian believers, especially in speech and knowledge (1:4–7), but also the divisions among them incited by rivalry and factionalism (1:10–17).

- He argues that worldly wisdom has been undermined and overturned by the cross of Christ, which is the power and wisdom of God (1:18–25). The Corinthians' boasting in their gifts, therefore, is misguided, since God chose them to belong to Christ. They should therefore boast in the Lord (1:26–31).
- Paul himself came to the Corinthians in human weakness in order to share the message of Christ crucified (2:1–5). He spoke with the wisdom of God, which is counter to human wisdom and can be revealed only by the Spirit (2:6–13). Thus, truly spiritual people are those who have God's Spirit and the mind of Christ (2:14–16).
- But the Corinthians are spiritual babies, being worldly in their envy and factionalism (3:1–4). In contrast, Paul and his fellow ministers are coworkers together in the work of God, who has given each their own responsibilities to build on the foundation of Christ (3:5–15).
- The Corinthians themselves are God's temple, with the Spirit living in them (3:16–17). There is no room for boasting or worldly wisdom, since they belong to Christ (3:18–23).
- Rather than being figureheads for Corinthian factionalism, Paul and his coworkers are servants of Christ and will be judged by God (4:1–5). And God has chosen to put the apostles in a humble position in the world's eyes, whereas the Corinthians exalt in their own "high" position (4:6–13).
- Corinthian arrogance even celebrates sexual immorality, including a man sleeping with his stepmother. Instead, they should be filled with grief, discipline offenders, and strive to keep the congregation clear of such influences (5:1–13).
- The Corinthians have been taking one another to court, and Paul says that they should have enough wisdom to arbitrate among themselves. They should rather be wronged than do wrong and cheat, and there is no room for the unrighteous in the kingdom of God (6:1–11).
- Believers must flee from sexual immorality and recognize that their bodies are part of Christ's body. Each body is a temple of the Holy Spirit, and each believer has been bought by God (6:12–20).
- Paul then responds to issues that the Corinthians wrote to him about. Apparently, they thought it good to abstain from sex, but Paul counters that sex should be enjoyed within the covenant of marriage, with husbands and wives seeking to serve each other. Not everyone should get married, but it is better to marry than to burn with passion

(7:1–9). Those already married should stay so, whether or not both partners are believers. But if an unbelieving spouse wants to leave the marriage, so be it (7:10–16). People in general ought to stay in the situation to which they have been called, because the time is short (7:17–24). Those who remain unmarried are freer to be devoted to the Lord without distraction (7:25–40).

- In response to the Corinthians' question about whether they should eat food sacrificed to idols, Paul says that the important thing is to act according to love. On the one hand, we know that idols are nothing and believers are free to eat whatever they want. But on the other hand, if others do not share this understanding, believers should not cause them to stumble by exercising their freedom (8:1–13).
- Paul sets an example for the Corinthians in the way he exercised his own freedom. Though as an apostle he had a right to receive financial support from them, he chose to preach the gospel free of charge (9:1–18). He fit in with whomever he was with—whether Jew or gentile—for the sake of the gospel, rather than insist on his own preferences (9:19–23).
- Learning from Israel's past mistakes, the Corinthians need to avoid temptation and flee from idolatry (10:1–14). When they come together to share the Lord's Supper, they participate in the body of Christ and therefore should not participate with those who effectively worship demons through their idolatry (10:15–22). Nevertheless, there will be some occasions when it is better to eat meat sacrificed to idols, and others when it should be avoided. The key is to do all for the glory of God, whatever the situation (10:23–11:1).
- Paul abruptly changes topic to address orderly conduct within the congregation. He makes a complex argument that women should pray with their heads covered and men should pray with heads uncovered, to reflect proper relationships (11:2–16). The Corinthians' factionalism is inappropriate for those who share in the Lord's Supper together, and all should examine themselves before participating in it (11:17–34).
- Rather than remaining divided, the Corinthians are to understand that they are members together of the same body of Christ, each with different gifts and roles, and each with concern for the others (12:1–31).
- But whatever gifts believers may have, love reigns above all. Of the three hallmarks of Christian character—faith, hope, and love—the greatest is love (13:1–13).

- In light of love, Paul encourages his readers to pursue the gifts that build up others, such as prophesy. Speaking in tongues serves the individual only if interpreted for others to understand (14:1–25). There should be order when the congregation is gathered (14:26–40).
- Resurrection from the dead is the last major issue Paul addresses, drawing attention to the fact of Jesus's resurrection and how it points to the general resurrection of all (15:1–34). The nature of Jesus's resurrection is also instructive, and believers will be raised with a glorious "spiritual" body that is immortal and incorruptible (15:35–58).
- Paul concludes the letter with mention of his collection for the saints, his travel plans, and final greetings (16:1–24).

Exploration

Although 1 Corinthians raises a variety of topics and themes, most of these can be grouped under the metathemes of the crucified Christ, the body of Christ, and the resurrected Christ. Broadly speaking, the believers in Corinth are to understand their relationship to the world through the lens of the cross, their present conduct in relation to the body of Christ, and their future through the lens of the resurrection.

The Crucified Christ

READ 1 CORINTHIANS 1:10–18

Addressing the factionalism within the Corinthian church, Paul states that Christ sent him to preach the gospel "not with wisdom and eloquence, lest the cross of Christ be emptied of its power" (1:17). The cross is foolishness to the wise of the world, both Jewish and gentile, but it is, in fact, the power and wisdom of God (1:18–25). Through the cross, Christ has become "our righteousness, holiness, and redemption" (1:30), demonstrating that God's power comes through means that appear weak and shameful in the eyes of the world.

Since the power of the cross comes through weakness, Paul characterizes his own ministry among the Corinthians as one of human weakness—without eloquence or persuasive words, but in fear and

HISTORICAL MATTERS

Greek and Jewish Wisdom

The importance of divine wisdom was stressed within Judaism. God revealed it in his Word, and wisdom sometimes was personified. The Hebrew Bible also contains books devoted to wisdom-related themes, known as Wisdom literature, such as Proverbs, Job, and Ecclesiastes. Ancient Greeks respected philosophy and rhetoric, the two main disciplines available for advanced study for the wealthy. Within Greek philosophy, wisdom acquired an almost religious significance. Its goal was happiness, as promoted by the Stoics and Epicureans. The key difference between Jewish and Greek conceptions of wisdom was its origin: for Jews, it came from God; for Greeks, it derived from human insight.

Portrait of John Calvin, 1550

RECEPTION HISTORY

John Calvin on 1 Corinthians 1:30

Commenting on Paul's statement that Christ "became wisdom from God for us—our righteousness, sanctification, and redemption" (1:30), the sixteenth-century Protestant reformer John Calvin sought to show how all those elements are integrated:

> For when it said that Christ is given to us for redemption, wisdom, and righteousness, it is likewise added that He is given to us for sanctification [1 Cor. 1:30]. From that it follows that Christ does not justify anyone whom He does not at the same time sanctify. For these benefits are joined together by a perpetual tie; when He illumines us with His wisdom, He ransoms us; when He ransoms us, He justifies us; when He justifies us, He sanctifies us. . . . So although [righteousness and sanctification] must be distinguished, nevertheless Christ contains both inseparably. Do we want to receive righteousness in Christ? We must first possess Christ. Now we cannot possess Him without being participants in His sanctification, since He cannot be torn in pieces. Since, I say, the Lord Jesus never gives anyone the enjoyment of His benefits except in giving Himself, He gives both of them together and never one without the other.[1]

trembling. His message was Christ crucified, and his manner matched the message, so that their faith would rest on God's power rather than on human wisdom (2:1–5). On the contrary, God's wisdom was hidden, revealed only by the Spirit of God. So, Paul's words are taught by the Spirit, and are understood and accepted only by the Spirit (2:6–16).

The counterintuitive, upside-down power of the cross of Christ remains important throughout the letter and is alluded to at various points. When Paul accuses the Corinthians of being "worldly" (3:1), it implies that they still have not understood the implications of the cross, which undermines worldly wisdom (3:18–20; cf. 1:18–25). While the apostles are

CANONICAL CONNECTIONS

Six Old Testament Texts

The argument of 1 Corinthians 1:18–3:23 is grounded in six Old Testament texts in which God acts to judge and save his people in ways that overturn human expectation. Isaiah 29:14, cited in 1:19, refers to God's judgment of the "wisdom of the wise," which Paul shows to be incompatible with the "word of the cross." Jeremiah 9:24, cited in 1:31, warns of boasting in human wisdom, strength, and riches, and Paul points to the Corinthians themselves as an illustration of how God will elevate the lowly rather than those who boast in their human strength. Isaiah 64:4, loosely cited in 2:9, claims that no human person can understand God's revelation unless he enables it, just as Paul affirms that the Spirit has revealed God's truth to the apostles and prophets. The Greek text of Isaiah 40:13, quoted in 2:16, asks, "Who has known the mind of the Lord?" to which Paul answers, "We have the mind of Christ" due to the presence of the Spirit. Job 5:13, quoted in 3:19, announces that God will catch the wise in their craftiness, just as Paul asserts the foolishness of the world in God's sight. Psalm 94:11, cited in 3:20, claims that the reasoning of the wise is futile, which suits Paul's overall argument in this section of 1 Corinthians. All told, these six Old Testament texts, along with their wider contexts, ground Paul's argument that the wisdom of God—expressed by the cross of Christ—overpowers and overturns the world's wisdom.

"fools for Christ," weak and dishonored, the Corinthians are "so wise in Christ," strong and honored (4:10). They further reveal their worldliness by taking one another to court, when they should rather be cheated than try to beat one another (6:1–8).

The overtones of the cross can also be felt in chapters 8–11 as Paul argues that the Corinthians should be willing to give up their freedom for the sake of love. Their (correct) understanding of food sacrificed to idols should not be used to tear down others; while knowledge puffs up, love builds up (8:1).

The Body of Christ

READ 1 CORINTHIANS 12:12–14

While discussing the problematic factionalism within the Corinthian church, Paul asks a rhetorical question: "Is Christ divided?" (1:13). Of course, the understood answer is no, and this undergirds much of Paul's argument to counteract their unholy factionalism. It also anticipates a major theme of the letter: the body of Christ—while the body consists of many parts, it is nevertheless a unified whole. Though Paul uses several metaphors to picture the church, the body of Christ is arguably the most central and significant. Thus, Paul's lengthy discussion of issues and problems facing the church in Corinth can be gathered under the rubric "the body of Christ."

In chapters 3 and 4, Paul addresses the various roles that apostles play in establishing the church, which is referred to as a field (3:6–9), a building (3:9–15), and a temple (3:16–17). All three metaphors imagine the church as being founded by God, with the apostles working simply as his servants and coworkers (3:5–9). Thus, the Corinthians ought to put little stock in their human leaders and avoid boasting in Paul, Apollos, or Cephas (Peter) (3:21–23). These servants must prove faithful and will be judged by the Lord (4:1–5), while the Corinthians must watch out for their arrogance and human strength (4:8–10, 18–21). Instead, they ought to follow Paul's example (4:11–17).

Within the body of Christ are those who have mistreated their own bodies (and others') through sexual immorality. In chapter 5, Paul acknowledges that this behavior has been reported about the Corinthians, to a degree even worse than found among unbelievers, including a man sleeping with his stepmother. But instead of grieving this lamentable situation, the Corinthians celebrated it (5:1–2). Paul exhorts the church to exercise discipline toward those indulging in immorality for the sake of their restoration and for the health of the body (5:2–13). Indeed, in chapter 6, Paul states that individuals' bodies are for the Lord, as an expression of the fact that the

> **RECEPTION HISTORY**
>
> **Famous Love**
>
> An extended exposition of love, 1 Corinthians 13 is one of the most widely cited biblical passages in history—and not only at weddings, as is seen in various recent cultural references. President Franklin D. Roosevelt took his inauguration oath in 1933 with his hand on his family Bible, which was open to 1 Corinthians 13. James Baldwin cited verse 11 at the end of his 1956 novel, *Giovanni's Room*. Singer Joni Mitchell used much of the passage in her song "Love," from her 1982 album *Wild Things Run Fast* and her 2002 album *Travelogue*. The 1986 film *The Mission* features a scene in which Rodrigo (played by Robert De Niro) reads from the chapter. British Prime Minister Tony Blair read the chapter at the funeral of Princess Diana in 1997. President Barack Obama referenced verse 11 in his inaugural address to the nation on January 20, 2009. And Macklemore used verse 4 in his 2012 song "Same Love."

church as a whole is the body of Christ. The Corinthians therefore should flee sexual immorality, since their bodies are temples of the Holy Spirit (6:12–20).

Instructions for the church community continue with respect to marriage, divorce, and remaining single (7:1–40). Marriage is the proper context for sexual relations, and husbands and wives are to care for each other's bodily needs in this regard (7:1–5). Married couples ought to stay together, but if an unbelieving spouse leaves the marriage, let it be so (7:10–16). Paul also counsels the unmarried to stay single for the sake of undivided devotion to the Lord, but if they want to get married, they should do so (7:25–40).

A major issue facing the body of Christ in Corinth is their attitude toward food sacrificed to idols. Through the complex argument that Paul mounts in chapters 8–10, his main point is that believers ought to take care of how their actions affect other people. If they act according to knowledge but not love, they might destroy their brothers and sisters (8:9–13). It is better to use their Christian freedom in service of others rather than for themselves (9:1–27; 10:23–33). Nevertheless, it is important to realize that when believers come together to share the Lord's Supper, they participate in the body of Christ and therefore should not participate with the demonic worship of idolatry. The cup of thanksgiving is a participation in the blood of Christ, and bread is a participation in the body of Christ. Believers are one body, for all share the one loaf (10:14–22).

The focus on the body of Christ shifts again as Paul issues instructions for corporate worship. Men and women are to be appropriately dressed when they gather together in the congregation (11:2–16), and the Lord's Supper is to be conducted in a manner worthy of the body of Christ—without divisions or petty behavior (11:17–34). Spiritual gifts are to be employed for the benefit of the body, as each part does its work. There is one body with many parts, and such diversity serves the unified whole (12:1–31). But the most important consideration for the service of the body is love (13:1–13).

The Resurrected Christ

READ 1 CORINTHIANS 15:50–57

While the majority of the letter has been occupied with the metathemes of the crucified Christ and the body of Christ, its most glorious chapter

CANONICAL CONNECTIONS

Resurrection in the Hebrew Bible

Some Old Testament texts employ resurrection imagery to point to a future national restoration of Israel (e.g., Ezek. 37:1–14). But at least two passages look forward to the bodily resurrection of individuals: Isaiah 26:19 promises a resurrection ("Your dead shall live") that is explicitly physical ("Their corpses shall rise"), and Daniel 12:1–3 speaks of the awakening of "many who sleep in the dust of the earth . . . , some to everlasting life, and some to shame and everlasting contempt." Other passages, such as Job 14:14; Psalms 16:10; 49:15; 73:24, also imply belief in life after death.

addresses the resurrected Christ. The resurrection of Christ is central to the gospel that Paul preached (15:1–11), and it is confirmation of the coming general resurrection of the dead (15:12–19). Christ will make alive those who belong to him and then will hand over his kingdom to God the Father once the last enemy—death—has been destroyed (15:20–28).

Fresco of the resurrection, Collegiata Santa Maria Assunta, Castell'Arquato

As the firstfruits of the resurrection of the dead, Christ's resurrection determines the nature of the resurrection of those who belong to him. Believers' bodies will be raised imperishable, glorious, and in power. They will be "spiritual" bodies, bearing the image of the heavenly man (15:42–49). Resurrection will occur in an instant at the designated time, and the perishable will be clothed with the imperishable. Then, death will be swallowed up in victory through our Lord Jesus Christ (15:50–58).

The glorious resurrection of the dead puts everything else that the letter addresses into perspective. The human body is perishable, but believers will be raised imperishable, which means that they should live not for passing accomplishments or pleasures but in light of their eternal future. The world's glory and its values are passing away, but the kingdom of Christ will never perish. While the wisdom of the cross appears as foolishness according to worldly wisdom, the resurrection of the dead in Christ will vindicate those who have lived in the shadow of the cross. As such, believers are to follow the pattern of Christ's death and resurrection in their own lives: death comes before resurrection; suffering before glory; self-denial before the riches of the kingdom.

Implementation

A striking feature of 1 Corinthians is that Paul does not question the genuine salvation of his readers—despite the church being a real mess, embroiled in immorality and worldly thinking. He describes his readers as "the church of God at Corinth," "those sanctified" and "called as saints" (1:2), and he reaffirms his love in Christ for them all (16:24). Thus, the Corinthians are regarded as genuine believers, even though some of their flaws and failures are quite shocking. This demonstrates that even grave moral and spiritual failure does not disqualify believers from what is promised to them in Christ. Of course, they need to repent and follow Christ with their whole lives, but Paul does not question their standing with God. The letter is therefore a remarkable encouragement to the contemporary church as it wrestles with its own failures and shortcomings.

The metatheme of the crucified Christ, seen especially in the first four chapters of the letter, points to the notion of *cruciformity*. This refers to a fundamental attitude of identification with the crucified Christ that shapes believers' way of life, thought, and perspective on the world around them. Paul's commitment to cruciformity explains his teaching on a variety of matters. The cross of Christ turns worldly wisdom and values upside down, so that the word of the cross is foolishness to the world, but is in fact the power of God. Believers are not powerful or impressive in the world's eyes but boast in the Lord. Paul did not employ showy rhetoric but ministered in weakness. God's servants are no one special, but he works through them to build his church. The human weakness of these themes demonstrates how the cross of Christ saves humanity, since it was through the weakness of Christ's suffering that God powerfully achieved his purposes.

The way of the cross has the power to undermine worldly structures of authority and control, since cruciformity demands that believers reassess the world's assumptions about wisdom, strength, power, and glory through the lens of the cross. Without such reassessment, believers today are likely to fall into errors similar to those that plagued the church in Corinth. Rather than succumb to the priorities and values of the world, cruciformity allows believers to submit themselves to self-denial and death—with the confident hope that the cross leads to resurrection and restoration.

A healthy dose of cruciformity also allows believers to adopt a loving posture toward the body of Christ. Each part of the body exists to serve the whole, which means that Christians ought to reflect on how they can serve the church rather than live for themselves and their priorities. Believers will understand that the choices they make have an effect on the whole body—including how they treat their own physical bodies. As cruciform members of the body of Christ, believers will want their intellect, knowledge, and gifts to be employed for the good of others rather than for their own gratification or glorification. Being "right" is not more important than being loving. In fact, lack of love makes being "right" wrong.

Believers must also take care to be loving and responsible when they gather together in worship. The gathered congregation is not the place to show off spiritual gifts, especially not the ones that don't benefit others. Rather, gifts are to be used in service to build others up, and meeting together should be done in such a way that benefits participants and even outsiders. Believers today are reminded that their meeting together should not be a consumerist, celebrity-driven performance that exists primarily for individuals' spiritual nourishment and gratification. We gather to love, worship, and serve God in Christ, and this works best when each member of the body contributes to the well-being of the whole.

Finally, the resurrection of Christ and the future resurrection of believers give ultimate meaning to life and faith now. Without the resurrection of Christ, believers' faith would be futile, and they would still be in their sins. Death would render everything meaningless, and hope for this life only would be utterly pitiable (15:17–19). Too many believers today have an anemic understanding of the significance of the resurrection—both Jesus's and their own. Churches would do well to beef up their theology of the resurrection so that believers would neither fear death nor despair of the meaninglessness of life. Moreover, a robust theology of the resurrection would enable believers to look forward to their forthcoming inheritance of the kingdom of God and to know that their work in the Lord now is not in vain (15:58).

Christian Reading Questions

1. Identify any elements of your culture that the church has unwittingly adopted. How does the message of 1 Corinthians 1–2 help you to reflect on these elements and to critique them?
2. In light of the argument of 1 Corinthians 8–10, how would you make the case that love is more important than freedom?
3. Read 1 Corinthians 10:1–22. What does the account of Israel's history mean (10:1–5), and how does it offer an example to Paul's readers (10:6–22)?

CHAPTER ELEVEN

2 Corinthians

Orientation

Difficult relationships can take a lot of work. A careful reading of 1 and 2 Corinthians reveals that Paul wrote *four* letters to the troubled church in Corinth, though only two survive. While the letter we know as 1 Corinthians is actually his second letter to Corinth, the letter we call 2 Corinthians is his *fourth* letter to that church (1 Cor. 5:9–11; 2 Cor. 2:3–4, 9; 7:8, 12). If the four letters are labeled A, B, C, D, then B = 1 Corinthians and D = 2 Corinthians, while A and C are lost.

While the historical reconstruction is a little complex, the main points are that after Paul wrote 1 Corinthians (letter B) from Ephesus in AD 53–54, the Corinthians wrote back to him. He wrote to them again (the lost letter, C), and they replied again. Then, after his three-year stint in Ephesus, Paul wrote a fourth time while in Philippi, around AD 56–57. As he indicates in this fourth letter, Paul is on his way to see the Corinthians again (2 Cor. 13:1–2), and the letter is intended to pave the way in anticipation of this potentially difficult visit.

The Composition of 2 Corinthians

Since the eighteenth century, some scholars have regarded 2 Corinthians as a compilation of different fragments of letters that Paul wrote to Corinth, rather than a unified original letter. This conjecture was based on an apparent lack of unity between various parts of the letter. However, there is no textual evidence that 2 Corinthians was ever anything other than a single united document. Moreover, several scholars have since sought to demonstrate the thematic coherence of the letter, offering explanations of its shifts in subject and tone at various points. Ultimately, the integrity of a letter must be tested by the question of whether its internal tensions are so great as to destroy the assumption of literary unity.

To make things even more complex, 2 Corinthians 13:1–2 also reveals that this will be Paul's *third* visit to Corinth, though Acts reports only *two* visits. Since all history is selective, it is not surprising that Luke left some of Paul's extensive travels out of his already complicated narrative. But the question is, When did the "missing" visit to Corinth occur? We know that the first visit was during Paul's second mission, in AD 50–52. His third visit to Corinth occurred during his third

Liturgical codex displaying 2 Corinthians 6:5–7 and portions of 2 Peter

mission in AD 57, after he had spent three years in Ephesus. So, the "missing" visit to Corinth must have occurred between AD 52 and 57. Many scholars think it most likely that Paul made a quick trip across to Corinth while he was stationed in Ephesus during AD 52–55. This was his "painful visit" (2:1), probably inspired by one of the many urgent crises experienced within the Corinthian church.

Despite Paul's repeated efforts to correct Corinthian worldliness, the letter reveals that the church in Corinth still uncritically adopted the wisdom and values of their unbelieving neighbors. In particular, the church had become enamored of "super-apostles" (11:5; 12:11), who wooed the Corinthians with their preaching of a different Jesus, different spirit, and different gospel. These "super-apostles" were, in fact, false apostles masquerading as the genuine article, as Paul points out. And rather than boast in worldly accomplishments, impressive speaking skills, or a fancy new (but false) message, Paul spends a major chunk of 2 Corinthians referring to his own weakness and human frailty in order to underscore the power and grace of God to accomplish his purposes.

RECEPTION HISTORY

The Humanity of the Apostle

The stark humanity of Paul's writing in 2 Corinthians has resonated with believers of every age. In 1879, James John Lias, chancellor of Llandaff Cathedral in Wales, wrote the following about Paul's self-disclosure in the letter.

> It has been universally remarked that the individuality of the Apostle is more vividly displayed in this Epistle than in any other. Human weakness, spiritual strength, the deepest tenderness of affection, wounded feeling, sternness, irony, rebuke, impassioned self-vindication, humility, a just self-respect, zeal for the welfare of the weak and suffering, as well as for the progress of the church of Christ and for the spiritual advancement of its members, are all displayed in turn in the course of his appeal, and are bound together by the golden cord of an absolute self-renunciation dictated by love to God and man.[1]

Overview of 2 Corinthians

- Paul begins by reflecting on God's comfort in the face of suffering (1:3–7). Even under threat of death, Paul's hope is in God, who raises the dead (1:8–11).

- Affirming his sincerity toward the Corinthians, Paul explains that he changed his plans to visit them for their own sake—not because he is fickle or two-faced (1:12–2:4).
- Paul and his fellow ministers share the aroma of Christ, which is the stench of death to some and the aroma of life to others (2:14–17), but their competence comes from God, not themselves (3:1–6).
- As ministers of the new covenant, Paul and his coworkers engage the glorious ministry of the Spirit rather than that of the law of Israel under Moses (3:7–11). While the Mosaic covenant maintains a "veil" that covers hearts, the Spirit brings freedom and unveils hearts. Being unveiled enables believers to face the Lord's glory and to be transformed into his image (3:12–18).
- Paul and his coworkers have renounced secret and shameful methods, acknowledging that God makes his light shine in believers' hearts (4:1–6). They carry in their bodies the death of Jesus so that life might be revealed to others, knowing that God will raise them from the dead. They therefore do not lose heart, fixing their eyes on eternal glory (4:7–18).
- Paul then reflects on the fact that the earthly body (or "tent") will pass away, but believers will be clothed with a heavenly body (5:1–5). Thus, he longs to be away from the present body and at home with the Lord but will seek to please him in the meantime (5:6–10).
- Compelled by the love of Christ, Paul and his fellow ministers try to persuade others to live for the one who died for them and was raised again (5:11–15). Anyone in Christ is a new creation, thanks to God reconciling the world to himself (5:16–19). Paul and his coworkers are God's ambassadors, appealing to others to be reconciled to God through Christ (5:20–21).
- Paul and his coworkers suffer all manner of hardships in order to commend themselves to others, and they have opened their hearts to the Corinthians—though the latter have not reciprocated (6:3–13).
- Paul then turns to exhort his readers not to be yoked with unbelievers, which is akin to mixing the temple of God with idols (6:14–7:1).
- Next, Paul reflects on his relationship with the Corinthians, his love for them and their longing for him. Though his previous letter caused them sorrow, this led to repentance, which made it worthwhile even while Paul acknowledges that it hurt the Corinthians (7:2–13).
- He draws on the example of the Macedonian churches to encourage the Corinthians to be generous with their resources (8:1–15). Titus is

coming to collect their offering to help those in need (8:16–9:5), and the Corinthians ought to give cheerfully, not under compulsion. This will lead to their enrichment and the praise of God (9:6–15).

- Paul hopes that the Corinthians will no longer live by the standards of this world or judge by appearances. He and his ministry coworkers do not compare themselves to others and boast only in the Lord. It is his commendation that matters (10:1–18).
- Sadly, the Corinthians can be led astray by a false Jesus and false gospel by "super-apostles." Paul is no way inferior to them, though the Corinthians think so. Rather, they are false apostles who work for Satan (11:1–15). In contrast, Paul "boasts" of his credentials, which include great suffering, danger, and toil for the sake of the churches (11:16–33). Actually, he will boast only in his weaknesses, including the "thorn in his flesh" that torments him. Paul asked the Lord to remove the thorn, but the Lord replied that his grace is sufficient, and his power is perfected in weakness (12:1–10).
- Paul will not be a burden to the Corinthians when he comes again, but he fears that he will find discord, sin, and lack of repentance (12:11–21). He will exercise God's power to discipline them, so the Corinthians should examine themselves while Paul prays for their restoration (13:1–10).

Exploration

The main themes of 2 Corinthians revolve around Paul's concept of new-covenant ministry—its glory, its weakness, its triumph, and its shame. Paul offers an account of the theological realities that have shaped his ministry and how they differ starkly from the values of the world and of false apostles.

New-Covenant Ministry

READ 2 CORINTHIANS 3:7–11

The key to understanding the new covenant is to grasp how it differs from the Mosaic covenant established with Israel through Moses. Paul treads a careful line, not denigrating the Mosaic covenant while also freely extolling the superiority of the new. He describes the Mosaic covenant as "ministry that brought death," "engraved in letters on stone"—referring to the Ten Commandments, which were inscribed on two stone tablets—and yet it "came with glory." The Mosaic covenant was transitory and brought death, so the ministry of the Spirit is even more glorious because it is permanent and brings righteousness (3:7–11).

Paul then draws on the story in Exodus 34:29–35, in which Moses's face became radiant as a result of speaking with the Lord on Mount Sinai. He put a veil over his face to hide this radiance from the Israelites, and it was renewed each time he spoke with the Lord. The story could be understood to imply that Moses's face gradually faded in radiance in between his visits with the Lord, and that's how Paul interprets it. He says that Moses's veil was used to hide the fact that his radiance was fading. He then uses this image metaphorically to refer to a veil that covers the hearts of those who remain under the Mosaic covenant (3:13–15). But in Christ the veil is taken away, the Spirit is present, there is freedom, and believers are able to gaze on the glory of the Lord, while being transformed into his image with increasing glory (3:16–18).

This series of contrasts demonstrates that the Mosaic covenant partially revealed the glory of the Lord, but that ministry was not intended to be permanent—just as the glory itself faded. It was a precursor to the full glory of the new covenant, through which each believer would be able to contemplate the Lord's glory (not just Moses), and such glory would be unfading.

Benjamin West, *Moses Receiving the Tablets of the Law*, after 1777

Paul then draws on the glory of the new covenant to undergird his philosophy of ministry. Rejecting deception and distortion, he and his coworkers are open and honest. Though some people have been blinded to the truth of the gospel, Paul and his partners preach Jesus Christ as Lord, since God has shone in their hearts the light of God's glory in the face of Christ (4:1–6). But this inner treasure is housed in "jars of clay," as Paul and his coworkers experience the frailty of their physical bodies through hardship and persecution. They carry in their bodies "the death of Jesus," enabling the life of Jesus to be revealed to others (4:7–12). The glory of the new covenant means that Paul and his coworkers do not lose heart, even though their physical experience is troubled and fading. They anticipate

CANONICAL CONNECTIONS

Mosaic vs. New Covenants

Paul demonstrates the superiority of the new covenant over the Mosaic covenant in at least three ways: it is shaped by the Spirit, who brings life, rather than the written code, which brings death; it offers righteousness rather than condemnation; its gifts of the Spirit and glory are permanent rather than diminishing.

an eternal glory that far outweighs their passing challenges, with eyes fixed on eternal rather than temporary realities (4:16–18). On that theme, Paul draws a stark contrast between the temporary earthly body and the eternal heavenly body. The former can be destroyed and experiences groaning, burden, and distance from God, while the latter is eternal, fashioned by God, and exists in his presence (5:1–10).

These eternal realities undergird Paul's ministry as he and his coworkers try to persuade others that Christ died for them so that they might live for him. No one is regarded from a worldly perspective, but those in Christ are nothing less than a new creation. Paul and his coworkers are Christ's ambassadors through whom God appeals to others to be reconciled to him through Christ (5:11–21). Paul is determined that the servants of God ought to commend themselves through enduring various kinds of sufferings and injustices, bearing the fruit of the Spirit, speaking the truth, rejoicing, and living in poverty while trusting in unseen eternal riches (6:3–10).

In the course of his new-covenant ministry among them, Paul asks the Corinthians to open their hearts to him (6:13; 7:2), to avoid idolatry that comes from being yoked with unbelievers (6:14–7:1), and to give to those in need out of sincere generosity (8:1–15; 9:6–14). He does not conduct his ministry according to the standards of this world, but rather draws on divine power to counter whatever opposes the knowledge of God, taking every thought captive in obedience to Christ (10:1–6). Paul appeals to the Corinthians not to judge by appearances, just as he does not compare himself to others or engage in self-commendation (10:7–18).

The glory of the new covenant profoundly shapes Paul's ministry so that it is grounded on eternal invisible realities, rather than the tricks of passing human cleverness or strength. Girded by the power of God, his ministry does not rest on himself or his abilities but serves as a conduit for God's call to humanity to be reconciled to him through Christ. Paul is able to retain a posture of humility and weakness because he anticipates an eternal glory bestowed by God that is not dependent on Paul's accomplishments and status in this world.

THEOLOGICAL ISSUES

God Made Christ "to Be Sin for Us"

In 2 Corinthians 5:21, Paul issues one of his most shocking statements: God "made the one who did not know sin to be sin for us, so that in him we might become the righteousness of God." Paul identifies Christ with sin, recalling the way in which a sacrificial offering for sin is identified with sinful people, as described in Leviticus. This means that it was not Christ's work alone that was offered for others, but it was Christ himself. And in the "exchange" that takes place, believers do not simply receive righteousness; they *become* the righteousness of God in Christ. This is therefore not a transactional exchange of sin for righteousness, like the transfer of funds from one account to another. Rather, Paul affirms that believers become the righteousness of God by virtue of their relationship to Christ, being found "in him." It is by their union with Christ that believers are able to share in his righteousness.

Generosity

READ 2 CORINTHIANS 8:7–9

In 2 Corinthians 8–9, Paul addresses the theme of generosity through the specific matter of his collection for impoverished believers. He begins by acknowledging the joyous generosity of the Macedonian churches (in Philippi and Thessalonica). Though they had been experiencing "a very severe trial"—probably referring to persecution for their faith—the Macedonian believers gave as much as they were able, and even more. They were not coerced or "guilted" into it, but did so of their own accord, even pleading for the privilege of serving in this way (8:1–4). It seems that Paul regards the Macedonian generosity as an outworking of the bigger picture, as "They gave themselves first of all to the Lord, and then by the will of God also to us" (8:5). Their giving was an expression of their full devotion to the Lord.

It seems that the Corinthians, on the other hand, had pledged to give to Paul's cause but failed to follow through. For that reason, Paul sent Titus to help the Corinthians to fulfill their pledge, knowing that they like to excel in everything and should also excel in the "grace of giving" (8:6–7, 16–24). Paul, however, is careful not to command them to give; rather, he sees this as an opportunity to test the sincerity of their love in comparison to others (8:8). Their level of generosity functions as a barometer of how much the Corinthians really care about their fellow brothers and sisters in need.

And though the comparison to other believers plays a role here (cf. 9:2–5), Paul ultimately wants the Corinthians to follow the example of Christ. He reminds them of Christ's grace and then offers a stunning articulation of the gospel in economic terms: "Though he was rich, yet for your sake he became poor, so that you through his poverty might become rich" (8:9). The metaphorical use of economic terms helps to articulate the generosity of Christ, who sacrificed himself for the sake of others. Ultimately, such self-sacrificial love is what ought to drive financial generosity. Paul then acknowledges the Corinthians' previous generosity, as they eagerly had given to the cause a year earlier (cf. 9:2). They simply need to follow through now, according to their means. The goal of their generosity ought to be a more equitable situation among believers so that no one goes without. The Corinthians have plenty, so they can supply what others need (8:10–15).

Finally, Paul encourages the Corinthians to give according to their heart, not reluctantly or under compulsion, because "God loves a cheerful giver" (9:6–7). God also blesses his people abundantly so that the Corinthians will have all they need. Their generosity will lead others to thank and praise God for his provision through them. And their beneficiaries will offer their heartfelt prayers for the Corinthians (9:8–15).

Though Paul does lean on the Corinthians to follow through on their pledge, his exhortation is not driven by moral obligation, guilt, or threat. Instead, Paul grounds his theology of generosity on the gospel. Jesus demonstrated extreme generosity in his loving self-sacrifice for the benefit of others, and Paul hopes that the Corinthians will have their hearts shaped by the same impulse. Financial giving is simply a practical outworking of a heart that has been shaped by the love of Jesus. While the Corinthians are bound to a certain extent by their own verbal commitment (cf. 1:18–20), that is not the primary issue here. The central concern is whether they love others from the heart and are willing to show it.

Weakness

READ 2 CORINTHIANS 6:4–10

A key distinguishing feature of 2 Corinthians is Paul's emphasis on weakness. Rather than presenting himself as strong, impressive, or accomplished, he takes the opposite route. This approach achieves several strategic goals. First, it underscores the fact that God's grace reveals his power and our powerlessness. Second, it reminds his readers that the new covenant is eternal and glorious precisely because it does not depend on human and earthly means. Third, it challenges the Corinthians' pride in their worldly status and smug self-reliance. Fourth, it reveals that genuine apostolic ministry depends on the power of God and does not rest on outward displays of human impressiveness.

The beginning of the letter sees Paul referring to his troubles, sufferings, and distress (1:4–6, 8). Such afflictions cause Paul and his coworkers to rely on God rather than themselves (1:9–10). Their bodies are mere "jars of clay," which can easily break and whose importance is determined solely by what they store inside. This shows that the surpassing power of the new covenant is from God and not them (4:7). Their physical decay and momentary

Medallion with Saint Paul from an icon frame, 1100

troubles are nothing compared to the unseen eternal glory that awaits them (4:16–18).

Rather than accepting a worldly assessment of their success, Paul and his coworkers view their hardships, beatings, imprisonments, hard work, and poverty as commending them as genuine servants of God. While they have nothing, they possess everything (6:4–10). They do not wield worldly weapons but engage divine power against the forces opposed to God (10:3–6).

As such, Paul does not regard himself as inferior to the "super-apostles," who have wooed the Corinthians with their preaching of a different Jesus, different spirit, and different gospel (11:4–5). They are, in fact, false apostles masquerading as the genuine article, as they serve their true master, Satan (11:13–15). Rather than boast in worldly accomplishments, as the false apostles do, Paul points to his frequent imprisonments, floggings, beatings, stoning, shipwrecks, danger, and hunger and thirst. If Paul must boast, he will boast in his weakness (11:18–30).

Paul even goes so far as to recount his struggle with "a thorn in the flesh, a messenger of Satan," that torments him. Though he pleaded with the Lord to take away this thorn in the flesh, the Lord affirmed that his grace is sufficient and his "power is made perfect in weakness" (12:7b–9a). This leads Paul to boast all the more about his weaknesses, so that Christ's power may rest on him. He delights "in weaknesses, in insults, in hardships, in persecutions, in difficulties. For when I am weak, then I am strong" (12:9b–10). But rather than recognizing the marks of genuine apostleship, the Corinthians did not commend Paul, showing preference for the "super-apostles" (12:11–12).

As with 1 Corinthians, this letter to Corinth completely inverts worldly thinking. Human strength, power, accomplishments, and status are irrelevant for the success of new-covenant ministry. In fact, they cut across the power of God's grace, which is perfected in human weakness. Paul's ministry among the churches is a fitting actualization of God's grace working through weakness, as his mortal body, lack of worldly acknowledgment, and chronic suffering are utilized for the eternal glory of God.

Implementation

Perhaps more than in any other letter, in 2 Corinthians Paul presents the inner heart of his ministry. The very existence of the letter—Paul is writing to the church in Corinth for the fourth time, in anticipation of his third visit there—demonstrates his unrelenting commitment to this group of challenging believers. The Corinthians had wielded personal insults against Paul, questioning his character, his authority, his giftedness, and his values. And they had consistently resisted Paul's exhortations to give up worldly ways of thinking. But rather than give in to the temptation to wield worldly defenses of himself and his message, Paul demonstrates what it means to reject the values of the world. Rather than boast of his strength, he revels in his weakness. Rather than celebrate his achievements, he highlights his sufferings. Rather than coerce the Corinthians to change, he models the worldview and values that he hopes to see in them.

Some believers and churches today are quick to celebrate flashy speakers, big preaching platforms, and ministry "success" (i.e., large numbers). And while the celebration of such "impressiveness" does not necessarily indicate a "Corinthianesque" infatuation with worldly values and thinking, it may well do so in certain situations. Paul's fourth letter to the Corinthians undermines worldly attitudes and values by pointing to the glory of God in Christ rather than human glory, the power of God that works through human weakness, and the eternal value of the new covenant in contrast to fading, fragile, and flawed human achievements. The letter requires believers to invert their natural instincts and to reinterpret everything in light of new-covenant spirituality.

Likewise, Paul hopes to see the Corinthians' hearts changed, as is evident in his discussion about generosity. Generosity is no good—nor is it genuine—if it does not come from the heart. Paul wants these believers to be generous because of what it reveals about their hearts, not because of whatever material benefit might result. Contemporary churches and ministries ought to keep this dynamic in mind: coercion and guilt-tripping are not godly ways to raise funds, nor are they in believers' best interests. If church and ministry leaders genuinely care about the spiritual well-being of their people, they ought to prioritize changed hearts, which will naturally result in generosity and myriad other godly characteristics.

Moreover, Paul sets an example for Christian leaders today by renouncing secret and shameful methods of power-wielding. Leaders ought to operate by persuasion, not coercion or manipulation, being compelled by the love of Christ. They must also be prepared to suffer hardship, mistreatment, and injustice, as they operate according to the upside-down values of cruciformity—in direct contrast to the culture and world around them. Leaders today, like Paul, are to carry in their bodies the death of Jesus, so that others might receive life. They ought not to lose heart because of their frailty, failures, or finitude but must fix their eyes on the eternal glory that is theirs in Christ.

Christian Reading Questions

1. In 2 Corinthians 4:10, Paul says that he and his coworkers "always carry around in our body the death of Jesus." What do you think this means, and how can it be applied to life today?
2. Take a closer look at 2 Corinthians 5:1–5, paying special attention to the terms "tent," "building," "house," and "clothed/unclothed." Try to put the passage into your own words.
3. Scan 2 Corinthians 10–12. Put into your own words Paul's position on "boasting."

PART 4

Paul’s Third Mission

CHAPTER TWELVE

Introduction to Paul's Third Mission

Chronology of Part 4: Paul's Third Mission (ca. 52–57)

ca. 52	From Syrian Antioch through Galatia to Ephesus
ca. 52–55	Three years in Ephesus
ca. 54	1 Corinthians written in Ephesus
ca. 55	Leaves for Macedonia
ca. 56	2 Corinthians written in Philippi
ca. 57	Three months in Corinth, where Romans was written
ca. 57	Bids farewell to the Ephesian elders in Miletus
ca. 57	Sails to Caesarea, then on to Jerusalem

The book of Acts wastes no space between Paul's second and third missions. After 18:22 reports that Paul arrived home in Syrian Antioch at the end of his second mission, the next verse simply says, "After spending some time there, he set out" on his third mission. It seems that Paul set out on his own this time, and once again visited the churches established on previous missions through Galatia and Phrygia in south central Türkiye today (18:23).

Ephesus

Paul kept his promise to return to Ephesus (Acts 18:21) and traveled west from Galatia to the western coast of Türkiye (19:1). He spoke in the

Paul's third missionary journey

synagogue in Ephesus for three months, but after Jewish opposition he began to speak every day in the lecture hall of Tyrannus for the following two years. This ministry was so effective that "all the residents of Asia, both Jews and Greeks, heard the word of the Lord" (19:8–10). Luke adds that God performed miracles through Paul, healing the sick and casting out evil spirits, which prompted some to try to copy him and others to become believers, renouncing their practice of magic (19:11–20).

READ ACTS 19:23–41

Paul spent roughly three years in Ephesus, but one major event dominates Luke's account of his Ephesian ministry. The silversmith Demetrius stirred up other craftsmen in the city because he could see that Paul's preaching of Christ would be bad for business, which depended on making shrines of the local deity Artemis. Paul's claim that gods made by hand were not gods at all had evidently made quite an impact in Ephesus

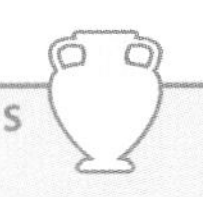

HISTORICAL MATTERS

Ephesus

Ephesus was the third-largest city in the Roman Empire, after Rome and Alexandria, and was the major hub of Asia Minor. The majestic temple of Artemis made Ephesus a major destination for spirituality and also for economy, as it also served as the bank for the region. With travelers constantly coming to and from Ephesus, and with its strong regional influence, Paul hoped that his ministry there would facilitate the rapid spread of his message throughout the eastern Roman Empire. Indeed, it seems that the church in Colossae, one hundred miles east of Ephesus, was planted exactly in this way.

Great Theater, Ephesus

HISTORICAL MATTERS

Artemis the Great

Artemis was goddess of the hunt, of wild animals, and of fertility, and was one of the most popular Greek deities. The Temple of Artemis in Ephesus was one of the Seven Wonders of the Ancient World. It was bigger than the Parthenon in Athens with 121 giant marble columns, only one of which is still standing today. The worship of Artemis was central to the religious, economic, and social fabric of Ephesus and drew visitors from around the Roman Empire.

Ephesian Artemis

POSTCARDS FROM THE MEDITERRANEAN

Ephesus

The ancient city of Ephesus is one of the most glorious Roman cities to visit today. The twenty-thousand-seat amphitheater featured in Acts 19 is spectacular, as is the Library of Celsus. It is great to walk the main street of the ancient city, lined with its temples, homes, and monuments. Located close to the western coast of Türkiye, Ephesus is one mile from the town of Selçuk, which is where the remains of the Temple of Artemis are located and where the apostle John is traditionally understood to have been buried.

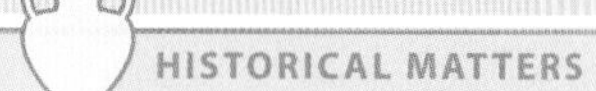
HISTORICAL MATTERS

***Ephesiaca*, by Xenophon of Ephesus**

Around the time when Paul lived in Ephesus, Xenophon of Ephesus wrote the work *Ephesiaca*, which portrays life in first-century Ephesus in vivid detail. It depicts the centrality of the worship of the goddesses Artemis and Isis in the life of wealthy Ephesians and their participation in social events such as leading processions and seeking oracles. The story also depicts certain expectations and obligations of wealthy Ephesians toward the gods. *Ephesiaca* illustrates the social rules and cultural fixtures of the ancient world as found in several other sources, including the importance of conformity to rules for maintaining honor, preserving identity, and ensuring social status in society.[1]

and the surrounding region, and Demetrius saw its risk to their livelihood as well as to the worship of their goddess (19:23–27). The whole city became embroiled, and the people rushed into the amphitheater. Paul was prevented from addressing the crowd, which chanted "Great is Artemis of the Ephesians!" for a full two hours. Finally, the city clerk calmed the commotion and explained that Demetrius and company could take the matter to the courts if they so wished. He then dismissed the assembly (19:21–41).

Macedonia, Achaia, Troas, Miletus

After Ephesus, Paul retraced the steps of his second mission through Macedonia and Achaia for a period of three months (Acts 20:1–3). Just as he had revisited churches in central Türkiye in order to encourage the believers, so now Paul revisited the churches begun on his first trip through this region. Acts is not specific here, but we can assume that this included Thessalonica, Berea, and Corinth. On his way back, Paul sailed from Philippi to Troas on the northwestern coast of Türkiye, where he spent a week. While Paul was speaking in an upper room at night, a young man named Eutychus fell asleep and fell out the window to his death. But Paul miraculously revived him, then went back upstairs to continue speaking until dawn (20:6–12).

Paul and his companions sailed from Troas to Miletus, deliberately bypassing Ephesus in order to avoid being held up there, since he was in a rush to reach Jerusalem in time for Pentecost. But he did ask the church elders in Ephesus to come south to meet him in Miletus for a final goodbye (20:13–17).

READ ACTS 20:18–38

Paul's farewell speech to the Ephesian elders demonstrates his determination to go to Jerusalem, in spite of certain risk, in order to complete the ministry given to him by the Lord Jesus (20:18–24). He sadly acknowledges that he will never see these dear friends again, while encouraging them to guard the flock under their care and reminding them of his example. Finally, after praying together, the elders embraced Paul, grieving the finality of their farewell (20:25–38). Paul and his companions then sailed their way through the Aegean and Mediterranean Seas to Syria, bringing his third mission to an end (21:1–3).

Paul's third mission did not involve any new locations, but he did establish the church in Ephesus, where he had only briefly visited on his second mission. He invested considerable time in that city—more than anywhere else on any mission—likely due to its strategic importance for the eastern part of the Roman Empire. From Ephesus, churches apparently sprang up through the surrounding region as people traveled in and out of the city, some carrying Paul's message with them. The church in Colossae was an example, begun by Epaphras after he had encountered Paul in Ephesus. Paul's third mission also reinforced the churches established during his first and second missions through Türkiye and Greece.

POSTCARDS FROM THE MEDITERRANEAN

Linford Stutzman and *Sailing through Acts*

As stated on its cover, Linford Stutzman's book *Sailing through Acts* is probably the first book—since the book of Acts—written by someone who actually sailed the entire routes of the apostle Paul. A professor of religion, Stutzman undertook a fourteen-month journey with his wife, touching land in eight countries, to visit every site where Paul stopped. He says, "Following the routes of Paul through storms, darkness, cold, and heat, listening to the roar of the waves or the flapping of sails, approaching the legendary islands of the Aegean, anchoring in ancient harbors with their ruins of theaters and temples along the Greek and Turkish coastlines, viewing the fascinating cultures of the Mediterranean from sea level, following the voyages that changed the world, it is as a traveler and especially as a sailor, that I have come to better understand and appreciate Paul."[2]

CHAPTER THIRTEEN

Colossians and Philemon

Colossians

Orientation

Of Paul's letters, only Colossians and Romans are written to churches personally unknown to him. Though he knew certain individuals associated with them, he did not plant these congregations, nor had he spent time among them (Col. 2:1). Unlike the church in Rome, however, there is no indication that Paul intended to visit the church in Colossae, nor was it a church or city of strategic importance. Nevertheless, the Letter to the Colossians (sent also by Timothy) reveals his evident concern for them, his commitment to pray regularly for them, and his desire to see them grow from strength to strength in their faith in Christ.

The letter reveals how the church in Colossae came into being: through the ministry of a Colossian native, Epaphras (1:7; cf. 4:12). Paul regarded Epaphras as a fellow servant and faithful minister of Christ (1:7), and through him the gospel came to Colossae. Epaphras likely came to know Paul in the context of his Ephesian ministry during his third mission (ca. AD 52–55). Ephesus was only about a hundred and twenty miles east of Colossae, and as the most significant city in the region, there would have been a variety of potential reasons for Epaphras to have traveled there from his hometown. In Ephesus, Epaphras met Paul, became acquainted with his ministry, and became a Christian. At some point within the next few years,

Epaphras then returned to Colossae, preached the gospel of Christ, and planted a church there.

Epaphras and Paul remained in touch, allowing Paul to hear how the church in Colossae was growing and maturing (1:4, 7–9; cf. 4:7–9). And as the opening thanksgiving of the letter indicates, Paul heard that the church in Colossae had become known for its faith, hope, and love and that the gospel had borne fruit among them (1:4–6).

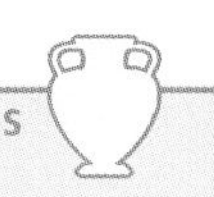

HISTORICAL MATTERS

Colossae

About a hundred and twenty miles east of Ephesus, the city of Colossae was located in the Lycus Valley in the Roman province of Asia (in west central Türkiye today). Though once an important city, by the time Paul (and Timothy) wrote to the Colossians its glory days had long faded, and it was now an insignificant and dwindling city, according to Pliny the Elder (AD 23–79). The city's two neighbors, Hierapolis and Laodicea, were bigger. The region was known for its wool—"Colossian wool" was dark red—fig, and olive production. Colossae was located on a major trade route and was enriched by its engagement in travelers' commerce and culture. Its population consisted of native Phrygians (Phrygia was located in today's west central Türkiye) and Greek immigrants. Around two thousand Jewish families were brought there from Mesopotamia and Babylon by Antiochus III in the second century BC. This led to a prominent Jewish influence in the area, mixed with other religious practices. For centuries, Colossae has been buried under sediment and earth, awaiting excavation. Plans are underway to excavate the site, led by Türkiye's Pammukale University.

The striking similarities between the Letters to the Colossians and Ephesians have long been noted. For instance, both letters share a similar structure and can be divided into two distinct halves (Col. 1–2; 3–4; Eph. 1–3; 4–6). Both emphasize the themes of participation with Christ, the supremacy of Christ, and the reconciliation of the cosmos in Christ. And most compelling are several similar phrases shared between the two letters, even with some parallels of exact wording.

A.Savin / Wikimedia Commons

Remains of the ancient city of Colossae

However, the similarities between the two letters should not be overplayed, and their differences are likewise instructive. For instance, Colossians (1,583 words) is considerably shorter than Ephesians (2,425 words), and the latter contains far more references to the Old Testament than does Colossians (partly accounting for the greater word count of Ephesians). If one letter relied on the other, it makes more sense that Ephesians was derived from Colossians—after all, why would the author *delete* Old Testament material that supports the argument? More likely, Colossians served as a template for Ephesians, which was bolstered with more supporting material.

While some scholars have argued that this means that one letter was written by a Paul imitator (or both letters were), it could also indicate that the letters were written by the same person during the same period. A compelling theory is that Colossians was written first to address the specific localized threat of the Colossian heresy. In so doing, Paul emphasized themes such as participation with Christ and the supremacy of Christ, which of course share universal significance. While the Colossian heresy apparently was limited to Colossae, the entire region was characterized by spiritual and magical beliefs and practices, and Paul believed that other churches in the region would benefit from the material originally addressed to the Colossians.

Though there are a few possible reconstructions, the letters were most likely written while Paul was imprisoned in Rome, before around AD 62, when an earthquake destroyed Colossae. Paul dispatched a coworker, Tychicus (Col. 4:7–8), to take the letter from Rome to Colossae, along with his Letter to Philemon (see below). Tychicus also likely delivered the Letter to the Ephesians around the churches of Asia Minor.

Overview of Colossians

Colossians falls neatly into two halves, with the major theological argumentation occupying chapters 1–2 and some of its practical and ethical implications teased out in chapters 3–4.

Colossians 1–2

- Paul thanks God for the Colossians, acknowledging their faith, hope, and love and how much the gospel has borne fruit among them (1:3–6).

- He prays that they will live worthily of the Lord, bearing fruit and joyfully giving thanks for their rescue from darkness, as they are now located in the kingdom of the Son and forgiven for their sins (1:9–14).
- Paul then launches into a glorious "Christ hymn," extolling him as the image of the invisible God and the one through whom the cosmos was created (1:15–17). He is the head of the church, the firstborn from the dead, with the fullness of God in him as he reconciles all things to himself (1:18–20).
- Paul reflects on the Colossians' reconciliation with God through Christ and rejoices in his sufferings for the church (1:21–24). It is his duty to declare the mystery now revealed in Christ so as to present everyone mature in him, regardless of whether he has met them or not (1:25–2:5).
- The fullness of God dwells in Christ, so believers are to live in him rather than be led astray by empty thinking (2:6–10). Believers have been spiritually circumcised, buried, and raised with Christ. Their sins, and all evil powers, have been conquered through his cross (2:11–15). As such, believers are not to fall into false worship (2:16–23).

Colossians 3–4

- Paul exhorts those raised with Christ to set their hearts and minds on things above, not on earthly things (3:1–4). Putting their vices to

Papyrus 46 showing the end of Philippians and the beginning of Colossians

death, believers are to be clothed with godly virtues, as the word of Christ dwells among them, with specific applications for households (3:5–4:1).

- Believers are to be devoted to prayer and wise in their interactions with outsiders, being graceful and winsome in conversation (4:2–6).
- The letter concludes with some lengthy greetings and an expression of Paul's desire that the Colossians would share the letter with the church in Laodicea and in turn read the (now lost) "letter from Laodicea" (4:7–18).

Exploration

The "Colossian Heresy"

READ COLOSSIANS 2:16–23

A major reason for writing the letter to the Colossians is to address the so-called Colossian heresy. It is "so-called" because it is not known to history outside this letter, so scholars do not know if Paul describes an actual religion or philosophy (perhaps unique to Colossae) or simply a mishmash of religious and spiritual practices that existed in Colossae at the time.

Paul begins to address the Colossian heresy in 2:8, as he warns his readers to avoid being taken captive by "hollow and deceptive philosophy" that is grounded on human and worldly elements rather than on Christ. He gets more specific in 2:16–23, referring to food regulations, religious festivals, religious days, and rules about worship and treatment of the body. It seems that the Colossian heresy involved specific religious and spiritual practices, including the worship of angels (2:18), in order that adherents might gain a greater degree of spiritual fulfillment.

Paul's chief problem with the Colossian heresy is that it implies that Christ is not enough. He offers the Christ hymn of 1:15–20 to demonstrate that Christ is supreme over all things and that the fullness of God dwells in him (1:19). If the very fullness of God dwells in Christ, and Christ dwells in believers (2:9–10), how can lesser elements achieve any greater spiritual fulfillment? Moreover, the belief that spiritual fullness can be found elsewhere implies that it is not found solely in Christ. In contrast to the Colossian heresy, Paul asserts that believers' spiritual identity and fulfillment are found by dying and rising with Christ.

As such, believers are to avoid being pressured into so-called spiritual practices that will undermine their sense of security and satisfaction in Christ. They are to avoid putting their confidence in fleshly and earthly elements as though those things can bring them into closer touch with the Divine. And they are to ignore pressure or judgment from others to do otherwise.

Public domain / Getty Center / Wikimedia Commons

Pompeo Batoni, *Christ in Glory with Saints Celsus, Julian, Marcionilla and Basilissa*, 1736

The Supremacy of Christ

READ COLOSSIANS 1:15–20

The Christ hymn of Colossians 1:15–20 is one of the most significant christological statements in the New Testament and is the highest expression of Paul's Christology. To begin with, Jesus the Son is described as "the image of the invisible God" (1:15a). While it is an oxymoron to describe something as the image of something invisible, this concept discloses some highly significant insights about Christ. First, he is the one able to reveal God. By definition, we cannot see the invisible God, but Jesus makes him known. Of course, it is not Jesus's physical appearance that is in view, as though that would help us to know what God looks like. It is his character, his mind, and his love that reveal who God is. Second, the "image" language evokes the creation of the first humans, who were made in God's image (Gen. 1:27). Jesus is the ultimate human, who fulfills the intention of humanity as God's image-bearers. Third, whereas Adam and Eve were made "in" the image of God, Jesus *is* the image of God. He is not merely a better expression of humanity than his forebears; he *is* the humanity in which they were formed. The full implications of these christological insights are seemingly unending.

Then Jesus is described as "the firstborn over all creation" (1:15b). The "firstborn" language has created some confusion, since it is easily read to support the false idea that Jesus came into existence at a certain point in time, rather than being of eternal existence, as orthodox Christology affirms. But it is important to appreciate the ancient significance of "firstborn" language. The firstborn of a family was given greatest honor and inheritance, and the point here is that Jesus is preeminent over all creation.

Jesus himself is not part of the creation, since "in him all things were created" (1:16a). Rather, he is the one through whom God created all things.

And this includes the entire sweep of creation—heavenly and earthly realities, whether visible or invisible, and all conceivable powers or authorities. Every element of creation was made "through him and for him" (1:16b). This means that Christ is not only the one through whom God created the cosmos but also the one *for* whom he created it. Moreover, he is the one in whom "all things hold together" (1:17). These are extraordinary claims that view Christ as the means, the sustaining power, and the goal of all creation.

The Christ hymn also describes Jesus as the head of the body—the church—and the firstborn from among the dead (1:18a). While the "firstborn" language could again be understood in a temporal sense (which makes more sense here, since Jesus *was* the first person to be permanently resurrected from the dead), again it should be understood in terms of preeminence, as the following phrase confirms: "so that in everything he might have the supremacy" (1:18b). Christ is supreme over the entire cosmos, and specifically he is supreme over the church.

Finally, the Christ hymn affirms that all the fullness of God dwells in Jesus, and through him God reconciles everything to himself (1:19–20a). This means that Christ is the means by which everything is put right; ultimately, everything will be restored and rectified through him. This includes earthly and heavenly things and is achieved "by making peace through his blood, shed on the cross" (1:20b). These brief statements are pregnant with significance, as Jesus is seen not only as the image of God but also as bearing his fullness. God is fully in Jesus, so that encountering Jesus is to encounter God. And his atoning work on the cross has cosmic significance, since it is the means through which all things in heaven and earth are reconciled to God. Jesus did not die solely to deal with humanity's sinfulness; he died for the entire cosmos so that peace and reconciliation with God would come through him.

Participating with Christ

READ COLOSSIANS 2:9–12

The focus on participation or union with Christ in this letter is second only to Ephesians. At the end of the first chapter, Paul affirms both that Christ is "in you" (1:27) and that he desires to see everyone fully mature "in Christ" (1:28). This highlights the mutual indwelling element of union with Christ, in which he is "in" believers and they are "in" him.

Believers are to live their lives in Christ, being rooted and built up in him (2:6–7). This means that the believer's entire life is defined by their union with Christ—they live in him and grow in him. They do not graduate or go beyond this fundamental reality of the Christian life. Moreover, the fullness

THEOLOGICAL ISSUES

What Is Union with Christ?

Several descriptions of union with Christ have been offered, but it is not easily defined. My own research describes it through the terms "union" (being joined to Christ), "participation" (sharing in Christ's death, resurrection, and ascension), "identification" (being located in the realm of Christ), and "incorporation" (inclusion in the body of Christ). In Colossians, the primary focus is on participation with Christ, as the concepts of dying and rising with Christ are highly significant for Paul's argument. The spiritual participation of believers in the death of Christ is seen as the way in which they escape the tyranny of opposing powers, while their spiritual participation in the resurrection of Christ enables believers to transcend earthly allegiances in preference for heavenly ones.

of God dwells in Christ, and Christ dwells in believers, so that "in Christ you have been brought to fullness" (2:9–10).

In Christ believers are spiritually "circumcised," meaning that the person formerly ruled by "the flesh"—or the sinful nature—was put off (2:11). The tyranny of the sinful nature is escaped through spiritual death, since believers have been buried with Christ in baptism and raised with him through faith in God (2:12). These tightly compressed statements reveal that the only escape from the dark powers that rule over human beings comes through spiritual death and resurrection with Christ. By participation with Christ, believers are given new life and freedom from their former captors.

Paul adds that believers were once dead in their sins and in "the uncircumcision" of their flesh, but God has made them alive with Christ (2:13a; cf. Eph. 2:1–5). Again, spiritual resurrection occurs through participation with Christ. And as spiritually resurrected people, believers' sins have been forgiven, with all obligation to the law canceled and purged through the cross of Christ (2:13b–14).

As he counters the so-called Colossian heresy (see above), Paul appeals to the fact that his readers have died with Christ and therefore ought not to submit to earthbound rules and expectations (2:20–23). Again we see that participation in the death of Christ releases believers from the control of competing forces. And participation in the resurrection of Christ allows believers to fix their hearts and minds on things above, rather than earthly things (3:1–2). Believers have died with Christ, and now their new lives are "hidden with Christ in God." When Christ comes again, believers will appear with him in glory (3:3–4).

These statements again underscore the essential significance of participation with Christ, as believers' death with Christ frees them from spiritual oppression. Their resurrection with him lifts them to a heavenly plane, and their close connection with Christ keeps them protected under his care until the point when they will share in his glorious return. Participation with Christ is therefore seen as the underlying principle that shapes the entire Christian identity and experience. It is the means through which believers escape the old, access the new, and remain secure for the future. Participation with Christ is a spiritual reality that constructs believers' destiny, regardless of whether or not they "sense" this element of their spiritual world. In this manner it is an "objective" reality, though unseen and intangible. And though participation with Christ is itself intangible, its implications for life today are deeply tangible.

Implementation

The message of the Letter to the Colossians is directly relevant for Christians living in the twenty-first century. Though we may not be subjected to the Colossian heresy per se, plenty of alternate spiritualities compete for our attention. Many of these are pseudo-Christian forms of worship that share some elements of orthodox belief while distorting it enough to no longer be considered authentic Christianity. Such variations can be tricky to navigate precisely because they draw on some elements of orthodox belief and might therefore seem legitimate. But any form of spirituality that effectively undermines the supremacy or sufficiency of Christ is not the orthodox faith. Colossians reminds believers that Christ is above all competing powers; that the fullness of God dwells in him; that he dwells within believers; and that he is therefore sufficient to share divine fullness with his worshipers. Not only is there nothing to be gained by the worship of angels or ascetic practices, but such things actually undermine the confession that Christ is supreme and sufficient.

The positive aspect of this is to impress upon believers how majestic, glorious, and centrally significant is Christ. He is nothing less than the Lord of the entire cosmos, the one holding all things together, and the source of life and reconciliation with God. With the fullness of God dwelling within him, it is also profoundly significant that believers are in union with Christ, having died and risen with him. We are in Christ and he is in us, so that it is accurate to claim that the fullness of God dwells within us, in Christ. In some quarters of the church today, these enormously significant elements are not deeply appreciated or embraced. Many believers hold to a thin vision of what Christ has achieved for them, focusing almost entirely on his death for our sins, while ignoring his cosmically reconciling impartation of the fullness of God.

Christian Reading Questions

1. Compare and contrast Colossians 1:15–20 and John 1:1–18. What similarities or parallels do you find? What differences can be detected between the two texts?

2. Drawing on Colossians 2–3, put into your own words the significance of dying and rising with Christ.
3. Compare and contrast the household codes of Colossians 3:18–4:1 and Ephesians 5:22–6:9. What is the effect of the differences between the two texts?

Philemon

Orientation

There is an inherent connection between Philemon and Colossians. First, Philemon was a prominent member of the church in Colossae. Second, both letters likely were written during Paul's Roman imprisonment (Col. 4:18; Philem. 1, 23). Third, Timothy is the coauthor of both letters (Col. 1:1; Philem. 1), and Paul mentions the same coworkers in both: Luke, Mark, Demas, Aristarchus, Archippus, and Epaphras (Col. 1:7; 4:10, 12, 14, 17; Philem. 2, 23, 24). Fourth, it is likely that both letters were sent to Colossae together at the same time.

Philemon lived in Colossae and apparently came to faith through Paul's ministry (v. 19). Since Paul never visited the town (cf. Col. 2:1), it is likely that Philemon encountered him in Ephesus—the major hub of Paul's third mission—which was situated near Colossae, about a hundred and twenty miles to the west. Philemon hosted the Colossian church in his home (v. 2), and Paul regarded him as a faithful believer who served others (v. 7).

Philemon was also a slaveholder, which is essential background for Paul's letter. It seems that Philemon's slave, Onesimus, had run away (though this is debated), met Paul, and become a Christian. Paul sent Onesimus back to his master along with this letter, which arguably urges Philemon to grant Onesimus his freedom.

The intent of Paul's letter has long been debated, but this is in part because Paul is relatively indirect (compared to his usual style!), which allows a degree of ambiguity. The traditional view is likely correct: Paul "hints" that he'd like Philemon to grant

HISTORICAL MATTERS

Did Onesimus Run Away?

Historically, the most common reconstruction of Paul's Letter to Philemon was that Onesimus was a runaway slave, but recent commentators have challenged that view. If Onesimus was a fugitive, Paul does not mention it, and there is no indication that Onesimus was in danger of punishment upon his return to Philemon. If Onesimus was not a runaway, it is possible that Philemon had sent him to assist Paul. On the other hand, if Onesimus had run away, Paul may have deliberately omitted mention of his fugitive status in order to avoid alerting the authorities, since fugitive slaves were a long-standing problem in the ancient world and laws allowed owners to punish their runaways.

Onesimus's freedom, and he does this indirectly in order to respect Philemon's position and legal rights as a slaveholder. He offers him due respect, while pushing the point fairly strongly without ever being explicit.

A core conviction that drives Paul's appeal to Philemon is the fact that Philemon's slave, Onesimus, is now also his brother in Christ. This extraordinary new reality transcends the legal, social, and economic substructures of the Roman world in which they live. Similarly, Paul's Letter to Philemon continues to hold explosive significance for today's world.

Overview of Philemon

Paul's shortest letter has a simple structure that falls into three sections: verses 1–7, 8–16, and 17–25.

Philemon 1–7

- Paul reports his thanksgiving for Philemon's love and faith (vv. 4–5).
- He prays that Philemon's participation in the faith may become effective for the glory of Christ, and Paul reflects on the joy that he experiences as a result of Philemon's love for others (vv. 6–7).

Philemon 8–16

- Paul appeals to Philemon on behalf of Onesimus, who has become attached to him (vv. 8–10).
- Paul has sent Onesimus back to Philemon, though he wanted to keep Onesimus with him during his imprisonment. But not wanting to do anything without Philemon's consent, Paul appeals to his free will (vv. 11–14).
- He suggests that Onesimus's separation from Philemon may have been part of a divine plan to lead Onesimus to Christ, so that Philemon might receive him back as a dearly loved brother rather than as a slave (vv. 15–16).

Philemon 17–25

- Paul asks Philemon to welcome Onesimus as he would Paul and to charge Paul for anything owing from Onesimus's account. Paul will be sure to pay it—even though Philemon owes him everything (vv. 17–19).

- He hopes his heart will be refreshed by Philemon, knowing that he will do even more than Paul asks (hint, hint!) (vv. 20–21).
- Finally, Paul asks Philemon to keep a guest room ready for him in the hope of a visit, and he extends greetings from mutual friends (vv. 22–24).

Exploration

Participation in the Faith

READ PHILEMON 5–6

Paul's Letter to Philemon, and whatever requests we might detect in it, is grounded in Philemon's shared participation in the faith (v. 6). Here "the faith" refers to the body of beliefs that all Christians hold, rather than someone's personal faith in God or Jesus. Someone's "participation in the faith" (CSB), or "partnership in the faith" (NIV), therefore refers to their active membership in and commitment to the group that holds such beliefs in common—that is, the church.

Paul prays that Philemon's participation in the faith would become effective for the glory of Christ (v. 6). He hopes to see Philemon act in a way that is consistent with the concerns of "the faith"—to act like a Christian—and to do so for the sake of Christ (rather than for Paul's or Onesimus's sake). It's not as though Philemon has not already been acting according to the faith, since Paul calls him his "coworker" (v. 1b), he hosts the church in his home (v. 2b), and he has already shown much love for his fellow believers (vv. 5, 7). So it seems that Paul is gearing up to ask something further of Philemon and prays that Philemon will be up to the task.

If the traditional view of the letter is correct and Paul hopes that Philemon will grant Onesimus his freedom, this is no doubt the special request that Paul prays about. He hopes that Philemon's participation in the faith will become (even more) effective as he considers Paul's forthcoming request. And the anticipated action will come through Philemon's appreciation of every good thing that God has given him through Christ (v. 6b). Since God has been so gracious to Philemon, will Philemon extend grace to Paul and Onesimus?

Asking, Not Commanding

READ PHILEMON 8–11

Paul does not hesitate to remind Philemon of his debt to him, portraying Onesimus as serving Paul in Philemon's place (v. 13), and stating that

HISTORICAL MATTERS

Slavery in the Roman World

Institutionalized slavery existed virtually everywhere in the ancient world. Slavery was a legal status rather than an occupation—slaves were regarded as property like animals. Though first-century slaves were granted certain rights, they nevertheless were vulnerable to violence and abuse, since they were expected to be absolutely obedient to their masters. But some household slaves could live comfortably compared to free but poor people. In the first century, up to 40 percent of Rome's population were slaves, with around 250,000 slaves sold each year within the empire. Slaves could perform a wide range of duties, including farming, mining, teaching, cooking, management, artistry, and whatever their owners wanted.

Photo by Jun / CC BY-SA 2.0 / Wikimedia Commons

Roman slaves

Philemon owes Paul his very self (v. 19). Clearly, Paul thinks Philemon owes him one!

While he is willing to mention this debt, however, Paul is also careful not to demand what he wants from Philemon. He treads a delicate line between obligation and favor. Paul explicitly says as much when he claims to have the boldness in Christ to command Philemon "to do what is right" but instead will appeal to him on the basis of love (vv. 8–9a). So, Paul—an elderly man—appeals to Philemon for his "son," Onesimus (vv. 9b–10). In sending Onesimus back to Philemon, he says, "I am sending my very own heart," and he would have preferred to keep Onesimus with him but did not want to do anything without Philemon's consent (vv. 12–14a). In this way, Paul hopes that Philemon will grant his request by his own free will, rather than out of obligation (v. 14).

Having said that, Paul is also clear that he does expect Philemon to grant his request, as revealed in verse 21: "I am confident of your obedience . . . , knowing that you will do even more than I say." The mention of "obedience"—though Paul has made an appeal, not a command—is strong language, and perhaps confusing for Philemon. And Paul "knows" that Philemon will do "even more" than he requests, suggesting that Philemon ought to read between the lines and do what Paul is really asking, though he has not laid out his request explicitly.

THEOLOGICAL ISSUES

Did Paul Support Slavery?

Paul neither endorsed nor condemned the institution of slavery—just as Jesus did not denounce it though he referred to slaves in several of his parables (e.g., Matt. 18:23–25; Mark 13:32–37; Luke 17:7–10). Unfortunately, this lack of indictment enabled the practice of slavery and the slave trade in Europe and the New World. In response to this, some contemporary scholars have suggested that the ancient practice of slavery was not as brutal or immoral as the race-based slavery seen in Europe and the Americas, but others have shown that ancient slavery could be devastatingly cruel. While it is true that Paul did not explicitly condemn slavery, and in fact he sent Onesimus back to his master, Philemon, his theological view that all people—including slaves and masters—are equal in Christ is radically subversive of the status quo of his day. Radical equality in Christ ultimately spelled the end of institutional slavery, as its implications eventually took hold in the intellectual and moral landscape of the Western world.

Brotherhood and Fellowship

READ PHILEMON 15–16

A major feature of the letter is the stress that Paul puts on the brotherhood and fellowship shared between him, Onesimus, and Philemon. From the beginning of the letter, Paul refers to Philemon as "our dear friend" (v. 1b), and he twice calls him "brother" (vv. 7, 20). On the basis of their partnership, Paul asks Philemon to welcome Onesimus as he would welcome Paul (v. 17). Their friendship is also evident in Paul's hope to be "restored" to Philemon (v. 22). Alongside Philemon, Paul's strong affection for Onesimus is also clear, referring to him as his "son" (v. 10) and his "very own heart" (v. 12). He expects Philemon to receive Onesimus as "a dearly loved brother," while Onesimus "is especially so" to Paul (v. 16). Paul's desire to advocate for Onesimus and to cover his expenses also reveals his affection.

While Paul's relationships with Philemon, on the one hand, and Onesimus, on the other, are not in doubt, he is eager to encourage a strong relationship between the two of them. Like someone who wants their two good friends to become friends with each other, Paul hopes to "matchmake" a friendship between Philemon and Onesimus. But Paul's goal is higher than simply friendship: he asserts and affirms that Philemon and Onesimus are brothers in the Lord. Philemon is to welcome Onesimus as a dearly loved brother and no longer regard him as a slave (v. 16). Their brotherhood in Christ is a fact; Paul simply wants to impress that fact upon Philemon so that he would act accordingly.

While the world around Philemon and Onesimus viewed them as belonging to different strata of society, with vastly unequal measures of respective worth and importance, in Christ they are brothers with equal status, value, and dignity before God. The concept that the relationship between a master and slave could transcend the legal, social, and economic substructures of the Roman world in which they lived is truly extraordinary.

Implementation

An interesting element to consider in Paul's Letter to Philemon is how to apply spiritual facts to specific situations. Paul regards Philemon's participation in the faith as an objective fact; so, too, Philemon's spiritual brotherhood with Onesimus. Yet while these facts are not in doubt, Paul does not lay down the law as to how they should be applied. Certainly, Paul has a clear preference for how he'd like such facts to be applied, but he does not impose that on Philemon. He lets Philemon know what he wants, but he does not demand it.

This dynamic is worth careful attention today, as believers sometimes put as much weight on specific applications of spiritual truths as they do on the spiritual truths themselves. To be sure, in some instances the application of certain spiritual truths is not in doubt, and there is a direct correlation between truth and action (e.g., worship of false gods is a direct and serious contravention of the truth that there is only one God). But in other instances the application of spiritual truth is not as direct and therefore not as certain. Participation in the faith and brotherhood in the Lord *might* lead a master to emancipate his slave, but not necessarily. Paul grasps this nuance and communicates with Philemon accordingly.

Issues that require similar nuance today might include how to vote, how to dress, how to regard alcohol consumption, or how to engage various other social issues. In many such instances there is no black-and-white Christian response. And even though certain spiritual truths speak to such issues, their application can vary depending on a range of factors. It's important that believers do not overplay their hand by insisting on set attitudes and behaviors that might represent only one perspective on how to apply spiritual truths.

Related to this is Paul's reluctance to use his spiritual authority to insist on what he wants. The term "spiritual abuse" has come into prominence in recent years, as pastors, preachers, or others with some measure of spiritual authority use their position to lord it over others. The "spiritual" nature of their leadership can be mistaken to mean that their personal opinions or whims come with the authority of God, when that is clearly not the case. A litmus test is to ask who will benefit from specific applications. Though his request to Philemon will primarily benefit Onesimus, Paul is aware that he stands to benefit too if Onesimus is granted his freedom. It would not be right to insist on something that is so much in his own interest. Likewise, pastors, preachers, and Christian leaders ought to check whether their demands are self-serving or are genuinely offered in the best interest of others.

Finally, socially constructed divisions of status are transcended by shared participation in the faith and brother- and sisterhood in Christ. While equality in Christ might not erase elements of worldly status from the world's eyes, in the church they are relativized if not erased entirely. All believers are brothers and sisters with equal dignity, value, and significance in the kingdom of God.

Christian Reading Questions

1. A traditional view understands Onesimus to be a runaway slave. What evidence can be found in Paul's Letter to Philemon to support this view?
2. If Paul really is asking Philemon to grant Onesimus his freedom, why does he seem unbothered by other Christian slaves remaining slaves (cf. Col. 3:22–25)?

CHAPTER FOURTEEN

Ephesians

Orientation

Along with the other "prison epistles," Paul most likely composed Ephesians while under house arrest in Rome within the last few years of his life, around AD 60–62 (Acts 28:16, 30–31). He adapted material from his Letter to the Colossians in order to produce a general letter that was to circulate around the churches in the cities of western Asia, of which Ephesus was the spiritual, commercial, and political hub. He sent Tychicus to deliver the letters to the Ephesians, the Colossians, and to Philemon around AD 62.

Ephesians is a "cosmic" letter, addressing the whole of creation—including physical and spiritual realms—and it offers an eternal view, addressing the mission of God before the foundation of the world through to

LITERARY NOTES

The Authorship of Ephesians

No one seriously questioned the Pauline authorship of Ephesians until the nineteenth century. Today, roughly 50 percent of Pauline scholars doubt its authenticity for reasons of (1) theology; (2) grammar, vocabulary, and syntax; (3) historical circumstances; and (4) its relationship to Colossians. In short, some scholars view Ephesians as being inconsistent in various ways with what we know about the "authentic Paul." Doubt about Pauline authorship is grounded on comparisons between this "authentic Paul" and the letter. But scholars who affirm the Pauline authorship of Ephesians argue that such negative comparisons are overstated and are not sufficient to overturn the unanimous opinion of the early church.

Gustave Doré, *St. Paul Writing Ephesians in Prison*, 1886

its ultimate fulfillment in the age to come. Ephesians presents a cosmic Christ, who is the central figure of the universe and the one through whom God is bringing all things together. He is supreme over all competing powers and yet operates in the hearts and lives of human beings. God has raised a people from the dead to be seated with Christ in the heavens, making him the reconciling centerpiece of God's plans for humanity and everything else. Christ is the head of his body, the church, which is to live out its calling by the power of God. He dwells in his people, transforming them into a new creation and a new humanity, all to the praise and glory of God.

Ephesus

Overview of Ephesians

Ephesians falls into two neat halves, with the major theological argumentation occupying chapters 1–3 and some of its practical and ethical implications teased out in chapters 4–6.

Ephesians 1–3

- Paul offers a doxology, which introduces a multitude of God's blessings, with the thread of union with Christ running through them (1:3–14).
- The doxology leads to Paul's thanksgiving prayer for his readers' faith in Jesus, praying that they would be enlightened as to their glorious inheritance and God's power, which is seen in Christ's elevation above all other powers (1:15–23).
- The letter's argument proper begins in chapter 2, as Paul describes how God has caused the spiritually dead to be raised with Christ (2:1–10).

RECEPTION HISTORY

The Enduring Significance of Ephesians

New Testament scholar Raymond Brown claimed, "Among the Pauline writings, only Romans can match Ephesians as a candidate for exercising the most influence on Christian thought and spirituality."[1] Given Paul's massive influence in the world's largest-ever religion, as one of his two most influential letters, Ephesians is regarded as one of the most significant letters ever written.

LITERARY NOTES

To Whom Is Ephesians Addressed?

Though it is known as Paul's Letter to the Ephesians, Ephesus is mentioned only in the first verse of the letter, and the earliest and most reliable manuscripts do not include "in Ephesus" in 1:1. It is also significant that the writings of the Apostolic Fathers do not give unanimous support to an Ephesian audience. These facts, along with the letter's lack of personal references, have led many scholars to doubt that Ephesians was originally written to the church in Ephesus. Instead, it may have been a circular letter intended for the churches in Asia Minor (western Türkiye today), including the church in Ephesus. Because of its significance for the region, the city of Ephesus became associated with the letter that would later bear its name.

- They are therefore saved by grace through faith, creating a level playing field between Jews and gentiles, who are now joined together in Christ (2:11–22).
- Paul's discussion of gentile inclusion with the Jews leads him to reflect on his own role as a prisoner of Christ (3:1–13) and to offer a prayer for spiritual power so that the gentiles might comprehend the extent of God's love in Christ (3:14–21).

Ephesians 4–6

- Paul states that there is one body, in which the various parts work together for its common growth and maturity (4:1–16).
- In order to express the oneness of the body of Christ, believers are to live out their new-for-old replacement, putting aside previous ungodly behaviors in favor of new godly ones (4:17–32).
- Having turned away from their previous lives in darkness, believers are to walk in the way of love according to the light of Christ (5:1–21). Such walking has implications for each member of the family, as elaborated in the household code (5:22–6:9).
- Finally, Paul reminds his readers that their whole lives are shaped by an invisible spiritual battle against the evil spiritual forces opposed to Christ. Wearing the full armor of God, believers will resist and be protected from evil while they await its final vanquishing (6:10–17).
- After encouraging his readers to pray for themselves and for him, Paul signs off (6:18–24).

Exploration

Thematically rich, Ephesians contains five main themes: union with Christ, the supremacy of Christ, salvation, Jew and gentile reconciliation, and the church.

Union with Christ

READ EPHESIANS 1:3–14

If there is one theological theme that Ephesians addresses more than any other Pauline letter, it is his theology of union with Christ. While it occurs frequently in his other letters, especially Colossians, the theme of union with Christ is deeply woven into the fabric of Ephesians. It is central to every other major theme in the letter, such as salvation, Jew and gentile reconciliation, and the church. It could be argued that union with Christ is the most essential theological ingredient for the argument of Ephesians.

Union with Christ is in view from the first verse ("To the faithful saints *in Christ Jesus*"), and it receives extended treatment in the opening doxology of 1:3–14. The doxology is introduced and summarized in 1:3: "Blessed is the God and Father of our Lord Jesus Christ, *who has blessed us with every spiritual blessing in the heavens in Christ*." The rest of the doxology articulates some of the spiritual blessings that are found "in Christ," including being chosen "in him" (1:4), being predestined for adoption "through Jesus Christ" (1:5), being lavished with God's grace "in the Beloved One" (1:6), and receiving redemption "in him" (1:7). God's good pleasure was purposed "in Christ" (1:9) to bring everything together "in Christ" (1:10). Believers have received an inheritance "in him" (1:11) and have put their hope "in Christ" (1:12), having been sealed with the Spirit "in him" (1:13). With such a concentration of "in Christ"–type phrases, the opening doxology of Ephesians is the richest collection of "union with Christ" language found anywhere in the New Testament.

The next major section of the letter that depends on union with Christ is 2:1–10, which argues that believers are saved by grace through faith. While salvation by grace is the inevitable outcome of the argument, union with Christ does the heavy lifting. The problem raised at the outset is spiritual death and alienation from God (2:1–3), and the solution is that God has made believers alive "with Christ," raised them up "with him," and seated them "with him" in the heavens "in Christ Jesus" (2:4–6). This "with" language indicates participation with Christ as Paul articulates the path to salvation through God's action to cause believers to participate in the resurrection, ascension, and exaltation of Christ.

Union with Christ also features in 2:11–22. The problem raised is gentile alienation from Judaism and all its divine privileges (2:11–12), and the solution is that "in Christ Jesus" those far away have been brought near (2:13), having been made one new person "in him" (2:15). Christ reconciled both Jews and gentiles to God "in one body" (2:16), so that "through him" both have access to the Father (2:18). "In him," Jews and gentiles are built into a temple for God's dwelling (2:21–22).

The next major employment of "union with Christ" theology is found in 4:12–16, in which the image of the body of Christ is a fundamental

THEOLOGICAL ISSUES

What Is Union with Christ?

Paul's theology of union with Christ can be understood by breaking it up into four broad concepts: "union" (being joined to Christ), "participation" (sharing in Christ's death, resurrection, and ascension), "identification" (being located in the realm of Christ), and "incorporation" (inclusion in the body of Christ). The theme of union with Christ can be identified through a range of idioms, such as "in Christ" (or "in him," "in whom"), "with Christ," "through Christ," and similar phrases. But there are also a variety of metaphors used, such as body, temple, building, clothing, and marriage, which convey significant elements of believers' union with Christ.

metaphor. The saints' ministry is to "build up the body of Christ" (4:12), so that believers together will "grow in every way into him who is the head—Christ" (4:15). The whole body grows from him as it builds itself up in love (4:16). Since the metaphor of the body of Christ is an essential image for Paul's teaching about union with Christ, it is clear that this union stands at the heart of the church's growth and ministry.

The extended address to wives and husbands in 5:22–33 also draws heavily on the theme of union with Christ. The body imagery again plays a significant role as Christ is described as the Savior of the body, the church (5:23), and husbands are to love their wives as their own bodies (5:28). The union inherent to the body imagery finds explicit mention with the phrases "He who loves his wife loves himself" (5:28b) and "We are members of his body" (5:30). But the climax of "union with Christ" theology comes after Paul's quotation of Genesis 2:24—the foundational biblical statement about marriage—when he says that the phrase "The two will become one flesh" ultimately applies to Christ and the church (5:32). In other words, Paul claims that Christ and the church share a profound "one flesh" union. Union with Christ, therefore, is viewed as an intimate marriage-type union in which Christ and the church have become one.

The Supremacy of Christ

READ EPHESIANS 1:20–23

Alongside its focus on union with Christ, Ephesians addresses the supremacy of Christ. While Ephesians does not have an equivalent to Colossians' Christ hymn of 1:15–20, it nevertheless asserts the universal supremacy of Christ over "every ruler and authority, power and dominion, and every title given, not only in this age but also in the one to come" (1:21). With Christ seated at the messianic position at the right hand of the Father, everything has been subjected to him, who has been appointed head over everything (1:20–22).

The supremacy of Christ is also implied in 6:10–17, in which believers are exhorted to "be strengthened by the Lord and by his vast strength" (6:10), where "Lord" refers to Christ. The vast strength of Christ is the means by which believers are able to stand against the schemes of the devil and all other evil spiritual powers (6:11–12).

Finally, Christ is pictured as the center of the entire cosmos, since God's purpose is "to bring everything together in Christ, both things in heaven and things on earth in him" (1:10). This idea relates to the supremacy of Christ as it demonstrates his preeminent significance for all creation. The universe literally revolves around him.

Salvation

READ EPHESIANS 2:1–10

The key passage addressing salvation is 2:1–10. As noted above, salvation by grace through faith is powered by union with Christ as believers are made alive with Christ, raised up with him, and seated with him in the heavens (2:5–6). Before being united with Christ, people were spiritually dead in their sins and under the influence of the forces of evil (2:1–2). Salvation, therefore, involves spiritual resurrection in order to overturn the state of spiritual death.

Salvation also involves being seated with Christ in the heavens (2:6). This is described as a present reality, having already been accomplished, rather than a future expectation (though it includes a future-oriented element [2:7]). As such, it may be a confusing notion for believers whose experience remains very much earthbound. But the heavens represent a spiritual dimension that believers are connected to by their union with Christ. Their connection to that dimension coexists with the reality of life on earth here and now. This means that believers are "with Christ" in a spiritual sense though he is physically absent. Being seated with Christ in the heavens also implies that believers share in his elevated status above every ruler and authority, power and dominion, over which Christ has been seated at God's right hand (1:20–21). Though believers will continue to battle the spiritual forces of darkness (6:10–17), they have already taken a seat at the victor's table.

Salvation also involves a fundamental change of orientation and conduct. Once spiritually dead in sins, believers "walked according to the ways of this world" and "according to the ruler of the power of the air" (2:1–3). But having been made alive with Christ, and therefore saved by grace through faith (2:5, 8), believers have been re-created in Christ Jesus. They now walk in the good deeds that God has prepared in advance (2:10).

It is clear, then, that the salvation presented in 2:1–10 is more sophisticated than a simplistic "removal of sins" view of salvation. Salvation begins with the recognition of spiritual death and the influence of evil powers over spiritually dead people. It recognizes their powerlessness to alter their situation and that it is up to God—motivated by mercy and love—to raise the dead to life with Christ. He seats them with Christ in the heavens, far above all competing spiritual forces, and gives them an eternal view of his grace and kindness in

CANONICAL CONNECTIONS

Isaiah and Psalms

Paul draws on Isaiah and several psalms to demonstrate that believers are united to God's anointed king in his victory over God's enemies. Christ is now enthroned in heaven, seated above competing rulers, authorities, and powers (Eph. 1:20–22; 4:8; cf. Pss. 8:6; 68:18; 110:1). When the people of Christ take their stand against such powers (Eph. 6:10–17), they do so with the armor of God and of his Messiah, as seen in Isaiah 11:5; 52:7; 59:17.

Christ. This entire picture is what Paul describes as salvation, which clearly comes by the grace of God, not by human effort, achievement, or any kind of works, leaving saved human beings entirely without boast before God. They are his workmanship and a new creation in Christ, now living anew under the influence of God.

CANONICAL CONNECTIONS

Peace between the Nations

In his discussion of the reconciliation of Jews and gentiles in 2:13–17, Paul alludes to Isaiah 57:19, which points to a future peace between the nations, Israel, and God. A common theme in Isaiah (2:2–4; 11:10; 19:24–25; 45:14, 22; 51:4–5; 52:10; 55:5; 56:6–7; 60:11; 66:18–23), it is sometimes connected to the idea of a new creation (66:18–23). Paul sees the union of Jew and gentile as the creation of a new person (2:15), while the new-creation theme is observed throughout Ephesians (2:10; 3:9; 4:13, 22, 24).

Peace among the Nations, stained-glass window, Canterbury Cathedral

Jew and Gentile Reconciliation

READ EPHESIANS 2:11–22

The first major application of salvation by grace through faith (2:1–10) is the reconciliation between believing Jews and gentiles in 2:11–22. The logic is that both Jews and gentiles rely on the mercy and love of God to raise them from spiritual death (2:1–5), and so salvation is a level playing field. There is no sense in which gentile believers are excluded from the privileges and blessings that Jewish believers enjoy. Paul reminds his gentile readers that they were once without Christ, excluded from the citizenship of Israel and its covenants (2:11–12). But in Christ, gentile believers have been brought near by his blood (2:13). Christ is the peace between the two factions, having made both groups one and having removed the elements that once stood to divide them (2:13–17). Gentile believers are now fellow citizens with Jewish believers and have been built together with them as the new holy temple in which God dwells by his Spirit (2:19–22).

The unification of Jews and gentiles in Christ marks a dramatic new chapter of salvation history, in which Paul has a unique and significant role. In 3:1–13, he discusses "the administration of God's grace that he gave me" for the gentiles (3:1–2). If God's grace has enabled all people to be saved through faith, it is Paul's job to make this grace known. As such, Paul has been given insight into "the mystery of

Christ"—a secret hidden for generations but now revealed to the apostles and prophets—that the gentiles are coheirs and partners in the promise in Christ through the gospel (3:4–6).

Paul was made a servant of the gospel by God's grace and therefore must proclaim the riches of Christ to the gentiles (3:7–8). And through gentile faith in Christ, God's profound wisdom is made known throughout the cosmos according to his eternal purpose accomplished in Christ (3:10–11). Paul's sufferings for the gentile cause, therefore, are not a reason for discouragement but rather lead to gentile glorification (3:1, 13).

The Church

READ EPHESIANS 4:11–16

If salvation by grace through faith leads to the unification of Jews and gentiles in Christ, so their reconciliation leads to Ephesians' teaching on the church. The new oneness between these two former factions underscores the oneness of the church. The letter presents a picture of a united "universal" church, rather than distinct congregations scattered throughout the Roman Empire. So, the first major section of the letter to address the church, 4:1–16, begins by strongly emphasizing its oneness. Believers are to strive for the unity of the Spirit because they are, in fact, already one. They share in the one body, one Spirit, one hope, one Lord, one faith, one baptism, and one God and Father of all (4:3–6).

But the oneness of the church is immediately qualified by an exploration of its diversity. Such diversity is undergirded by "the measure of Christ's gift" (4:7), producing "some to be apostles, some prophets, some evangelists, some pastors and teachers" (4:11). The people who occupy these roles for the church are Christ's gifts for its equipment and edification. But it is clear that the church grows through all its members, rather than by a "professional elite," for the real task of church leaders is to prepare the whole for its own works of service (4:12). The all-member service of the church is to enhance the unity in the faith, knowledge of Christ, and growth to maturity. Such maturity is to protect believers from false teaching as the church speaks the truth in love and grows further into Christ. From Christ, every part of the body works toward the growth of the whole (4:13–16). In order for the church to live out its maturity and growth, believers must replace their previous ungodly behaviors with those that are consistent with love and unity (4:25–32).

The final major section to address the church is the husband-wife part of the household code in 5:22–33. Here wives are metaphorically likened to the church, of which Christ is head (5:23). The church submits to Christ,

THEOLOGICAL ISSUES

The *Missio Dei*

A major concern of Ephesians is the *missio Dei*—the mission of God—which has the ultimate fate of the entire cosmos in its scope. God is bringing all things in heaven and earth together in Christ. His plan to do so has been worked out through the history of Israel, the reconciliation of Jews and gentiles, the formation of the church as the body of Christ, and the overthrow of competing cosmic powers. Finally, the *missio Dei* leads to the ultimate praise of God's glory.

who loved her by giving himself for her (5:24–25; cf. 5:2). Christ has made the church holy, presenting her to himself without imperfection (5:26–27). After citing Genesis 2:24, the foundational biblical text about marriage, Paul claims that it refers to Christ and the church (5:31–32).

Ephesians' teaching about the church has three major stages. First, it is built on the new unity of Jews and gentiles in Christ. Second, the church is characterized by unity and diversity and grows as a body in maturity and conformity to Christ, its head. Third, the church is the bride of Christ, having a loving bond with her husband, who gave himself for her.

Implementation

Ephesians has been one of the most influential of Paul's letters in the history of the church, and its contribution is no less potent today. It has obvious significance for the doctrine of salvation by grace through faith but offers so much more besides. First, salvation by grace is dependent on Paul's theology of union with Christ, which permeates the letter. While the modern Western church has tended to sideline this vital concept, Ephesians is central to contemporary efforts to recapture the importance of union with Christ. Believers can turn to no more instructive part of the Bible to explore the riches of their union with Christ.

While the modern Western church has tended to focus on the sin and salvation of individuals, Ephesians presents a much bigger picture. Sin is a cosmic force with reach and implications far beyond the individual, and the work of Christ includes his overthrow of the forces of evil. Moreover, the "vertical" salvation of believers has immediate "horizontal" implications, as those who have been reconciled to God through Christ are also reconciled to one another. Modern individualism is challenged by the letter's focus on the reconciliation of people groups (Jews and gentiles) and on the church as the body of Christ. While Ephesians has plenty to say to individual believers, its corporate social and cosmic dimensions are highly instructive for the church today.

Speaking of the church, Ephesians presents a model of corporate service and love that stands in strong contrast to the experiences and attitudes of many contemporary churchgoers. To begin, it is clear that the leaders of the church are to equip all its members to serve one another, so that all believers are the "ministers" of the church. Church is not meant to be a production performed by a few professionals, while everyone else consumes the product or takes in the show. Church, according to Ephesians, is a body in which all the parts serve the whole. There are to be no passive observers or consumers, since the body thrives when all its parts work together in harmony.

Ephesians reminds the Western church that it is engaged in ferocious and dangerous spiritual warfare. The real enemy is not flesh and blood, and the real battle is fought with spiritual armor and weaponry, not the tools of the material world. Too often the contemporary church defaults to the strategies, methods, and agendas of this world, forgetting the unseen forces that wage war against us. The letter also reminds us that, in Christ, we have everything we need to stand our ground in such spiritual warfare.

Finally, Ephesians presents a cosmic and glorious image of the enthroned Christ. Too often the church today keeps Jesus on the cross, sometimes forgetting to remember his resurrection, and often neglecting his current enthronement over the forces of the entire cosmos. He is the glorious Lord over all creation, in whom the entire universe is reconciled and restored. Ephesians reminds us that our Jesus is often too small.

Christian Reading Questions

1. Compare and contrast Ephesians 2:1–10 with 2:11–22. What similarities and differences do you find in argument, structure, and content?
2. Find all the "walking" language in Ephesians (this may be obscured in some English translations). What does such "walking" language convey, and what role does it play in the letter?
3. Read Colossians and make a list of similarities and differences between it and Ephesians.

PART 5

Paul on Trial for Christ

CHAPTER FIFTEEN

Introduction to Paul on Trial for Christ

Chronology of Part 5: Paul on Trial for Christ (ca. 57–??)

ca. 57–59	Imprisoned by the governor Felix in Caesarea
ca. 59–60	Sails for Rome, spends three months in Malta
ca. 60–62	House arrest in Rome
ca. 61	Philippians, Ephesians, Colossians, Philemon written
ca. 63–??	Visit to Spain?
ca. 63?	1 and 2 Timothy, Titus written
64	Great fire of Rome and persecution of Christians
ca. 65?	Paul is executed

Returning from his third mission, Paul and his companions arrived at Tyre, on the Syrian coast, where some believers warned him not to go to Jerusalem (Acts 21:1–6). After a week in Tyre, they sailed to Caesarea, on the coast of Judea (Israel today), and stayed with Philip the evangelist, who lived there. During their time there, a prophet known as Agabus warned Paul that he would be captured by Jews in Jerusalem and handed over to the Romans. As a result, everyone, including Luke, the author of Acts, begged Paul not to go to Jerusalem. But Paul refused to be deterred, expressing his willingness to die for Christ if need be (21:7–14).

Jerusalem

Paul and company received a warm welcome from the believers in Jerusalem. Paul met with the apostle James and other leaders, to whom he reported about his ministry to the gentiles. They responded with joy, but also informed Paul that he might encounter some tension with Jewish believers who had heard that he encouraged gentile believers to dispense with the law of Moses (Acts 21:15–25). While Paul was taking measures to mollify any offense he may have caused believing Jews in Jerusalem, some Jews from Asia (the region surrounding Ephesus) spotted him in the temple and created a ruckus. Claiming that Paul had opposed the Jewish people, law, and temple, the mob dragged Paul out of the temple with the intent to kill him (21:26–30). However, the Roman regiment intervened and took Paul into their custody. As they were about to enter the Roman barracks, which towered above the northwestern corner of the temple complex, Paul asked if he could address the mob. He was granted permission from the commander and spoke to the Jews in Aramaic (21:31–40).

READ ACTS 22:1–21

In his address to the angry mob at the steps of the Roman barracks, Paul basically gave his testimony. He recounted his birth in Tarsus, his upbringing in Jerusalem, and his study with the great Gamaliel. Paul was zealous for God, persecuting the followers of Jesus ("the Way")—some to death and others to imprisonment. But on his way to Damascus to persecute believers there, he encountered the risen Jesus, who told him to continue into Damascus to await instructions. Blinded by the light of his vision, Paul was met by Ananias, who explained Saul's commission to be a witness for Jesus to all people. Later in Jerusalem this commission was reaffirmed in a vision that Saul experienced while praying in the temple (22:1–21).

Paul's claim that the Lord had sent him to the gentiles sent the mob into a frenzy. The Romans again intervened and took Paul into their barracks with the intention of interrogating him by the whip. But Paul informed them of his Roman citizenship, which guaranteed protection from such treatment—especially without trial. Upon hearing this, the Roman commander backed off (22:22–29). The next day, the commander presented Paul before the Sanhedrin in order to discover why the Jews were accusing him.

CANONICAL CONNECTIONS

Paul's Testimonies

Paul's encounter with the risen Jesus on the road to Damascus is recorded three times in Acts (9:1–9; 22:1–21; 26:4–18). Although Acts 22:1–21 is the second account of the event, this is the first time it is presented in Paul's own words. Thus, the chief difference between this account and that of Acts 9:1–9 is that it is Paul's testimony, including his former way of life as a persecutor of Jesus's followers. The third account of Paul's encounter with Jesus—and his second testimony (26:4–18)—gives more attention to his commission from Jesus to minister to the gentiles.

After clashing with the high priest, Ananias, Paul cleverly sparked a dispute within the group by appealing to the resurrection of the dead. Since the Sanhedrin consisted of Pharisees (who believed in resurrection) and the Sadducees (who did not believe in resurrection), Paul's reference to resurrection was divisive, and the dispute became violent. Paul was again whisked away to the safety of the Roman barracks (22:30–23:11).

The next day, more than forty Jews swore that they would abstain from food and drink until they had killed Paul. They implicated the chief priests and elders in their conspiracy, but the plan was foiled when Paul's nephew tipped him off. The nephew informed the Roman commander of the murderous plot, and he organized 470 soldiers to accompany Paul to Caesarea overnight. Paul was thus safely delivered to Felix, the Roman governor of Judea, in the coastal port city of Caesarea (23:12–35).

HISTORICAL MATTERS

What Was the Sanhedrin?

The Sanhedrin were assemblies of twenty-three elders (the Lesser Sanhedrin) or seventy-one elders (the Great Sanhedrin), which functioned as a tribunal and supreme court, respectively. The Great Sanhedrin met in a dedicated building within the temple complex in Jerusalem every day of the year except for festivals and Sabbaths. Since Acts 22:30 refers to "all the Sanhedrin," it is most like the Great Sanhedrin that heard Paul.

HISTORICAL MATTERS

Who Were Felix and Festus?

Antonius Felix was the procurator (the imperial governor) of Judea during AD 52–59 and was known for his cruelty and corruption. His rule was marked by a great increase in crime and internal feuds. In AD 58, Felix arranged the assassination of Jonathan the high priest, who had been a critic of Felix and threatened to report him to Caesar, and Felix tried to bribe Paul (Acts 24:26). Felix was succeeded by Porcius Festus, who was procurator of Judea during AD 59–62. His administration was troubled by problems he inherited from Felix, which led to the inflammation of Jewish hostility toward Rome. This ultimately contributed to the outbreak of the Jewish War in AD 66.

Caesarea

After receiving a letter concerning Paul from the Roman commander in Jerusalem, Felix put him under guard in Herod's palace and waited for Paul's accusers to arrive (Acts 23:33–35). When Ananias the high priest, some elders, and a lawyer arrived from Jerusalem, they accused Paul of being an agitator and ringleader of "the sect of the Nazarenes" (the followers of Jesus of Nazareth), who tried to desecrate the temple (24:1–9). Paul denied being an agitator, insisting that he has simply worshiped the God of his ancestors and held hope in the resurrection of the dead (24:10–21). Felix delayed deciding Paul's case and kept him in prison for two years as a favor to the Jews, until Felix was replaced by Festus (24:22–27).

Festus went to Jerusalem to hear from the Jewish leaders, then heard from Paul in Caesarea. Paul invoked his privilege as a Roman citizen to appeal to Caesar, and Festus agreed to send Paul to Rome in order to stand trial before the emperor himself (25:1–12). Several days later, King Agrippa and his sister Bernice visited Festus and asked to hear Paul after discussing his matter together (25:13–27).

POSTCARDS FROM THE MEDITERRANEAN

Paul's Caesarea

Caesarea Maritima was a Judean city on the Mediterranean coast built by Herod the Great around 22–10 BC and later became the capital of Judea under Rome. Its ruins make for a wonderful visit by the sea, with its preserved Roman aqueduct, impressive theater, hippodrome, and several columns and mosaics. It also includes a plaque that marks Paul's likely location during his trials before Felix, Festus, and Agrippa and records his appeal to Caesar in Acts 25.

Photo by Zairon / CC By-SA 4.0 / Wikimedia Commons

Caesarea Maritima

HISTORICAL MATTERS

Who Was King Agrippa?

Herod Agrippa II (AD 27–100) was the son of the Herod Agrippa mentioned in Acts 12 and was the last king in the Herodian line. Bernice was his sister who lived with him after the death of her husband and uncle, Herod of Chalcis. Because of his youth, Agrippa II did not automatically assume his father's kingdom upon his death, but eventually he gained power over the same regions.

READ ACTS 26:1–23

Paul again recounted his testimony—how he had lived as a Pharisee, persecuted the followers of Jesus, and then was confronted by the risen Christ on the way to Damascus. Jesus himself sent Paul to the gentiles that they might turn from darkness to light and receive the forgiveness of sins (26:1–18). Paul did just as he had been instructed by Christ, and for this reason the Jews had tried to kill him. But Paul affirmed that everything he had preached was supported by the prophets and Moses, who foretold the sufferings and resurrection of the Messiah, offering light to all peoples (26:19–23).

Festus declared Paul to be out of his mind because of his great learning, but Paul calmly replied that he was speaking publicly the truth about things that had happened, not in a corner (26:24–26). He then challenged King Agrippa about his own beliefs, receiving a swift rebuff from the king. Paul, however, declared his desire for all those listening to him to believe (26:27–29). Finally, the king told the governor that Paul had done nothing deserving death and could have been released had he not appealed to Caesar (26:30–32).

Toward Rome

Paul and some other prisoners were put under the supervision of a Roman centurion named Julius, who was responsible for getting them all to Rome

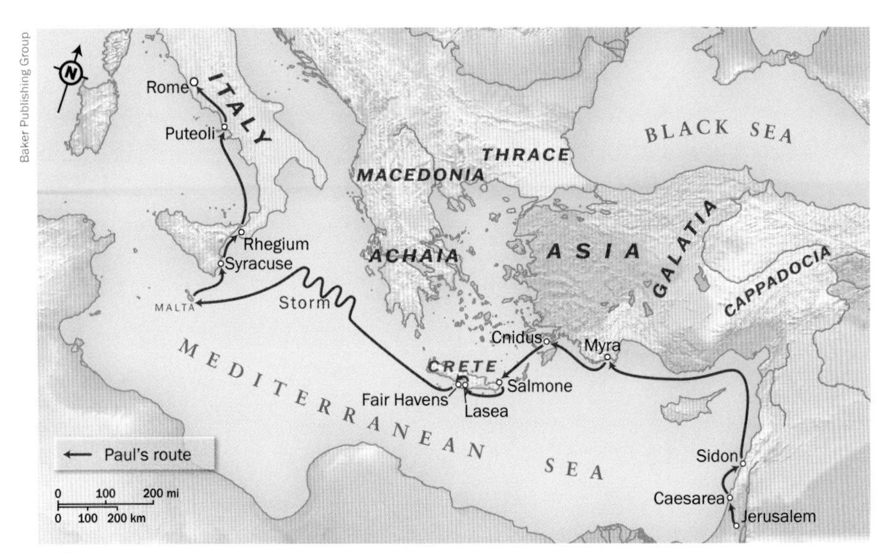

Paul's journey to Rome

(Acts 27:1). After stopping at various ports along the Mediterranean coastline and changing ships, the party sailed into some extremely difficult weather in the open sea. For many days they could see neither sun nor stars as the storm raged on, and they began to despair for their lives (27:2–20). Paul, however, was able to offer some hope because of a vision in which an angel told him that it was God's plan for him to appear before Caesar and that all sailing with him would be spared (27:21–26). After two weeks adrift in the Adriatic Sea, Paul encouraged all 276 people on board to eat, since they had gone without food during that time. Then they threw the remaining grain overboard to lighten the ship as they finally approached land. After running aground on a sandbar, they jumped overboard, and everyone eventually made it safely to the shore (27:27–44).

The shipwrecked survivors learned that they had landed on the Mediterranean island of Malta, and they were shown extraordinary kindness and hospitality there. But after Paul was bitten by a viper, the

POSTCARDS FROM THE MEDITERRANEAN

Paul's Malta

One of the most striking things about Malta today is how much Paul's visit made a permanent imprint on the island. In a restaurant on St. Paul's Bay (where he was shipwrecked), the menu contains the whole account of Paul's visit to Malta from Acts 28. Paul is literally on the menu! And his presence can be felt throughout the island, not least at the twelfth-century cathedral built in his honor, with its Paul-themed museum standing adjacent, in Medina. According to tradition, it was built on the site of Publius's home, where Paul stayed briefly (Acts 28:7–8).

Paul statue in St. Paul's Bay

people concluded that he was a murderer condemned to death by the gods. When Paul shook off the viper and suffered no ill effects, they changed their minds and decided that he was a god (28:1–6). The key leader of the island, Publius, showed Paul and Luke hospitality, and Paul healed his ill father. After this, all the sick of the island came to Paul for healing. After a pleasant and restful spell on Malta, the voyagers continued on to Rome (28:7–10).

Rome

After three months on Malta, Paul and his traveling companions made their way to Puteoli, on the Italian coast, then walked to Rome. Paul's imminent arrival in Rome was known to the Roman believers, some of whom met and encouraged Paul and Luke on their way into the city. Once he arrived in Rome, Paul was put under house arrest (Acts 28:11–16). He called together the leaders of the Jews in Rome and recounted the most recent parts of his story to them. Paul then proclaimed his message of Jesus Christ to them, leading to some being persuaded and others not. In the face of Jewish resistance, Paul affirmed the salvation of

HISTORICAL MATTERS

1 Clement

Clement was the bishop of Rome in the late first century, and his letter known as 1 Clement was written to the Corinthian church in AD 96 or 97. In a passage discussing Peter's and Paul's sufferings for their proclamation of Christ, Clement says that Paul taught righteousness to the whole world, "having reached the farthest limits of the West" (1 Clement 5:7). In Clement's day, the "bounds of the West" would have been understood to mean Spain (as the westernmost point of Europe), as the famous Greek geographer Strabo called it. Thus, according to Clement, Paul did indeed visit Spain as he intended (Rom. 15:24, 28), though it is not recorded in the New Testament. Since Clement lived in Rome, it is reasonable to presume that he had first- or secondhand knowledge of Paul's movements in and out of Rome.

Mamertine Prison in Rome

gentiles who would listen. Paul remained under house arrest for two years, continuing to proclaim the kingdom of God and the Lord Jesus Christ (28:17–31).

Luke concluded the narrative here, without indicating what happened to Paul after his Roman house arrest. It's possible that Luke died before he finished writing his account of Paul's ministry. It's also possible that, because Paul had made it to Rome, Luke's narrative was complete, since Acts 1:8 had been fulfilled. Regardless, we know that Paul underwent a more severe imprisonment before being beheaded at the command of Emperor Nero in the mid-60s. This might have happened immediately after Paul's two-year house arrest, or it might have occurred after an intervening period in which Paul regained his freedom. According to 1 Clement 5 (AD 96), Paul fulfilled his ambition to preach in Spain (Rom. 15:24, 28). If Clement's account is reliable, Paul's journey to Spain must have happened after his arrest and before his more severe imprisonment.

POSTCARDS FROM THE MEDITERRANEAN

From Paul's Final Imprisonment to His Resting Place

Tradition holds that Paul's final days were spent in the Mamertine Prison, next to the ancient Roman Forum. It is very sobering to visit the underground dungeon, which has little natural light, and imagine the harsh conditions. Prisoners were chained naked to the wall, with no toilet or washing facilities, and they relied on friends for food and blankets. Paul was beheaded elsewhere in Rome, now marked by the Church of St. Paul at the Three Fountains. The church complex today is quite attractive and peaceful. He was buried outside the ancient Roman city walls at a location now marked by the glorious Basilica of Saint Paul outside the Walls, which is my favorite location in Rome. The sarcophagus containing Paul's remains sits below a marble tombstone in the basilica's crypt. The beautiful architecture, artwork, and light-filled interior are truly moving when one considers where Paul spent his final days.

Constantine R. Campbell

St. Paul outside the Walls

CHAPTER SIXTEEN

Romans

Orientation

Of Paul's surviving letters, Romans is one of only two that are addressed to churches he did not know personally (Colossians is the other). At the time of writing, Paul had not yet visited Rome. Obviously, he did not plant the church there. And while Paul knew some individuals, he had not lived among the church in Rome and did not know its culture from the inside. However, Paul had every intention to visit Rome, unlike Colossae. As the letter itself indicates, it had long been his desire to go there on his way to Spain (Rom. 15:22–29). Though there is no biblical indication that Paul made it to Spain, there is some historical evidence that he went there before his execution in Rome in the mid-60s. But regardless of whether he made it to Spain, Paul certainly went to Rome. This was the result of his appeal to Caesar while under arrest in Caesarea Maritima (Palestine), which granted him as a Roman citizen the right to make his case personally to the emperor. After a harrowing journey across the Mediterranean, including a

Photo by BeBo86 / CC BY-SA 3.0 / Wikimedia Commons

The Roman Forum

shipwreck and a three-month respite in Malta, Paul finally achieved his intention to go to Rome.

Paul's Letter to the Romans was written before all of this happened, but it was part of his long-term strategy to go to Rome on his way to Spain. He wanted to make his gospel known to the believers in Rome before meeting them in person, and, as a result, he penned the longest, richest, and arguably most important letter he would ever compose. Paul was on his third mission when he wrote the letter around AD 57. He likely was near Corinth at the time and was on his way back to Jerusalem before somehow finding a way to get to Rome and then Spain.

RECEPTION HISTORY

Ideological Readings of Romans

Alongside traditional approaches to reading Romans are a range of sociopragmatic and liberationist approaches, such as feminist, Black, Latinx, Asian, and political readings. These approaches to Romans can radically affect how it is understood for the sake of supporting contemporary expressions of justice and liberation. The ideological underpinnings of Romans are examined in order to apply them to contemporary contexts in which various struggles toward justice continue.

The origins of the church in Rome remain unclear. Paul gives no hint that he was aware of how the church was founded there—unlike the church in Colossae, which was established by his disciple Epaphras. It is possible that the first Christians in Rome were Jews returning from the Pentecost celebration in Jerusalem. As Acts 2 records, three thousand Jews from around the Roman Empire came to faith in Jesus after hearing Peter's Pentecost speech, including some from Rome (Acts 2:10, 41). These new followers of Jesus may have returned home and established the first church in Rome.

Overview of Romans

Romans is traditionally understood to consist of four main sections, and for good reason. While scholars debate which section is the most significant for understanding the message of the letter, its four-part structure is generally accepted. These sections address the themes of justification by faith (chaps. 1–5), union with Christ (chaps. 6–8), Israel (chaps. 9–11), and church life (chaps. 12–16).[1]

Romans 1–5

- Paul defines the gospel of God as foretold by the prophets, concerning Jesus, a descendant of David, who was appointed Son of God through his resurrection (1:1–4).
- After acknowledging the Roman believers' faith and his desire to visit them (1:8–15), Paul states that he is not ashamed of the gospel, which is the power of God for salvation to all who believe—both Jew

and gentile (1:16). In the gospel, the righteousness of God is revealed (1:17).

- God's wrath is also revealed against all unrighteousness, causing people to lose the knowledge of God and be given over to sinful desires (1:18–32).
- But anyone who judges such sinners falls under the same judgment, since God does not show favoritism (2:1–11). Jews and gentiles alike will be judged according to what they do, regardless of whether or not they have the law of Moses or were circumcised (2:12–29).
- So Paul concludes that all people alike are subject to God's judgment, since all people are under sin (3:1–20).
- Having established the universal guilt of humanity, Paul announces that the righteousness of God is available through faith in Jesus Christ to all who believe. Redemption comes through Christ, whose blood was shed to atone for sins (3:21–26). There is therefore no room for boasting, since no one is justified by their works; they are justified through faith (3:27–31).
- Paul then appeals to the experiences of Abraham and David to support his thesis, that righteousness comes by faith, not works or circumcision (4:1–12). Those who have the faith of Abraham are his true descendants, and therefore the heirs of his promise (4:13–25).
- Paul then draws conclusions from his argument: since believers are made righteous by faith, we have peace with God and a hope that will not disappoint (5:1–5). God's love is proved by Christ dying for his enemies, bringing justification, salvation, and reconciliation with God (5:6–11)
- Finally, Paul contrasts Adam and Christ and their respective contributions to the fate of humanity. Sin and death were introduced to the world through Adam, but righteousness and life have come through Christ (5:12–21).

Romans 6–8

- Paul argues that believers have died with Christ and therefore will be raised with him. As such, death and sin no longer rule over them; they are alive to God in Christ and should live accordingly (6:1–23).
- Paul turns to discuss the law of Moses and believers' complex relationship with it. Having died with Christ, believers are no longer bound to the law but serve in the Spirit (7:1–6). The law pointed out

sin and created an impossible wrestle for the flesh, but it ultimately led to God's rescue in Christ (7:7–25).

- He then celebrates that there is no condemnation for those in Christ Jesus, who have been set free from sin and death (8:1–2). Rather than living according to sinful flesh, believers are enabled by the Spirit of Christ living in them to live as God's children (8:3–17).
- Present sufferings cannot be compared to future glory, when the whole creation will be set free from decay and will be renewed. Believers also will be renewed with the redemption of their bodies (8:18–25).
- In the meantime, the Spirit helps believers in their weakness, and they know that God works everything for the good of those who love him, leading to their glorification (8:26–30). With God for them, there is nothing to fear. Nothing can separate them from the love of God in Christ (8:31–39).

Romans 9–11

- Paul addresses Israel's rejection of Jesus as the Christ. While he acknowledges that to Israel belong the covenants, the law, the temple, and the promises of God, only those who belong to the promise of Abraham are his children (9:1–13).
- God retains the right to choose on whom he will have mercy from among Jews and gentiles, as the prophets have said. For both Jew and gentile, righteousness comes through faith (9:14–10:13). But faith comes from hearing, and so the gospel must be proclaimed—though many from Israel have not accepted what they heard (10:14–21).
- But Paul insists that God has not rejected his people but has selected a remnant to belong to him while others have been hardened against him (11:1–10). Through Israel's hardening, gentiles have been blessed, but this does not change Israel's status as the root of the tree. Ultimately, "all Israel" will be saved (11:11–36).

Romans 12–16

- Paul seeks to apply the teaching of the previous eleven chapters. In view of the mercies of God, he says, believers are to present themselves as living sacrifices as worship of God, being transformed in mind to know and do the will of God (12:1–2). Right thinking will lead to humility, love, service, hope, and harmony and away from hypocrisy, evil, pride, and vengeance (12:3–21).

- Believers ought to submit to governing authorities, recognizing them as established by God. Being a good citizen is to be done as God's servants (13:1–7). They are to love one another in fulfillment of the law and eagerly await their coming salvation (13:8–14).
- Paul instructs his readers not to argue about disputable matters, such as whether a believer should eat this or that food, or whether one day is more important than another (14:1–12). Rather than judge one another, believers ought to build up one another, seek peace, live in harmony, and welcome one another (14:13–15:13).
- Paul then reflects on his role of preaching Christ to the gentiles and his desire to visit the church in Rome on his way to Spain. He asks for prayer that he might escape danger and make it to Rome (15:14–33).
- Paul ends the letter with a long set of greetings to believers in Rome, some concluding remarks, and a final doxology (16:1–27).

Exploration

While Romans addresses a great number of themes and concepts, its major themes follow the overarching structure of the letter: righteousness through faith (chaps. 1–5); dying with Christ (chaps. 6–7) and life through the Spirit (chap. 8); Israel (chaps. 9–11); and life together (chaps. 12–16). Rather than reiterate the contents of these major sections (see the overview above), the following will draw together their lines of argumentation in order to better understand their themes.

Righteousness through Faith

READ ROMANS 3:21–26

The *gospel*, or good news, is clearly in mind as Paul begins his letter (1:1–4, 9, 15–17), and it serves to launch his discussion of righteousness, since in the gospel "the righteousness of God is revealed" (1:17). There has been considerable debate about what "the righteousness of God" refers to through Romans 1–3 (specifically in 1:17 and 3:21–26). Does it refer to God's own righteousness (i.e., he is righteous), or does it refer to God's gift of righteousness to sinful human beings (i.e., the righteousness that comes *from* God)? The translation "the righteousness of God" leaves this question open, since it can be taken either way. At stake is whether Romans 1–3 is primarily a discussion about God's righteousness or about the righteousness he gives to believers in Christ.

Luis de Morales, *Christ Carrying the Cross with the Virgin and Saint John*, 1570

But whichever way the phrase "the righteousness of God" is understood, Romans 1–3 addresses both God's own righteousness and the righteousness he bestows on believers. Both ideas are seen together in 3:21–26, in which Paul says that sinners are *justified* freely by God's grace (3:24)—*justified* means *made righteous*—and that God demonstrated his righteousness in presenting Jesus as the "mercy seat" or atoning sacrifice by his blood (3:25–26). Indeed, both types of righteousness are summed up in 3:26: "God presented [Jesus] to demonstrate *his* righteousness at the present time, *so that he would be just and justify the one who has faith in Jesus.*" Or, to rephrase, *so that God would be righteous and make righteous the one who has faith in Jesus.* So, it is clear that God's own righteousness and the righteousness he gives to believers are both part of the argument in Romans 1–3.

With that in place, we can look more closely at Paul's argument about the righteousness of God. In order to understand how the righteousness of God is revealed in the gospel (1:17), we must also see that his wrath is being revealed against

THEOLOGICAL ISSUES

Grace within Judaism

Paul's concept of grace features in Romans (e.g., 3:24; 4:16; 5:2, 15, 17, 20, 21; 6:1, 14, 15; 11:6) and has often been interpreted as the antithesis of Judaism, which is characterized as "works based." But biblical scholar John Barclay has explored Paul's conception of grace against the context of Second Temple Judaism and arrived at a different conclusion. According to Barclay, in Judaism good relations were maintained by the giving of a benefit or favor, which elicited some form of reciprocation that fostered the continuation of the relationship. Thus, for Paul, God's grace requires a reciprocal response of devotion and obedience. The popular idea of grace being a "free gift" without obligation or expectation is therefore potentially misleading, as is "works-based righteousness," since God's grace opens a relationship with its recipients who in turn maintain their relationship with God through their reciprocal transformation.

all unrighteousness (1:18). Paul's description of such unrighteousness in 1:18–32 is typical of Jewish ways of talking about sinful gentiles. They have turned away from a natural knowledge of God, and God's ensuing judgment is to give them over to an increasing lack of knowledge of God, expressed in false worship, sexual impurity, and various sorts of wickedness. At this point, Paul's Jewish readers would all be nodding in agreement with this apparent condemnation of godless gentiles.

But Paul turns the tables on his imagined Jewish readers, arguing that they too fall under God's judgment. Though not ignorant of God or his law, and sharing in his covenant with his people—marked by circumcision—Jews nevertheless fail to live up to their knowledge (2:1–29). Indeed, Jews with a hardened and unrepentant heart will also experience the wrath of God (2:5). This move enables Paul to conclude that all people—Jews and gentiles—are under sin (3:9). Through 1:18–3:20, then, Paul establishes his case for the universal sinfulness of humanity and the appropriateness of God's just judgment.

It is at this bleak juncture that Paul turns the tables again, but this time it is to announce good news. Returning to the theme of the righteousness of God being revealed, Paul states that all are justified (= made righteous) freely by God's grace through the redemption that is in Christ Jesus (3:24). Through the death of Christ, God dealt with all sins, thus proving his own righteousness as the one who does not let evil go unchecked (3:25). God presented Christ "so that he would be just and justify the one who has faith in Jesus" (3:26).

At this point, Paul has demonstrated humanity's need for God to intervene in order to make sinners righteous, and he has demonstrated that God's way of doing this was itself just. Rather than sweep humanity's sin under the carpet, he presented Jesus as an atoning sacrifice for sin. That way, God can justify sinners while remaining just himself. Sin is checked while sinners may go free.

Since God makes sinners righteous through faith, Paul points out that there is no room for boasting of any kind. People are not made righteous through obedience to the law of Moses, or through being Jewish, or through circumcision (3:27–31). Righteousness comes through faith for both Jew and gentile, which means that no one has grounds to see themselves as superior to anyone else.

Paul then supports his overall argument about justification by faith by appealing to the examples of Abraham and David, demonstrating that both were justified by faith, not by works of the law (4:1–8). David was regarded as righteous even though he had gravely sinned (4:6–8). Abraham was credited with righteousness *before* he was circumcised

(4:9–12). Moreover, the grand promise made to Abraham—that his descendants would inherit the world—makes sense only if justification comes by faith rather than by the law. If the promise comes by faith, it will be according to God's grace rather than human merit (4:13–16a). As such, the promise is open to those who have faith, whether Jew or gentile, since it is not dependent on the law of Moses. This is how Abraham becomes the father of many nations, since the promise extends to all those who have faith (4:16b–18). Abraham himself demonstrated faith that God would fulfill his promise and was thus credited with righteousness (4:19–22). The same applies to those of us who also have faith in God, the one who raised the Lord Jesus from the dead, who died for our trespasses and was raised for our justification (4:23–25).

Paul then spells out the implications of believers' justification by faith. Having been justified by faith, believers now experience peace with God, enjoy access to his grace, and share in the hope of the glory of God (5:1–2). Their situation has been entirely reversed: no longer regarded as sinners under the wrath of God, believers have been reconciled to God and will be saved from his wrath (5:9–10). The final piece in Paul's argument about righteousness is his contrast between Adam and Christ as two representative heads of humanity. Sin, death, and condemnation came into the world through Adam, while grace, righteousness, and eternal life have come through Jesus Christ (5:12–21).

THEOLOGICAL ISSUES

Raised for Our Justification?

In Romans 4:25, Paul states that Christ "was delivered up for our trespasses and raised for our justification." Since it is common to associate justification (the declaration of righteousness) with the death of Christ, many struggle to explain in what sense Jesus's resurrection was "for our justification." In order to understand this phrase, it is important to recognize the connection between resurrection and the final judgment of God in Jewish thought (e.g., Dan. 12:2–3; John 5:25–29). The Jewish expectation was that the dead would be raised for judgment—some to the resurrection of life, others to the resurrection of condemnation. Jesus's own resurrection was the sign that he had been judged righteous by God—though he was raised in the "middle" of time, rather than at the end. As Paul goes on to explain, believers are united with Christ in his death and resurrection (6:4–5, 8–11), which means that his declaration of righteousness (seen in his resurrection from the dead) is shared with those united to him by faith. As such, Jesus was "raised for our justification."

THEOLOGICAL ISSUES

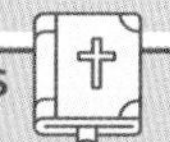

Adam vs. Christ

In Romans 5:12–21, Paul develops a pivotal contrast between Adam and Christ, in which each is representative of two opposite domains for human existence. Under the domain represented by Adam, humans are subjected to death and sin, which are understood as cosmic powers that keep people under their power. Under Adam, people are powerless to alter their destiny, resulting in condemnation. But under the domain represented by Christ, people are the recipients of God's grace, which enables their escape from captivity to sin and death, resulting in justification. This contrast of domains represented by Adam on the one hand and Christ on the other establishes the framework for much of Paul's argumentation to follow in Romans 6 and 7.

Dying with Christ

READ ROMANS 6:5–11

The discussion in 5:12–21 sets up the theme of dying with Christ by establishing a corporate and representative relationship between Christ and believers. As the new head of humanity (in contrast to Adam), Jesus establishes justification for everyone through his "one righteous act" (5:18).

This introduces the notion that a corporate entity (the body of Christ, the church) can share in deeds performed by its representative, Christ.

In chapter 6, Paul presses into this corporate-representational concept to speak of believers dying and rising with Christ. The discussion addresses the question of how believers should now think about sin—since it is by the grace of God that they have received righteousness (5:15–16). He asks if believers should "continue in sin so that grace may multiply" (6:1). His short answer is no (6:2a)! His long answer takes the rest of the chapter to unpack as Paul explains that believers have died with Christ and therefore have already died to sin and can live in it no longer.

Paul argues that if someone has been baptized into Christ, they have been baptized into his death (6:3). And those baptized into his death will also receive new life by sharing in his resurrection (6:4–5). This means that the old self—who was ruled by sin—has been crucified with Christ and therefore is dead. Thus, the believer is no longer enslaved to sin, since death releases a person from sin's hold over them (6:6–7). Having died with Christ, the believer will now live with him through his resurrection from the dead and will no longer be subjected to (the finality of) death (6:8–10). The believer therefore is to consider themselves dead to sin but alive to God in Christ Jesus (6:11).

The implication of this is that believers are not to obey the leading of sin but to offer themselves to God as "weapons for righteousness" (6:12–14). Though once slaves to sin, believers have now been set free from its rule and are enslaved to righteousness and produce its fruit, resulting in eternal life (6:15–23). Believers' participation in the death of Christ, then, is Paul's theological answer as to why they are no longer to continue in sin. Their old self has been crucified with Christ and their new self belongs to God, not sin

In chapter 7, Paul explores how dying with Christ changes one's relationship to the law of Moses. Since the law applies to someone only while they're alive, those who've died with Christ are no longer under the law (7:1–6). Though sin was made more potent through the law, the law is not guilty of making people more sinful; it simply pointed out people's sinfulness, which relished the opportunity to become even more sinful in the process (7:7–13). In the remainder of chapter 7, Paul adopts a hypothetical Jewish identity that gives voice to what it's like to want to obey the law but not be able to do so (7:14–25).

LITERARY NOTES

Who Is Speaking in Romans 7:14–25?

Paul's use of the first person in this passage naturally makes him sound like he is talking about himself. But what he says about himself, such as calling himself a slave to sin (7:14), seems to contradict his own arguments in Romans 6 and 8—in 6:17 he says that believers are no longer slaves to sin (cf. 8:2). Other examples in 7:14–25 jar with Paul's affirmations in chapters 6 and 8, which suggest that the "I" in 7:14–25 is *not* the Christian Paul. Whether it represents Paul before he knew Christ or someone else, the testimony provides an account of how life under the law only condemns the sinner to death. But the Christian Paul can offer thanks to God for his rescue through Jesus Christ our Lord (7:25).

Life through the Spirit

READ ROMANS 8:14–17

In contrast to the bleakness of life under the law, compromised by the flesh, Paul celebrates the Spirit of life. He boldly declares that there is no condemnation for those in Christ Jesus, "because the law of the Spirit of life in Christ Jesus has set you free from the law of sin and death" (8:1–2). Unpacking this claim, Paul explains that the law was not able to provide life, since it was compromised by the flesh and ultimately only served to condemn humanity. Instead, God condemned sin by making Jesus a sin offering so that the law's requirement to condemn sin would be fulfilled (8:3–4). In this way, the law is fulfilled by those who walk according to the Spirit rather than according to the flesh (8:4–5). Those who live according to the flesh cannot please God, but believers are in the Spirit, since the Spirit lives in them because they are in Christ (8:8–10a). With Christ in them, believers' bodies are dead due to sin but will be raised to life by God through the Spirit, just as he raised Christ from the dead through the Spirit (8:10–11). In short, the law kills but the Spirit brings life. Thus, Paul urges his readers to be led by the Spirit rather than the flesh, as appropriate for God's children (8:12–14). By the Spirit, God's adopted children cry out to him as Father and as his heirs with Christ, with whom they suffer and with whom they will be glorified (8:15–17).

The mention of suffering leads Paul to reflect on the future glory that will far outweigh present sufferings (8:18). Indeed, the entire creation has been subjected to futility—including various kinds of suffering—but will be set free from its bondage to decay and will experience glorious freedom. Just as the creation presently "groans" under its current burden, so believers internally groan as they await the promised redemption of their bodies (8:19–23). This hope for things not yet seen saves believers while they patiently await its fulfillment (8:24–25). In the meantime, the Spirit works within believers to intercede for them, since they don't always know what to pray (8:26–27). Through all of this, believers know that God brings about the good of those who love him, as God predestines, calls, justifies, and glorifies his people (8:28–30).

Knowing that God has secured all this for his people—from predestining them to belong to him through to their ultimate glorification—believers can rest assured that he will grant everything to them and that no one can bring an accusation against them. God is the one who judges and justifies, and the risen Christ intercedes for them. Believers are "more than conquerors" through Christ, and nothing in all creation can separate them from the love of God in Christ (8:31–39).

Public domain / Wikimedia Commons

Pietro or Ambroglio Lorenzetti, *Triumph of Death*, 1342

Throughout Romans 8, Paul puts to rest the existential insecurities and struggles raised in chapter 7. While the law leaves people uncertain of their standing before God, rendering them guilty before him because of their sinful flesh and inability to keep the law, the Spirit assures believers that they are God's children, secure in his calling, justification, and glorification. Nothing at all can separate God's children from his love. In significant ways, this represents the high point of the entire letter and brings together the major themes of chapters 1–8.

Israel

READ ROMANS 11:1–6

After chapter 8 and all it entails, chapters 9–11 abruptly change tack as Paul addresses the plight and place of Israel in the plan of God. From the outset it is clear that Paul's heart burns for his fellow Israelites, as he even claims that he would give up his own salvation for their sake. To the Israelites belong the covenants, the law, the temple, the promises of God, the patriarchs, and the Christ (9:1–5).

Paul addresses a major apparent problem that the argument of chapters 1–8 raises: If everything that Paul says is true, what's gone wrong, since the majority of Israelites have not accepted Jesus as their Messiah? First, he argues that not all of Abraham's children are his physical descendants. The children of God's promise are Abraham's (and therefore God's) true children (9:6–13). This notion of promise will be addressed again later, but for now Paul engages the problem of whether or not it is fair for God's promise to apply to some people and not others. In short, Paul argues that God is God and has mercy on whom he wants to have mercy (9:14–18).

Public domain / The Yorck Project / Wikimedia Commons

Giotto, *Isaac Blessing His Son*, ca. 1292

CANONICAL CONNECTIONS

Election in Israel's History

Throughout Romans 9, Paul draws on three key eras of Israel's history to demonstrate that God has always operated through election. God did not choose all of Abraham's offspring to be God's children but chose only those according to his promise. So of Isaac's sons, God chose Jacob not Esau (Rom. 9:7–13; cf. Gen. 21:12; 18:10, 14; 25:23; Mal. 1:2–3). The next era is God's rescue of the Israelites from captivity in Egypt, when he tells Moses that his mercy is shown to whomever he chooses while he hardens Pharaoh for his own purposes (Rom. 9:14–18; cf. Exod. 33:19; 9:16). The third era is the prophets' expectation of the future work of God in gathering a people for himself. According to Hosea, God will call people who are not his people, and according to Isaiah, only a remnant from within Israel will be saved (Rom. 9:25–29; cf. Hosea 2:23; 1:10; Isa. 10:22–23; 28:22; 1:9).

Paul then anticipates the possible objection that human beings ought not to be held accountable for their choices, given that God's choices determine ultimate reality, including who will receive his mercy. Paul simply rebukes the reader who thinks that way for talking back to God. After all, what authority, power, or rights belong to the "clay" over the "potter"? God, the potter, does what he likes with the clay, and this might include preparing some for honor and others for dishonor (9:19–21). In fact, Paul speculates, God may allow some to experience his wrath so as to highlight the richness of his mercy for those he has called—from among the Jews and the gentiles (9:22–32). All of this functions to support the claim that God is God and can choose whomever he wants to belong to him, whether Jew or gentile.

But Paul reiterates his desire that God would save his fellow Israelites. Though they have zeal for God, they have not understood God's righteousness, which comes not through the law of Moses but through faith in Jesus the Lord, regardless of whether one is a Jew or a gentile. Everyone who calls on the Lord will be saved (10:1–13). But the Israelites cannot call on the Lord they don't believe in, and they can't believe in him without hearing about him. Faith comes from what is heard through the message about Christ. But then again, some did hear but did not listen due to their defiance (10:14–21).

But God has not rejected his people. Instead, there is a faithful remnant within Israel, just as there was in times past. Some Israelites were elect and others were not (11:1–10). But their plight is not irreversible. Salvation has

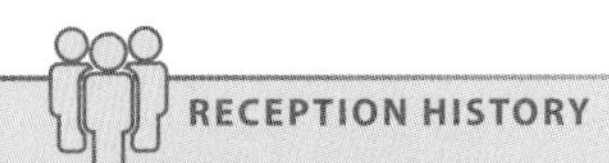

RECEPTION HISTORY

The Problem of Supersessionism

Supersessionism is the view (or a spectrum of views) that regards the church as the replacement of Israel in God's purposes. Supersessionism has contributed to Western anti-Semitism, including the horrific Holocaust of the twentieth century. Admittedly, in Romans 9–11 it sometimes sounds as though Paul thinks that ethnic Israel has been rejected. Yet he explicitly rules out the idea that the gentile church can replace Israel, since the gentiles were grafted into the olive tree of Israel as wild branches and cannot become the tree itself (11:19–24). However, it is clear that there is no salvation for Jews (or gentiles) outside Christ, and Paul retains hope that ethnic Israel will one day be reconciled to God through faith (11:23).

come to the gentiles, and this may in turn lead to Israelites returning to God. Israel is the root of the olive tree, and the gentiles are the branches. So the gentiles have nothing to boast about, since the root is the foundation and branches can be broken off just as they can be grafted in. If wild gentile branches can be grafted in, how much more so can the natural branches be grafted into their own olive tree (11:11–24). In God's sovereign plan Israel has been partially hardened so as to make way for believing gentiles to enter the fold. Just as the gentiles had been alienated from God but now have received mercy, so Israelites are not beyond God's mercy (11:25–36).

Paul's discussion in Romans 9–11 underscores Israel's importance in the plan of God, combating the erroneous assumption that Israelite unbelief somehow undermines Paul's message or the plan of God. On the contrary, it is part of the plan, as Israelite unbelief opened a way for gentiles to enter God's family. But such unbelief is not permanent, nor does it exclude Israelites from God's mercy.

Life Together

READ ROMANS 15:1–6

The "So what?" part of the letter occupies its last five chapters, as Paul spells out some of the implications of the argument mounted in chapters 1–11. This is perfectly initiated with the first sentence of chapter 12: "Therefore, brothers and sisters, in view of the mercies of God, I urge you to present your bodies as a living sacrifice, holy and pleasing to God; this is your true worship" (12:1). The "mercies of God" is a fitting summary of what Paul has been discussing throughout the letter, and true worship is the fitting response. Such worship is holistic, involving believers' bodies offered as living sacrifices and their minds transformed and renewed (12:1–2).

A major thrust of this section of the letter is how believers are to live and love together. This will require humility (12:3–8, 16), genuine love for one another, empathy, generosity, and harmony. Believers must not avenge themselves but rather are to conquer evil with good (12:9–21). Living well includes submission to the governing authorities, whose authority is granted by God. Believers should pay their taxes as good citizens (13:1–7). Living well requires love for one's neighbors, which fulfills the law (13:8–10). All of

this is conducted in the knowledge that the time is short—"The night is nearly over, and the day is near" (13:11–14).

Life together requires wisdom in how to deal with debatable matters. Instead of looking down on those whose conscience prevents them from eating certain foods or who think that certain days are more important than others, believers should seek to build others up and promote peace. Believers are not to judge one another and must remember that all will stand before the judgment seat of God (14:1–23). Again, the principles here are humility and love, rather than being "correct" or insisting on one's own point of view to the detriment of others. Believers have an obligation to please their neighbors rather than themselves, as Christ did, and to live in harmony with one another so that God is glorified with one mind and voice. This means welcoming one another, just as Christ went to great lengths to welcome the gentiles into God's people (15:1–13).

Is Romans 13 a Subversive Text?

In Romans 13:1–7, Paul instructs his readers to submit to the governing authorities because these have been installed by God for the orderly conduct of society. There is no authority except from God, and followers of Christ therefore ought to pay their taxes and show honor and respect to those in authority. On the other hand, the text is grounded on the fact that Caesar and all other authorities stand under the authority of God, and in that sense the rule of the empire is relativized. Often contrary to their own beliefs, ruling authorities do not exercise absolute power, nor is their authority beyond scrutiny. They are under the authority of God and therefore subject to judgment for the way they fulfill the responsibilities delegated to them. So, while Romans 13:1–7 should be read at face value as it instructs Christians to obey the authorities, it also subverts any claim of absolute authority, recognizing that only God rules absolutely, according to his own authority.

The most prominent theme through Romans 12–15 is love for one another. This is deeply significant, given that this part of the letter answers the "So what?" question that lingers over all that has been argued through its first eleven chapters: the proper response to God's mercies is that believers should love one another. Love is also believers' true worship of God, as their minds and bodies are renewed so as to be able to love truly. Finally, love is at the center of life together. Christian community, church, relationships with neighbors, and all the variegated dealings with others in various contexts are to be conducted in love. Love is the mark of Christian maturity and worship in response to the mercy and love of God.

Implementation

Romans is a favorite book of the descendants of the Protestant Reformation, with its strong focus on the gospel and its teaching about justification by faith. However, Paul's letter contains much beyond that theme (it is largely confined to chaps. 1–5) that often is not given equal weight by contemporary Protestants. For instance, the application of the letter's entire argument is *love*, along with humility, harmony, and peace. Sadly, many

Protestant believers have used Romans to more or less "wage war" against other types of believers in the name of justification by faith. Though the importance of that doctrine should not be downplayed, it has, unfortunately, sometimes been "defended" without much in the way of Christian charity, gentleness, or respect. Without tangible expressions of love for brothers and sisters within the body of Christ, those who wage war using Romans 1–5 are at risk of being condemned by Romans 12–15. Instead, a proper appreciation of Romans 1–5 (along with Rom. 6–11) will yield Paul's desired result: believers will love one another in view of God's extravagant mercies toward humanity.

Paul's significant discussion about Israel also does not jibe well with some contemporary expressions of Christianity that overlook the central significance of Israel in God's plans, in salvation history, and in the Scriptures. If believers are not led to wrestle with the big questions that evoke pain in Paul's heart regarding his fellow Jews, we may rightly question how much they have really understood Paul's message and mission. Occupying the entirety of Romans 9–11, Paul's unpacking of the relationship between God's promises and contemporary Israel's rejection of their promised Messiah raises questions about God's goodness and faithfulness, the meaning of election, God's sovereignty, and the priority of Israel among the people of God. Paul warns his gentile readers not to take for granted their current status as ingrafted members of God's people, nor to disrespect the rightful place of Israel—the natural-born root of the vine. Sadly, however, many (gentile) Christians today barely give a thought to the priority of Israel—except, perhaps, for a misguided focus on its political and national concerns in a contested geographical region. Paul does not seem to care about national Israel's political fortunes. He cares, rather, about its spiritual health and its covenantal relationship with God. At a very basic level, there is absolutely no excuse for Christian anti-Semitism, which, regrettably, has a ubiquitous presence in church history and is still present among some believers today.

At the heart of the Letter to the Romans is the extraordinary theology of union with Christ, seen especially in the language of "dying with Christ" in chapter 6. Though this theology gives insight into how justification by faith actually works, it has long been neglected among certain quarters in the contemporary church. Without an understanding of union with Christ, it is not possible to fully apprehend Paul's teaching in this letter—or most of his other letters. Perhaps ironically, however, union with Christ was strongly championed by the major voices of the Protestant Reformation, such as Martin Luther and John Calvin. Somewhere along the way, however, it became of secondary importance to many Protestant Christians, who today are relatively ignorant of its riches. To be united to Christ in his death and resurrection is a profoundly important concept not only for theological formation but also for personal formation, as believers are invited to grasp the deeply personal implications of an identity conformed to Christ.

Finally, the extraordinarily good news that there is now no condemnation for those in Christ Jesus rings like a bell from Romans 8. The Spirit of God dwells among and within believers so that we are able to live in a manner pleasing to God. He intercedes for us and declares believers to be the sons and daughters of God—his heirs, destined to be glorified with Christ. With God *for* his people, there is no one who can condemn them and nothing that can separate them from the love of God in Christ. By the power of the Spirit and in union with Christ, believers are more than conquerors as we live with and for God. Romans 8 stands as a pinnacle of glory over the entire letter, and indeed arguably over all of Paul's writings. Christians today would do well to soak in its glorious message, which has enormous implications for every individual, every believing community, and the worldwide body of Christ. Rather than being entangled in comparatively trivial debates, shallow Christian moralism, or overly worrisome consciences, believers may marvel in this good news and allow it to permeate our souls, our relationships with others, and our churches.

Christian Reading Questions

1. In Romans 1:18–32, Paul says some confrontational things about homosexual practice. Is Paul antigay? Think about the argument of this passage in its context and how it applies today.
2. Put into your own words the argument of Romans 6 and its answer to the question "Should we continue in sin?"
3. Read Romans 13:1–7. Discuss how this passage might apply to the church today. Is it ever appropriate for the church to resist the authority of government? If so, when and why?

CHAPTER SEVENTEEN

The Pastoral Epistles

Orientation

Known as the Pastoral Epistles, 1 and 2 Timothy and Titus stand alongside Philemon as the only existing letters that Paul wrote to individuals rather than to churches. There are few clues within the letters themselves to indicate Paul's situation as he wrote. He urges Titus to visit him in Nikopolis, on the western side of modern-day Greece, since Paul had decided to spend the winter there (Titus 3:12). This reveals that Paul was not under arrest at the time of writing the letter to Titus, but we don't know when he was in Nikopolis. It is possible that he was there at some point during his missionary activities, though it is not recorded in Acts. We already know that Acts is selective in its account of Paul's activities, so it is entirely possible that he wintered in Nikopolis without us knowing about it (apart from its mention here). It is also possible that Paul wintered in Nikopolis during the period between the end of Acts and his death. One theory posits that Paul resumed missionary activities after his Roman house arrest recorded in Acts 28. If so, it is not known where he went—though Spain is usually regarded as one of his destinations—and Nikopolis would be another possible destination.

LITERARY NOTES

Authorship Issues

For more than two centuries, many New Testament scholars have questioned or outright denied the Pauline authorship of the Pastoral Epistles. This began with observation of vocabulary and syntactical differences between 1 Timothy and 2 Timothy/Titus, leading some scholars to conclude that the letters were not written by the same author. Soon after, however, others affirmed similarities among the three letters and concluded that they were written by the same author, but not Paul. Modern corpus linguistic theory, however, brings serious challenge to language-based conclusions about authorship, since Paul's corpus is far too small to make any meaningful conclusions (as is the entire New Testament).

Another reason proposed to doubt the authenticity of the Pastoral Epistles is the perceived difficulty of fitting them into Paul's historical timeline. However, the evidence used to reconstruct Paul's life has various gaps, as seen in Luke's account in Acts. While such gaps do not constitute evidence that the Pastoral Epistles were written by Paul, they permit a reconstruction of his life that may account for them. Given this possibility, and the unreliability of claims about language and style, we are left to consider whether there is enough evidence to overturn the early and unanimous attestation that the Pastoral Epistles were written by Paul, as they claim.

The three Pastoral Epistles are addressed to two individuals: Timothy and Titus, who were located in Ephesus and Crete, respectively, when Paul wrote to them. In Acts 16:1, Timothy is introduced as a disciple with a Jewish mother and Greek father whom Paul took with him on his second mission (16:3). He is mentioned on other occasions in Acts as Paul's traveling companion and coworker (17:14–15; 18:5; 19:22; 20:4). Timothy is also a cosignatory of several of Paul's letters (Phil. 1:1; Col. 1:1; 1 Thess. 1:1; 2 Thess. 1:1; Philem. 1).

Titus is not mentioned in Acts, but he is named in three of Paul's letters, most frequently in 2 Corinthians (2:13; 7:6, 13–14; 8:6, 16, 23; 12:18), but also in Galatians (2:1, 3) and 2 Timothy (4:10). The Corinthian references reveal that Titus was Paul's coworker on his second (and possibly third?) mission. But the references in Galatians show that Titus was involved in Paul's ministry much earlier too, accompanying him to the Jerusalem council, recorded in Acts 15 (see Acts 15:2; Gal. 2:1). If 2 Timothy was written after the Letter to Titus (as held here), it would seem that after Titus wintered with Paul in Nikopolis (Titus 3:12), he ventured a little farther north to Dalmatia (2 Tim. 4:10).

Given this history, it is clear that Paul knew Timothy and Titus very well, having traveled and ministered with both of them over several years. As trusted coworkers and brothers in Christ, Timothy and Titus had been appointed by Paul to continue their ministry in his absence, leading churches, teaching the Scriptures, and encouraging believers to live in Christ.

HISTORICAL MATTERS

When Was Paul in Crete?

The only record of Paul in Crete is during his journey to Rome as a prisoner (Acts 27:7–12). Though the ship's crew planned to spend the winter in Crete, it is unclear if that's what they did, but it seems they did not (27:21). So, on that particular voyage Paul either spent a winter in Crete or spent little or no time there at all. Even if they wintered there, it is unlikely that Paul was able to establish the churches in Crete (Titus 1:5), since he was a prisoner under centurion guard (Acts 27:1). There are two other possibilities. First, Paul may have visited Crete during one of his missionary journeys, though Luke did not record it—after all, Luke did not tell us everything he could have (since all history is selective). Second, Paul may have visited Crete after being released from his house arrest in Rome (AD 62) but before his second, more severe, imprisonment, which led to his death.

TIMOTHY
"Instructed from childhood to read the scripture, and to lead a pure life."

Public domain / Wikimedia Commons

Timothy from David O. McKay, *Ancient Apostles*, 1918

Overview of the Pastoral Epistles

1 Timothy 1–3

- Paul warns Timothy of false teachers who have turned to fruitless discussion rather than promote God's plan (1:3–11).

- He offers himself as an example of God's mercy and grace to give hope to all and instructs Timothy to fight the good fight of faith (1:12–20).
- He urges orderly prayer for those in authority, with men being an example of peace and women an example of modesty, learning quietly (2:1–15).
- Paul lays out qualities to seek in potential church leaders, both overseers and deacons, reminding Timothy of the importance of good conduct in God's household (3:1–16).

1 Timothy 4–6

- Paul warns again of false teachers and urges Timothy to be a good servant of Christ Jesus, paying attention to his teaching and godly conduct (4:1–16).
- Timothy is to treat his fellow churchgoers as family members, giving special attention to the care of widows, and to honoring church elders (5:1–25).
- Once again Timothy is to set an example in contrast to false teachers as he fights the good fight of the faith in anticipation of the appearing of Jesus. He is to urge the rich to hope in God, do good, and share their wealth (6:3–19).

Titus

- Paul reminds Titus to appoint elders in every town who are qualified to lead, while watching out for false teachers who lead people astray (1:5–16).
- Titus is to teach others to live godly lives, reminding them of God's grace, salvation, and the coming appearance of Jesus (2:1–3:11).

2 Timothy

- Paul thanks God for Timothy and exhorts him to share in suffering for the gospel in the power of God, as Paul has. Like Paul, Timothy is to guard the gospel entrusted to him, though others may fail (1:3–18).
- Timothy is to be strong in grace as he serves as a good soldier of Christ Jesus, reminding himself and others of the risen Jesus, as an approved worker in contrast to false teachers (2:1–26).

- In the face of false teachers who corrupt others, Timothy is to follow Paul's example, enduring persecutions and holding fast to the Scriptures breathed out by God (3:1–17).
- Finally, as Paul faces the end of his journey, he charges Timothy before God to preach the word in season and out of season, though people may turn away from the truth (4:1–18).

Second Timothy as Paul's Farewell Letter

It is generally agreed that the style of 2 Timothy reads as a farewell discourse or as Paul's "last will and testament" as he self-consciously neared the end of his life. While the letter contains various hints of this purpose, 4:6–8 explicitly points to Paul's impending death—the time for his departure is near, he has finished the race, and he now anticipates the nearing day on which he will receive the crown of righteousness from the Lord, the righteous Judge. In view of his imminent death, Paul charges Timothy to preach the word in all its facets and functions and to discharge the duties of his ministry, as Paul has done.

Rembrandt, *St. Paul in Prison*, 1627

Unknown artist, *The Martyrdom of Saint Timothy*, Byzantine, between 1025 and 1050

Exploration

Leadership Responsibilities

■ READ 2 TIMOTHY 4:1–5 ■

Arguably, the most central theme of the Pastoral Epistles is their repeated exhortation that Timothy and Titus fulfill their responsibilities as leaders of the church. No doubt Timothy and Titus are well aware of these responsibilities, and the letters give the impression that Paul is reminding them of what they already know. In this sense, the Pastoral Epistles remind us that it is good to be reminded of one's responsibilities. The task of church leadership is an ongoing struggle, and it is all too easy to lose direction. Paul's letters implicitly and explicitly acknowledge these difficulties.

Leadership responsibilities are frequently contrasted with the destructive ministry of false teachers (addressed below). Instead of false teachers' preoccupation with meaningless, distracting, or just plain erroneous themes, Timothy and Titus are to hold on to what they've been taught, retaining the centrality of the Scriptures and the gospel message. A good summary of Paul's exhortation to Timothy is found in 1 Timothy 1:18–20, in which he urges Timothy to fight the good fight with faith and good conscience, in contrast to others who have rejected and shipwrecked their faith.

Paul lays out his expectations for overseers and deacons, which informs Timothy of the characteristics he should look for in church leadership candidates, while also reinforcing what is expected of Timothy himself (1 Tim. 3:1–13). It is telling that nearly all the qualifications for overseers concern character, while the capacity to manage one's own household and to teach are the only mentioned abilities. For deacons, only household management is mentioned, implying that they are not required to teach. It is clear that church leadership is primarily concerned with *who* the leaders are, how they live, and how they set an example for others to follow.

In contrast are those who will depart from the faith, and Timothy's responsibility is to point out such dangers to the brothers and sisters (1 Tim. 4:1–6). He is to have nothing to do with misleading myths but is to train himself in godliness, which holds promise for this life and the one to come (4:7–8). Timothy is to command and teach these things, setting an example for other believers in his speech, conduct, love, faith, and purity. He is to be devoted to the public reading of Scripture, exhortation, and teaching. He is to commit himself to such things, making use of the gift within him and making evident progress. Timothy is to watch his life and his teaching, which will be of benefit to himself and others (4:11–16).

THEOLOGICAL ISSUES

Women, Teaching, and 1 Timothy 2

In possibly the most controversial New Testament passage today, Paul appears to forbid women from teaching men within the church (2 Tim. 2:9–15). As scholars ponder possible explanations of Paul's statement, "I do not allow a woman to teach or to have authority over a man; instead, she is to remain quiet" (2:12), various historical reconstructions tend to raise more questions than answers. However the passage is understood and applied today (or not applied), it is worth stating that Paul is not fairly regarded as a misogynist, since he regularly upheld the dignity of women and their essential ministry alongside him (e.g., Rom. 16:1–3, 6–7, 12). He also countered his own culture's expectations by elevating certain women and by recognizing wives' agency within their households (e.g., Eph. 5:22, where the fact that wives are addressed directly stands out against Roman culture).

It must be asked how Paul's statement about Adam and Eve in 2:13–15 relates to the prohibition of 2:12. While it appears that 2:12 is theologically grounded in Genesis 2–3 (the textual referent of 2 Tim. 2:13–15), scholars debate how this background shapes the interpretation of Paul's text. Importantly, it is unclear whether Paul's appeal to Genesis means that his prohibition should be interpreted as universal, regardless of culture and context. Certainly, a case can be made to take Paul's prohibition as culturally informed irrespective of its connection to Genesis, since Paul might simply have applied that biblical text in a way fitted to his contemporary context.

Timothy is to treat his fellow believers as family members: older men as fathers; younger men as brothers; older women as mothers; and younger women as sisters (1 Tim. 5:1–2). He is to make sure that the vulnerable (widows, in this case) are looked after by the church (5:3–10). Timothy is also to ensure that those who serve as elders and leaders within the church are treated with proper respect, but without favoritism (5:17–21).

Timothy is to flee the trappings of falsehood and instead pursue righteousness, godliness, faith, love, endurance, and gentleness. He is to fight the good fight, taking hold of eternal life (1 Tim. 6:11–12). Paul charges him in the presence of God and of Christ Jesus to keep this command without fault or failure until Jesus comes again (6:13–14). In light of the age to come, Timothy is to warn the rich not to trust in their worldly riches but to rely on God, who provides all we need. They should be rich in good works, generous and sharing, and storing up treasure for the coming age (6:17–19). Finally, Timothy is to guard what has been entrusted to him while he avoids false speech and knowledge (6:20).

We see similar emphases in Paul's Second Letter to Timothy, in which he is encouraged not to be ashamed of the testimony about the Lord (2 Tim.

1:8) but to hold on to the sound teaching he heard from Paul and to guard "the good deposit" he received (1:13–14). To fulfill his responsibilities, Timothy is to draw strength from the grace that is in Christ Jesus as he entrusts ministry responsibilities to persons who will faithfully teach others (2:1–2). Timothy is to share in suffering as a good soldier of Christ Jesus (2:3) as he keeps Paul's gospel in mind: Jesus Christ is risen from the dead and descended from David (2:8).

Timothy is to present himself to God as an approved worker who correctly handles the word of truth and avoids empty speech and false teaching (2 Tim. 2:15–16). He is to continue in what he has learned and believed, trusting in the God-inspired Scriptures, which are fit for teaching, rebuking, correcting, and training in righteousness so that God's people are fully equipped for every good deed (3:14–17). Paul again charges Timothy before God and Christ Jesus to preach the word; to be ready at all times to do so; and to correct, rebuke, and encourage his hearers with great patience (4:1–2). Timothy must be prepared for a time when people will prefer false teaching and turn away from the truth. But he must be self-controlled, endure hardship, and fulfill his ministry (4:3–5).

Like Timothy, Titus is entrusted with the responsibility to appoint other church leaders—in this case, in every town in Crete (Titus 1:5). As in 1 Timothy 3, Paul describes to Titus the characteristics of potential leadership candidates, again focusing mainly on character (1:6–9). Titus is to proclaim the truth with sound teaching, helping other believers to live in harmony with one another, offering himself as a good example (2:1–10; 3:1–2, 9–11).

Beware the False Teachers

READ 1 TIMOTHY 1:3–7

One of the major themes of the Pastoral Epistles is their repeated warnings about the dangers of false teachers and false teaching. Clearly, Paul regards false teaching as an existential threat to the health of the first- and second-generation churches.

The opening salvo of 1 Timothy reminds Paul's young apprentice to remain in Ephesus to dissuade would-be false teachers (1 Tim. 1:3–4). Paul wants them to steer away from myths, endless genealogies, empty speculations, fruitless discussion, and misapplications of the law of Moses (1:4–11). These things impede the goal of Paul's instruction, which is love, purity of heart, good conscience, and sincerity of faith (1:5).

Paul addresses the problem of false teachers in more detail in 1 Timothy 4. The Spirit predicted their departure from the faith as they allowed themselves to be led astray by deceitful spirits, demons, and hypocritical liars

(1 Tim. 4:1–2). Part of their message appears to involve a type of asceticism in which the self-denial of good gifts from God is perceived as a desirable spiritual practice. This includes forbidding marriage and demanding abstinence from certain foods. But Paul regards such things as good gifts of God's creation, to be received with thanksgiving (4:3–4). In contrast to the false teachers, Timothy is to have nothing to do with pointless and silly myths. Instead, he is to train himself in godliness (4:7).

HISTORICAL MATTERS

Asceticism

The false teachers whom Paul opposes apparently promoted a type of asceticism, which was an avoidance of material entanglements and pleasures. There were various groups associated with asceticism, such as some forms of Judaism—though the rejection of marriage does not fit Judaism—and Gnosticism. The latter involved the idea that the visible material world is evil, and thus it is more spiritual to abstain from pleasures of the flesh. While Gnosticism is generally regarded as a second-century phenomenon, it is possible that an early type of Christian Gnosticism already existed by the time of Paul's writing in the first century.

In 2 Timothy, Paul reiterates some of the same emphases. He warns Timothy to avoid irreverent and empty speech, which produces godlessness that spreads like gangrene (2 Tim. 2:16–17). Hymenaeus and Philetus are examples of those who have departed from the truth and ruined others' faith by claiming such errors as the belief that the resurrection from the dead has already happened (2:18).

In the last days—from the ascension of Jesus until his return—Paul expects ungodly false teachers to appear like the real deal, while they are in fact counterfeits (2 Tim. 3:1–5). They manage to deceive gullible people who are easily led astray in their passions, while seeking knowledge but not coming to a knowledge of the truth (3:6–9). In contrast, while impostors will become worse, deceiving and being deceived, Timothy is to continue in what he has learned and believed, holding fast to the sacred Scriptures, which are inspired by God and equip his people for every good work (3:13–17).

THEOLOGICAL ISSUES

The Last Days

Throughout the New Testament, "the last days" refers to the period between Jesus's ascension and his eventual return. That is, the last two thousand years have been the last days. So, Paul's statement about the hard times that will come in the last days (2 Tim. 3:1) simply refers to difficulties that will take place as we await Jesus's return. One of these difficulties is the presence of false teachers.

Paul also warns his disciple Titus of rebellious people who are full of empty talk and deception. Titus is to silence such people, as they ruin households for the sake of dishonest gain (Titus 1:10–11). Paul hopes that, given a sharp rebuke, they might return to sound faith and leave aside myths and false commands, but as it stands, they claim to know God but deny him by their works (1:13–16).

Life and Doctrine

READ 1 TIMOTHY 4:11–16

At the heart of Timothy's and Titus's responsibilities as leaders of churches is their duty to live a certain way and to teach a certain way. In

Sixth-century Byzantine Church of St. Titus

short, they are to watch their *life* and *doctrine* (1 Tim. 4:16). This simple summary captures the positive and negative aspects of their roles: by watching their life and doctrine they set a positive example for believers to follow and counteract the dangerous lifestyle and teaching of false teachers.

As mentioned above, overseers and deacons are to set an example for believers in their character and conduct. Faithful in marriage and family life, self-controlled, respectable, gentle, and having a good reputation among outsiders, overseers and deacons are simply Christians living well (1 Tim. 3:1–13). As an overseer himself, Timothy is to train himself in godliness as an expression of his hope in the living God (4:7–10). He is to command and teach the truth and set an example in speech, conduct, love, faith, and purity. He is to give attention to the public reading of Scripture, to exhortation, and to teaching, so that his progress is evident to all. Timothy is to pay close attention to his life and teaching, which will result in the salvation of himself and his hearers (4:11–16). Both the content of his teaching and the quality of his character are essential for Timothy's ministry success. Bad character would undermine his teaching, and bad teaching would lead himself and others astray. Unlike the false teachers, Timothy is to flee from error and sin, pursuing righteousness, godliness, faith, love, endurance, and gentleness. He is to fight the good fight for the cause of the faith, and take hold of eternal life. Timothy is charged by Paul to keep his command without fault until the appearing of the Lord Jesus Christ (6:11–14).

Timothy should not cower from the "shame" associated with following Christ but instead share in suffering for the gospel by the power of God

(2 Tim. 1:8; 2:3–4). He is to hold on to the sound teaching he received and guard the good deposit of the gospel (1:13–14), while also looking out for others who might be qualified to do likewise (2:2). Timothy is to be a dedicated soldier, a fair athlete, and a hardworking farmer (2:3–6) as he keeps in mind the center of his message: Jesus Christ, risen from the dead and descended from David—Paul's gospel message (2:8). Timothy is to make sure that he is approved by the one whose approval matters—without fear of shame—because he rightly handles the word of truth (2:15). He should aspire to be God's special instrument, set apart for his use and for every good work (2:21). As such, Timothy needs to flee unhelpful instincts and pursue godliness, gentleness, and patience (2:22–25). Timothy has followed Paul's teaching, conduct, and love—along with his persecutions and sufferings—and he is to continue in what he has learned and believed (3:10–14). Paul charges him to preach the word with patience, while exercising self-control in everything, enduring hardship, doing the work of an evangelist, and fulfilling his ministry (4:1–5).

HISTORICAL MATTERS

Shame in the Ancient World

When Paul exhorts Timothy, "Don't be ashamed of the testimony about our Lord, or of me his prisoner" (2 Tim. 1:8), he draws on one of the most powerful social elements in Paul's world: the concept of honor and shame. These sociopsychological categories provided measures of worth in the Roman world. While honor was ascribed to things or deeds regarded noble, shame was associated with ignoble behavior or rank. Here Paul points to the potential shame associated with the message about Jesus and with his own imprisonment. Being imprisoned was, naturally, a matter of shame in the ancient world (much like today), but Paul urges Timothy to reject society's association of shame with his imprisonment, since Paul is in chains for a noble cause. Likewise, it is likely that the message of Jesus—mocked by outsiders—was also considered shameful, but Timothy is to resist the social pressure of shame associated with it.

Likewise, Titus is to offer sound teaching while setting an example of good works with integrity and dignity. His message is to be beyond reproach so that his opponents will be ashamed, with nothing bad to say about him (Titus 2:1–8). Titus is to proclaim the truth with authority, making it impossible for others to disregard him (2:15).

Implementation

The Pastoral Epistles remain a chief go-to source for Paul's teaching about ministry service and church leadership. While they should not be regarded as exhaustive—as though they contain everything Paul might say on the subject—the repetition of themes across the three letters demonstrates his main concerns at the time of writing. However, it should also be recognized that Paul's extant thinking about ministry is not limited to the Pastoral Epistles. Second Corinthians, for example, is chock-full of insight and wisdom about sacrificial new-covenant ministry and includes several themes unaddressed in the Pastoral Epistles. So, while the Pastoral Epistles are go-to resources for Paul's ministry priorities, they should be supplemented with an appreciation of Paul's wider teaching.

In an age when many church leaders are influenced by big-name preachers, the seduction of Christo-entertainment, and the goal of ever-larger congregations, it is sobering to reflect on the priorities that Paul impresses on Timothy and Titus. These priorities have nothing to do with achieving celebrity, entertainment, or megachurch status. Instead, Timothy and Titus are to know, teach, and protect the truth. They are to exemplify this truth through the conduct of their lives and the content of their teaching. No thought is given to people-pleasing, and instead their responsibilities include warning, rebuking, and instructing those under their care. Clearly, such things should be conducted with gentleness and respect, with the overarching goal of protecting the people of Christ from harmful falsehoods and deceptions.

An obvious incompatibility with megachurch culture is that church leaders must know the people under their care in order to protect and defend them from external (and internal) threats. By the same token, it is not possible for pastors to set an example to others through their life and doctrine if their congregation barely knows them in person. Rather, the responsibilities of church leadership require pastors and their flock to engage in a shared life together, in which mutual knowledge and care are possible.

The threat of false teaching is as real today as it was in Paul's day. Though his warnings about false teaching are frequent in these letters, it is unlikely that Paul would encourage a fearful or hypochondriacal attitude about it. False teaching is just a part of the world we live in—it is to be expected—and church leaders need to watch out for it, while not going overboard finding error under every rock. One of the most pernicious falsehoods circulating through the church today is the so-called prosperity gospel. The belief that God's biggest desire is to bless believers with all health, wealth, and success is misleading, to say the least. And it is even worse to suggest that any lack of blessing is sure evidence of faulty or deficient faith. A clear contradiction to such thinking is found within the Pastoral Epistles, as Paul predicts that all who want to live a godly life in Christ Jesus will be persecuted (2 Tim. 3:12). In other words, the godly will suffer rather than prosper. God may choose to bless believers in various ways—and living wisely often results in good things, just as foolish living reaps its own reward—but God does not promise to reward the faithful with health, wealth, and success (at least, not in this life). Nor does God promise to keep believers away from trouble—quite the opposite. The false gospel of prosperity distorts the teaching of the Bible, misinterprets God's intentions for us, and undermines the faith of those who experience suffering through no fault of their own. It is false teaching that must be corrected.

According to the Pastoral Epistles, the best protection from false teaching is good teaching. If pastors and church leaders properly handle the word of truth (2 Tim. 2:15), they will enable believers to discern truth from falsehood, to hold on to the good and to reject the bad. This also means that pastors are to avoid destructive tendencies in their *own* lives if they are to be of much use to others. Timothy is to avoid irreverent and empty speech, which produces godlessness (2:16), and to avoid being quarrelsome (2:24). These exhortations demonstrate that the trappings of false teaching are not only "over there" but can be found closer to home too. Good leadership begins with the leader.

Christian Reading Questions

1. A key perspective throughout the Pastoral Epistles is the importance of pastors' lives matching their message (e.g., 1 Tim. 4:11–16). What are some ways pastors today might struggle to live up to this standard?
2. One of the most controversial passages in the New Testament is 1 Timothy 2:8–15. Work through the details of this text and think through how it might (or might not) be relevant today.
3. Given that the Pastoral Epistles could not possibly anticipate every issue that a pastor might face today, what issues might have been included if Paul could update these letters?

PART 6

Paul's Theology

CHAPTER EIGHTEEN

Paul's Theology (1)

After Jesus, Paul is the most significant theologian of the New Testament and the most influential theologian in the history of the Christian church. Every serious theologian and thinker within Christianity has been influenced by Paul's writings, which continue to stir rigorous debate, reflection, and inspiration. Paul's theology of justification by faith was directly linked to the birth of the Protestant Reformation, and his thinking in general has profoundly shaped Western culture and its intellectual tradition. Paul's influence continues unabated within the contemporary church, with his New Testament letters being a staple of preaching series, public and private Bible reading, and academic studies. It is impossible to overestimate Paul's impact and significance for Christianity and, through it, the world.

While Paul remains the premier theologian in the history of Christianity (after Jesus), it is important to appreciate that he was primarily a missionary and pastor, not an academic or systematic theologian. The purpose of Paul's theological activity was always to address pastoral and missionary concerns, rather than to produce theological output for its own sake. He was steadfastly committed to the spiritual health of the various congregations associated with him, as well as certain individuals who played a key role in the leadership of these churches. While it could be argued that all modern theology is offered in service of the church, it is generally not produced with specific church needs in mind—at least not with the specificity and urgency with which Paul wrote.

Even though Paul was not a systematic theologian in today's sense, it would be a mistake to claim that his theology was not "systematic." His thinking is strongly logical, following a tight structure of argumentation, and is shaped around core principles that drive his commitments. Paul's writings can be systematized in the sense that his thinking on various topics can be pieced together into a coherent whole (though some commentators debate this). Thus, we might claim that Paul's theology is systematic without being presented as systematic theology—if that distinction makes sense. In the end, it is inescapable that Paul's writings have been packaged as missionary and pastoral documents, and this fact remains universally relevant for understanding his contribution and how it might apply today.

Since we have already worked through Paul's letters—their context, historical situation, and teaching—we are now in a position to pull together the threads of his theological thought. While we can never fully extract Paul's thinking out of the occasional and idiosyncratic nature of his letters, what follows is a theological distillation of the insights outlined in previous chapters of this book. As such, this cannot be a comprehensive account of Paul's theological mind, since it is highly unlikely that his letters captured everything he ever thought. But the following summary seeks to outline the main themes of what *was* captured in his letters.

This overview of Paul's theology is organized across two chapters. This chapter addresses Jesus the Messiah, sin and death, humanity, the cross of Christ, resurrection, union with Christ, justification by faith, salvation, gospel, the Spirit, and eschatology. Since all of Paul's themes are interrelated, it is impossible to separate them fully, just as it is impossible to establish much of an order of priority. The topics that follow are, therefore, not given in any order of importance (except for the first theme: Jesus the Messiah); rather, they are organized to best facilitate the reader's movement through them.

Jesus the Messiah

At the center and heart of Paul's theology is the person and work of Jesus, the Messiah—God's anointed King. Paul's conviction that Jesus is the Messiah (or Christ) was, for him, the fulfillment of God's promises that a descendant of David would rule forever at God's right hand. Jesus is, thus, God's anointed king of Israel but also the appointed ruler over the entirety of humanity. Jesus was appointed Messiah through his resurrection from the dead and ascension into the heavens. But in contrast to contemporary messianic expectations, Paul affirmed that the powerful, ruling King is also the humble servant who died for the sake of his enemies. The Messiah is the very demonstration of God's love for humanity, enabling all people—both Jews and gentiles—to be reconciled to God.

Christ is pictured as the center of the entire cosmos, since God's purpose is to bring everything together in Christ—both things in heaven and things on earth—affirming his preeminent significance for all creation. Jesus himself is not part of the creation, since in him all things were created; rather, he is the one through whom God created all things. And this includes the entire sweep of creation—heavenly and earthly realities, whether visible or invisible, and all conceivable powers and authorities. Every element of creation was made through him and for him. This means that Christ is not only the one through whom God created the cosmos but also the one *for* whom he created it. Paul views Christ as the means, the sustaining power, and the goal of all creation.

Christ Pantocrator mosaic in Church of the Holy Sepulchre, Jerusalem

Paul describes Jesus as the image of the invisible God. He is able to reveal the invisible God and make him known. The "image" language also evokes the creation of the first humans, who were made in God's image. As such, Paul views Jesus as the ultimate human who fulfills God's intention for humanity as his image-bearers. But whereas Adam and Eve were made "in" the image of God, Jesus *is* the image of God. He is not merely a better expression of humanity than his forebears; he *is* the humanity in which they were formed.

Paul also describes Jesus as the firstborn over all creation. Rather than support the heterodox notion that Jesus came into existence at a certain point in time, such language is used to evoke the honor and inheritance that the firstborn enjoyed within the family setting. To Jesus is ascribed all honor and inheritance within the cosmos. As head of the body, the church, Jesus is also the firstborn from among the dead. "Firstborn" language should again be understood in terms of preeminence—so that in everything he might have the supremacy. Christ is supreme over the entire cosmos, and specifically he is supreme over the church.

According to Paul, all the fullness of God dwells in Jesus and through him God reconciles everything to himself. This means that Christ is the means by which everything is put right; everything will ultimately be restored and rectified by the making of peace through his blood, shed on the cross. Jesus is seen not only as the image of God but also as bearing his fullness. God is fully in Jesus, so that to encounter Jesus is to encounter God. And his atoning work on the cross has cosmic significance, since it is the means through which all things in heaven and earth are reconciled to

God. Jesus did not die solely to deal with humanity's sinfulness; he died for the entire cosmos so that peace and reconciliation with God would come through him.

Sin and Death

Paul presents sin as personal, social, and cosmic. It can therefore refer to specific sinful acts by individuals, to an interrupting force that corrupts social relationships and groups, and to a cosmic power—Sin, with a capital *S*—that keeps the world under captivity. All three aspects of sin interact with one another so that the inherent sinfulness of individuals operates in concert with the priorities and inclinations of the dominant cosmic rule of Sin, effecting damaging consequences within and across communities.

All people are born "in Adam," who is the figurehead for the realm of Sin and Death. Everyone under this realm is governed by their own sinful flesh in concert with the rule of Sin. For Paul, the "flesh" represents human corruption, desires, and inclinations that are focused on self rather than God's intentions. The flesh, therefore, is the power that ensures that individuals continue to live under the influence of the cosmic power of Sin. The cosmic power of Sin is in effect the handmaiden of Death, since the former guarantees the latter: everyone guilty of sin will be subject to death. In this sense, Sin and Death are cosmic powers who cooperate to rule together over the realm represented by Adam.

Peter Paul Rubens, *Christ and the Penitent Sinners*

As long as people live under the realm of Sin and Death, they are powerless to resist the inclinations of the flesh. There is no hope for humanity in Adam, and the only escape is death itself. However, Paul proclaims that by participation in the death and resurrection of Christ, believers exit the realm of Adam through death with Christ and are given new life in the realm of Christ through participation in his resurrection. This is why Paul proclaims the resurrection of

Christ as the final defeat of Death: by conquering Sin through his death and by conquering Death through his resurrection, Jesus has overcome both cosmic powers. Faith in Christ joins believers to his victory and sets them free from their captivity to Sin and their sentence of Death.

Believers, then, are no longer hapless victims of their sinful flesh, since they are no longer under the sway and influence of the cosmic power of Sin. They can resist the inclinations of the flesh and choose to live by the Spirit instead. As such, Paul exhorts believers to put off the flesh, which means that they are to engage in the daily reconfirmation of their identification with the realm of Christ and their rejection of the realm of Sin and Death represented by Adam.

Humanity

Paul portrays a bleak vision of humanity apart from Christ. Without the Spirit of God, people follow the desires of the flesh, making them deceptive, self-serving, treacherous, hateful, violent, proud, and ignorant of God. They are under the rule of Sin and Death, following the ways of the world and the ruler of the air, and they are spiritually dead. As such, humanity is condemned to death and destruction and is subjected to God's wrath. Despite this bleak appraisal of humanity, Paul affirms God's love for all people in the strongest possible terms. God demonstrated his love for sinners through Jesus's death on their behalf. Because of God's mercy and love, he makes them alive with Christ, raising them to be seated in the heavens with him. God imparts his Spirit to live among his people and to renew and transform them. Putting these two elements together, we see that Paul affirms both the total depravity of humanity and our incredible value and dignity as God's beloved creatures made in his image. Jesus himself has shared in our humanity, bearing human flesh while being without sin.

A key element of Paul's understanding of human beings is the distinction between their inner and outer persons. For Paul, the former is permanent while the latter is temporary. Both are necessary for a living human being. The outer body is the physical or material aspect of a person, which is weak and deteriorates, is susceptible to human desires and temptations, and ultimately will be subjected to death. The inner person is housed by the outer body and includes a person's mind, heart, spirit, soul, and will. Transformation of actions and behaviors evident in the outer body is tangible evidence of change within the inner person by the power of the Spirit of Christ.

The distinction between the inner and outer persons is paralleled by the distinction between the old person and the new person. Believers have been crucified with Christ and have been raised with him. Dying with Christ spells the death of the old person, who was a slave to sin, subjected to death, and sentenced to condemnation. When a believer is raised with Christ, they become a new person, a new creation in Christ, no longer enslaved to sin or subjected to the finality of death, and set free from condemnation.

Though the new person in Christ has come and the old has passed away, our existence within the overlap of old and new ages means that believers are still susceptible to reverting to the ways and priorities of the old person. Empowered by the Spirit, believers are to continue to put off the old self and to put on the new self, who has been created to be like God in righteousness and holiness.

The Cross of Christ

The cross of Christ was central to Paul's preaching: "We preach Christ crucified" (1 Cor. 1:23). The death of Christ is a declaration of God's love for sinful humanity, for it was while we were God's enemies that Christ died for us. He was delivered to death for our transgressions, and Paul regards himself as cocrucified with Christ. Through the cross, God erased the certificate of debt against us and disarmed the rulers and authorities. The cross therefore represents the intersection of the reality of human sin, the supreme love of God, the willing sacrifice of the Son, and the rule of God over all powers and authorities.

The cross of Christ is foolishness to the wise of the world, both Jewish and gentile. Though crucifixion was associated with intense shame in the Roman world, the crucifixion of Christ is, for Paul, the power and wisdom of God. The cross reveals God's glorious plan for redemption, which could not be derived from human calculation. Through the cross, Christ has become our righteousness, holiness, and redemption, demonstrating that God's power comes through means that appear weak and shameful in the eyes of the world.

Ultimately, the cross of Christ achieves reconciliation between God and rebellious human beings. God reconciles all things to himself by making peace through the blood of Christ, shed on the cross. This reconciliation achieves the restoration not only of vertical relationships (humans with God) but also of horizontal ones as the implications of the cross reach into human relationships with one another.

The cross of Christ also connects to the eschatological kingdom of God, since it is the central turning point in the story of salvation history and allows the future kingdom to break into history. Related to this ultimate rule of God is his victory over the powers of evil, which are disarmed and conquered by means of the cross. The irony of the cross is that although Jesus was mocked, humiliated, and crucified by Roman power, God was working to triumph over all competing powers—including Roman—through this act of outward weakness, shame, and apparent defeat.

Public domain / Metropolitan Museum of Art / Wikimedia Commons

El Greco, *Christ Carrying the Cross*, 1577–87

Paul's frequent use of the language of crucifixion may have been intended to remind his readers of the shame and brutality of the cross. It is deeply ironic that the rulers of this age crucified the Lord of glory. While crucifixion had been used by Romans to enforce their brutal Pax Romana (Roman peace) over their enemies, it was through the cross of Christ that God defeated his enemies and achieved the possibility for genuine peace between him and those opposed to him.

The cross of Christ is also integral to Paul's teaching about justification. The death of Jesus is presented as a sacrifice of atonement or propitiation through which his blood facilitates redemption. This aspect of the cross is commonly known as penal substitutionary atonement, in which Christ willingly died as a substitute for guilty sinners in order to satisfy the righteous wrath of God. As such, the cross holds together God's mercy and his justice, since sin must receive judgment but sinners are spared it because Jesus suffered on their behalf.

Finally, the cross of Christ is part of Paul's theology of union with Christ, since believers participate in his death so that their old self has been crucified with Christ. The ongoing identification of believers with the death of Christ defines their lives through the ongoing practice of putting to death their sinful impulses. Being crucified with Christ was a centrally defining aspect of Paul's own identity so that his life and ministry could be described as cruciform.

Resurrection

The resurrection of Christ is central to the gospel that Paul preached, as it declared that Jesus is the Christ and that he was raised for our justification.

The resurrection of Jesus is also confirmation of the coming general resurrection of the dead. Christ will make alive those who belong to him and will then hand over his kingdom to God the Father once the last enemy—Death—has been destroyed.

Paul affirmed the Jewish belief that God will raise the dead at the end of history, when the faithful will be restored and granted eternal life with God. The resurrection of the dead went hand in hand with Jewish thinking about justification, since the righteous would be declared right with God on judgment day, with the resurrection from the dead serving as their vindication and reward. But Paul believed that the resurrection of Jesus had ushered in the new age, which now overlaps with the old, so that justification and spiritual resurrection are possible now through participating with Christ.

In keeping with messianic expectation, Paul regards the resurrection of Jesus as the confirmation and declaration that he is the Son of Man, the Messiah. God had promised that his chosen one would not be abandoned to the grave nor see decay, so the resurrection confirmed Jesus's messianic status and, together with his ascension, positioned Jesus at God's right hand to rule as his co-regent, as was anticipated of the Messiah.

Those in Christ share in his resurrection from the dead, so that Paul says that believers have already been (spiritually) raised with him and seated with him in the heavens. They are therefore to seek things above, where Christ is, and to live as new people made alive with Christ. Believers' spiritual resurrection with Christ anticipates their future bodily resurrection, which will take place upon his return. Resurrection with Christ is also the sign that believers share in his justification, since resurrection from the dead to eternal life is the result of vindication on the day of judgment.

As the firstfruits of the resurrection of the dead, Christ's resurrection determines the nature of the bodily resurrection of those who belong to him. Believers' bodies will be raised imperishable, glorious, and in power. Each will have a "spiritual" body, bearing the image of the heavenly man. Resurrection will occur in an instant at the designated time, and the perishable will be clothed with the imperishable. Then, death will be swallowed up in victory through the Lord Jesus Christ.

Union with Christ

"Union with Christ" is the phrase we use to refer to Paul's theology of being joined to Christ. It is reflected in his very common idioms "in Christ," "with Christ," "through Christ," and so forth. It is also seen through various metaphors such as the body of Christ, clothing, the temple, and the church as the bride of Christ. Union with Christ is best understood through four images: union, participation, identification, incorporation. "Union" refers to a profound spiritual connection to Christ through mutual indwelling by the Spirit. "Participation" refers to sharing in the key events of Christ's narrative, such as his suffering, death, burial, resurrection, ascension, and glorification. "Identification" refers to shifting our allegiance from Adam and the realm of sin and death to Christ and his realm of righteousness and peace. "Incorporation" refers to being members together in a corporate entity shaped by Christ. All of God's blessings are bestowed on believers through our union with Christ.

While the ascended Christ is seated in the heavens with his heavenly Father, he is not a remote figure. In fact, Paul affirms that all who believe in Christ have become one with him by the power of the Spirit. Believers are "in Christ," and Christ is in them. This means that our relationship with Christ is intensely personal rather than mechanistic, and that our fellowship with God is one of mutual indwelling. It also means that all believers are connected to one another too, since each person in union with Christ is a member of his body.

Believers are to live their lives in Christ, being rooted and built up in him. This means that the believer's entire life is defined by their union with Christ—they live in him and grow in him. They do not graduate or go beyond this fundamental reality of the Christian life. Moreover, the fullness of God dwells in Christ, and Christ dwells in believers, so that in Christ the believer has been brought to fullness. In Christ believers are spiritually "circumcised," meaning that the person formerly ruled by "the flesh"—or the sinful nature—was put off. The tyranny of the sinful nature is escaped through spiritual death, since believers have been buried with Christ in baptism and raised with him through faith in God. The only escape from the dark powers that rule over human beings comes through spiritual death and resurrection with Christ. By participation with Christ, believers are given new life and freedom from their former captors.

Paul argues that if someone has been baptized into Christ, they have been baptized into his death. And those baptized into his death will also receive new life by sharing in his resurrection. This means that the old self—who was ruled by sin—has been crucified with Christ and therefore is dead. The believer is therefore no longer enslaved to sin, since death releases a person from its hold over them. Having died with Christ, the believer will now live with him through his resurrection from the dead and will no longer be subjected to (the finality of) death. Believers therefore are to consider themselves dead to sin but alive to God in Christ Jesus.

The implication of this is that believers are not to obey the leading of sin but to offer themselves to God as weapons for righteousness. Though once slaves to sin, believers have now been set free from its rule and are enslaved to righteousness and produce its fruit, resulting in eternal life. Believers' participation in the death of Christ, then, is Paul's theological answer as to why they are no longer to continue in sin. Their old self has been crucified with Christ, and their new self belongs to God, not sin.

Believers' death with Christ frees them from spiritual oppression. Their resurrection with him lifts them to a heavenly plane, and their close connection with Christ keeps them protected under his care until the point when they will share in his glorious return. Participation with Christ is therefore seen as the underlying principle that shapes the entire Christian identity and experience. It is the means through which believers escape the old, access the new, and remain secure for the future. Union with Christ is a spiritual reality that constructs believers' destiny, regardless of whether or not they "sense" this element of their spiritual world. In this manner it is an "objective" reality, though unseen and intangible. And though participation with Christ itself is intangible, its implications for life today are deeply tangible.

Justification by Faith

Paul argues that both Jews and gentiles are declared to be right with God (or justified) by means of faith in Christ. Justification does not come through being born a Jew or by maintaining Jewish identity markers, such as keeping the law of Moses, circumcision, food customs, or other stipulations of the old covenant. Paul argues that, irrespective of whether one can claim Jewish identity, God's promise to bless the children of Abraham extends to all his children—those who share in the faith of Abraham, both Jews and gentiles. Paul states that all are justified (= made righteous) freely by God's grace through the redemption that is in Christ Jesus. Through the death of Christ, God dealt with all sins, thus proving his own righteousness as the one who does not let evil go unchecked. God presented Christ so that he would be just and justify the one who has faith in Jesus. Rather than sweep humanity's sin under the carpet, he presented Jesus as an atoning sacrifice for sin. That way, God can justify sinners while he himself remains just. Sin is checked while sinners may go free.

Paul points out that since God makes sinners righteous through faith, there is no room for boasting of any kind. People are not made righteous through obedience to the law of Moses, or through being Jewish, or through circumcision. Righteousness comes through faith for both Jew and gentile, which means that no one has grounds to see themselves as superior to anyone else.

Paul then supports his overall argument about justification by faith by appealing to the examples of Abraham and David, demonstrating that both were justified by faith, not by works of the law. David was regarded as righteous even though he had gravely sinned. Abraham was credited with righteousness *before* he was circumcised. Moreover, the grand promise made to Abraham—that his descendants would inherit the world—makes sense only if justification comes by faith rather than by the law. If the promise comes by faith, it will be according to God's grace rather than human merit. As such, the promise is open to those who have faith, whether Jew or gentile, since it is not dependent on the law of Moses. This is how Abraham becomes the father of many nations, since the promise extends to all those who have faith. Abraham himself demonstrated faith that God would fulfill his promise and was thus credited with righteousness. The same applies to those of us who also have faith in God, the one who raised from the dead the Lord Jesus, who died for our trespasses and was raised for our justification.

Having been justified by faith, believers now experience peace with God, enjoy access to his grace, and share in the hope of the glory of God. Their situation has been entirely reversed: no longer regarded as sinners under the wrath of God, believers have been reconciled to God and will be saved from his wrath. Paul's argument about righteousness includes his contrast between Adam and Christ as two representative heads of humanity. Sin, death, and condemnation came into the world through Adam, while grace, righteousness, and eternal life have come through Jesus Christ.

Salvation

"Salvation" is an umbrella term that includes various inner workings such as justification and reconciliation. Because Christ sets his people free from the dominion of sin and death, he is their savior. By dying for sins on the cross, he canceled the debt that stood against us, and by rising from the dead, he secured our righteous status before God. He has inaugurated a new age of righteousness and peace into which believers have access by rising with Christ. Dying with Christ ends their allegiance to the old age, and rising with him secures their eternal life in the new age and delivers them from future divine judgment. Because of this, salvation is most assuredly by God's grace and cannot be achieved by human works or boasting.

Salvation by grace through faith is powered by union with Christ as believers are made alive with Christ, raised up with him, and seated with him in the heavens. Before being united with Christ, people were spiritually dead in their sins and under the influence of the forces of evil. Salvation, therefore, involves spiritual resurrection in order to overturn the state of spiritual death. Salvation also involves a fundamental change of orientation and conduct. Once spiritually dead in sins, they walked according to the ways of this world and according to the ruler of the power of the air. But having been made alive with Christ, and therefore saved by grace through faith, believers have been re-created in Christ Jesus. They now walk in the good deeds that God has prepared in advance.

Salvation begins with the recognition of spiritual death and the influence of evil powers over spiritually dead people. It recognizes their powerlessness to alter their situation and that it is up to God, motivated by mercy and love, to raise the dead to life with Christ. He seats them with Christ in the heavens, far above all competing spiritual forces, and gives them an eternal view of his grace and kindness in Christ. This entire picture is what Paul describes as salvation, which clearly comes by the grace of God, not by human effort, achievement, or any kind of works, leaving saved human beings entirely without boast before God. They are his workmanship and a new creation in Christ, now living anew under the influence of God.

Gospel

Paul's gospel announces that Jesus is the long-awaited Messiah, the promised king of Israel. Since Jesus is a descendant of King David, his resurrection from the dead establishes his credentials as the Son of God (= Messiah). Christ died for our sins according to the Scriptures and was raised on the third day according to the Scriptures.

Paul's statements about the gospel include the following elements. The gospel is that Jesus the King

1. preexisted as God the Son,
2. was sent by the Father,
3. took on human flesh in fulfillment of God's promises to David,
4. died for our sins in accordance with the Scriptures,
5. was buried,
6. was raised on the third day in accordance with the Scriptures,
7. appeared to many witnesses,

8. is enthroned at the right hand of God as the ruling Christ,
9. has sent the Holy Spirit to his people to effect his rule,
10. will come again as final judge to rule.[1]

Paul claims that the gospel he preaches has come *straight from Jesus himself*. It is not of human origin. It was not passed on to him by another human being. Rather, it came by a revelation of Jesus Christ. The gospel affirms that justification comes not through keeping the law of Moses but by faith in Jesus Christ. This was foretold by Scripture when it proclaimed the gospel ahead of time to Abraham, saying, "All the nations will be blessed through you." All who have faith like Abraham are blessed.

Paul bears a God-given responsibility to proclaim the gospel, especially to the gentiles. It is Paul's apostolic duty to proclaim the gospel to all people—regardless of opposition—that they might hear the good news and come to faith in the promised Messiah, by which they will be saved from divine judgment and receive eternal life. Paul also exhorts his readers to live lives worthy of the gospel of Christ, which will involve their standing firm together to contend for the faith of the gospel in the face of opposition.

The Spirit

If the center of Paul's theology is the person and work of Christ, then the Spirit is the one through whom Christ is joined to his people. Where the Spirit dwells, there dwells Christ. The presence of the Spirit among believers is also evidence that God does not show partiality and thus dwells among all those who confess Christ as Lord. The Spirit intercedes for us with groans that words cannot express, and he produces his fruit in the lives of believers, taking the place of the law of Moses of the old covenant. The Spirit is also a deposit guaranteeing an inheritance to come, meaning that through the Spirit believers are connected to a glorious future in the presence of God.

Paul celebrates the Spirit of life in contrast to the bleakness of life under the law, compromised by the flesh. He boldly declares that there is no condemnation for those in Christ Jesus because the law of the Spirit of life in Christ Jesus has set us free from the law of sin and death. Paul explains that the law was not able to provide life, since it was compromised by the flesh and ultimately only served to condemn humanity. Instead, God condemned sin by making Jesus a sin offering so that the law's requirement to condemn sin would be fulfilled. In this way, the law is fulfilled by those who walk according to the Spirit rather than according to the flesh. Those who

Gian Lorenzo Bernini, *Holy Spirit as a Dove*, St. Peter's Basilica, 1660

live according to the flesh cannot please God, but believers are in the Spirit, since the Spirit lives in them because they are in Christ. With Christ in them, believers' bodies are dead due to sin but will be raised to life by God through the Spirit, just as he raised Christ from the dead through the Spirit. In short, the law kills but the Spirit brings life. Thus, Paul urges his readers to be led by the Spirit rather than the flesh, as appropriate for God's children. By the Spirit, God's adopted children cry out to him as Father and as his heirs with Christ, with whom they suffer and with whom they will be glorified.

God put the Spirit of his Son into the hearts of believers, who have been born by the Spirit. As such, believers are to "walk by the Spirit" rather than carry out the desires of the flesh. The flesh is in conflict with the Spirit; they are opposed to each other, so that we don't do what we want to do. Being led by the Spirit, however, means that believers do not rely on the law to know what to do. The fruit of the Spirit includes love, peace, and gentleness. The Spirit takes the place of the law as the guide for the sons and daughters of God to live by. Living by the Spirit will prevent believers from falling into fleshly vices. Indeed, the one who sows according to the flesh will reap destruction, but the one who sows according to the Spirit will reap eternal life.

Eschatology

The resurrection of Christ inaugurated an overlap of the ages, since it signaled that the new age had already dawned—before the old age has yet passed. This is because resurrection belongs to the end of time, to judgment day. Christ's resurrection from the dead declares him righteous in the face of judgment, and it secures God's verdict now of all who are in Christ. Thus, the resurrection has created a "now and not yet" eschatological framework that gives shape to all of Paul's theology. Believers are to live as new creations in Christ, who belong to the new age, no longer enslaved by the powers that dominated the old age.

Finally, the goal of all things is the glory of God in Christ. In the end, Christ will be glorified by all creation to the glory of his heavenly Father. And an astonishing hope awaits us as Christ will share his glory with his people. We will be glorified with him, if indeed we have suffered with him.

Paul's teaching about the coming of the Lord has three main concerns. First, his coming will inaugurate the promised day of the Lord. Second, the day of the Lord will bring judgment alongside salvation. Third, his coming will occur as an expected surprise. In light of these elements, believers are to live in hope while keeping themselves ready for that great day.

Waiting for God's Son to come from heaven is a central characteristic of believers' behavior, and Paul anticipates that they will be his joy and crown when the Lord Jesus comes. He prays that the Lord would make believers' hearts blameless before God at the coming of Jesus. Paul affirms that those brothers and sisters who have died (or are "asleep") will be raised from the dead, just as Jesus was. When the Lord comes, God will bring with him those who have fallen asleep, and those who are still alive at that time will be caught up together with them in the clouds to meet the Lord in the air. The pastoral significance of this affirmation is that believers need not grieve like the rest, who have no hope. While believers will grieve for deceased loved ones, their hope of the resurrection of the dead will enable them to grieve with hope. They will be reunited when the Lord comes.

The coming of Christ will announce judgment and salvation and will occur in a clear, public, and undeniable fashion. Believers are to be ready for the coming of the Lord whenever he comes, but they are not to be troubled by prophecies alleging that the day of the Lord has already come.

Christian Reading Questions

1. Think about the themes raised in this chapter. How do they connect to one another? Can you write out the "logic" of their connectedness?
2. Which of these themes do you understand the least? What parts of Paul's writings can help you to understand it better?

CHAPTER NINETEEN

Paul's Theology (2)

This chapter continues our overview of Paul's theology by addressing the themes of promise-fulfillment, new covenant, Jew-gentile reconciliation, faith-works-law, Israel, church, Christian living, spiritual warfare, ministry, and false teaching.

Promise-Fulfillment

The theme of promise and fulfillment runs throughout Paul's writings as he regularly presents Christ, and life in Christ, as the fulfillment of the plan of God as revealed in the Scriptures—beginning with the gospel, which was promised beforehand through the prophets. Jesus is presented as the long-awaited Messiah promised by God. Paul draws on Psalms, Isaiah, Deuteronomy, Hosea, and Genesis in particular to affirm the authority and rule of Jesus over God's enemies, to make sense of his suffering, resurrection, and exaltation, the inclusion of the gentiles, and Paul's mission to the nations.

Jesus is God's yes to all his promises and inaugurates a new covenant that replaces the Mosaic covenant. Although the new covenant replaces the old, it stands in continuity with the promises to Abraham that predate Moses. According to Paul, the inclusion of the gentiles into the new-covenant people of God fulfills the promise to Abraham that all peoples would be blessed through him. Abraham's true children are those who share his faith in God, regardless of whether they are circumcised—just as Abraham was justified by faith before he was circumcised. And many Jews' rejection of Jesus as their Messiah is understood as fulfillment of prophecy.

New Covenant

The key to understanding the new covenant is to grasp how it differs from the covenant established with Israel through Moses. Paul treads a careful line of not denigrating the old covenant while also freely extolling the superiority of the new. He describes the old covenant as "ministry that brought death," "engraved in letters on stone"—referring to the Ten Commandments, which were inscribed on two stone tablets—and yet it "came with glory." The Mosaic covenant was transitory and brought death, so the ministry of the Spirit is even more glorious because it is permanent and brings righteousness.

Paul states that the law belongs to the Mosaic covenant, which has been fulfilled in Christ. While works of the law indicated participation in the Mosaic covenant, faith in Christ indicates participation in the new covenant. Paul argues for the legitimacy of the new covenant by demonstrating its continuity with God's covenant with Abraham, which precedes the giving of the law. God promised Abraham, "All the nations will be blessed through you" (Gen. 12:3; 18:18), and Paul concludes that those who share the faith of Abraham will share in his blessing. The law, however, came 430 years later and does not invalidate a covenant previously established by God and thus cancel the promise.

God's promises that the nations would be blessed through Abraham and that Abraham's descendants would receive an inheritance rely not on the law but on God's faithfulness to keep his promises. Before Christ came, the law—and the Mosaic covenant to which it belonged—functioned as a guardian, or babysitter. But once he came, the guardian is no longer necessary. The law and the Mosaic covenant were not,

Lorenzo Monaco, *Abraham*, 1408–10

therefore, opposed to the plan and promises of God but rather played a vital role. However, the two covenants lead to very different outcomes for those under them. Those under the Mosaic covenant are slaves, while those under the new covenant are God's sons and daughters.

Jew-Gentile Reconciliation

The first major application of salvation by grace through faith is the reconciliation between believing Jews and gentiles. Both Jews and gentiles rely on the mercy and love of God to raise them from spiritual death, and so salvation is a level playing field. There is no sense in which gentile believers are excluded from the privileges and blessings that Jewish believers enjoy. Paul reminds his gentile readers that they were once without Christ, excluded from the citizenship of Israel and its covenants. But in Christ, gentile believers have been brought near by his blood. Christ is the peace between the two factions, having made both groups one and having removed the elements that once stood to divide them. Gentile believers are now fellow citizens with Jewish believers and have been built together with them as the new holy temple in which God dwells by his Spirit.

The unification of Jews and gentiles in Christ marks a dramatic new chapter of salvation history, in which Paul has a unique and significant role. If God's grace has enabled all people to be saved through faith, it is his job to make this grace known. As such, Paul has been given insight into the mystery of Christ—a secret hidden for generations but now revealed to the apostles and prophets—that the gentiles are coheirs and partners in the promise in Christ through the gospel.

Paul was made a servant of the gospel by God's grace and therefore must proclaim the riches of Christ to the gentiles. And through gentile faith in Christ, God's profound wisdom is made known throughout the cosmos according to his eternal purpose accomplished in Christ. Paul's sufferings for the gentile cause, therefore, are not a reason for discouragement but instead lead to gentile glorification.

Faith-Works-Law

Paul's understanding of the law of Moses can appear self-contradictory, since he proclaims that believers are not under the law (Rom. 6:14) while also saying that we uphold the law (Rom. 3:31). While Paul clearly does not expect gentile believers to maintain the customs of the Mosaic law (Gal. 5:1–6), he also sometimes quotes the law directly as authoritative for all (e.g., Eph. 6:2). The most likely resolution of these apparent tensions is as follows. Paul believes that Christ has fulfilled the righteous requirements of the law (Rom. 10:4; Gal. 3:13); believers uphold the law by being in Christ. When a new covenant is created, it is accompanied by a new law, and the new covenant of Christ is ruled by the law of love, not the law of Moses (Gal. 6:2). Nevertheless, the law of Moses reflects God's moral character. For this reason, it is profitable to know the law and sometimes even to apply it directly.

Paul frames the "faith versus works" discussion in terms of Jew-gentile relations. The modern tendency to interpret "works" as any good deed is not so much wrong as it misses the immediate point. Paul is primarily interested in showing that Jews and gentiles are justified the same way, and it's not by keeping the law of Moses—a central marker of Jewish identity. In other words, gentile believers do not need to become Jews in order to be right with God.

Since Abraham was credited with righteousness by believing God, so too those who have faith are Abraham's sons and daughters and are blessed as he was. But those who rely on the works of the law are under a curse because "everyone who does not do everything written in the book of the law is cursed" (Gal. 3:10; cf. Deut. 27:26). In other words, if you are going to try to keep the law, you have to keep *all* of it, and since no one can do that, you will find yourself under the curse of the law. No one can be justified before God by the law, since righteousness comes by faith (Gal. 3:11).

The law condemns everyone under it, since no one can keep it, and therefore all are under its curse (Gal. 3:10). But being "crucified with Christ" means that the curse on all has been borne by Christ, and since believers have been cocrucified with Christ, they have died, meaning that the law no longer has any claim on them. Its curse has been fulfilled and taken away, so believers have "died to the law."

Being crucified with Christ, and therefore no longer being under the curse of the law, goes deep into Paul's theology of the gospel. It also explains why works of the law are now irrelevant for justification and why relying on them is dangerous. It can only be by faith in Christ—the one who suffered the law's curse through crucifixion—that believers can avoid the curse of failing to keep the law and maintain a right standing with God.

Israel

Paul's heart burns for his fellow Israelites, so much so that he even claims that he would give up his own salvation for their sake. To the Israelites belong the covenants, the law, the temple, the promises of God, the patriarchs, and the Christ. But if everything that Paul says is true, what's gone wrong, since the majority of Israelites have not accepted Jesus as their Messiah? He argues that not all of Abraham's children are his physical descendants. The children of God's promise are Abraham's (and therefore God's) true children. This notion of promise will be addressed again later, but for now we will look at how Paul engages the problem of whether or not it is fair for God's promise to apply to some people and not others. In short, Paul argues that God is God and has mercy on whom he wants to have mercy. God can choose whomever he wants to belong to him, whether Jew or gentile.

Though the Israelites have zeal for God, they have not understood God's righteousness, which comes not through the law of Moses but through faith in Jesus the Lord, regardless of whether one is a Jew or a gentile. Everyone who calls on the Lord will be saved. But the Israelites cannot call on the Lord they don't believe in, and they can't believe in him without hearing about him. Faith comes from what is heard through the message about Christ. But then again, some did hear but did not listen due to their defiance.

But God has not rejected his people. Instead, there is a faithful remnant within Israel, just as there was in times past. Some Israelites were elect and others were not. But their plight is not irreversible. Salvation has come to the gentiles, and this may in turn lead to Israelites returning to God. Israel is the root of the olive tree and the gentiles are the branches. So the gentiles have nothing to boast about, since the root is the foundation and branches can be broken off just as they can be grafted in. If wild gentile branches can be grafted in, how much more so the natural branches can be grafted into their own olive tree. In God's sovereign plan, Israel has been partially hardened so as to make way for believing gentiles to enter the fold. Just as the gentiles had been alienated from God but now have received mercy, so Israelites are not beyond God's mercy.

Church

Though Paul uses several metaphors to picture the church, the body of Christ is arguably the most central and significant. Spiritual gifts are to be employed for the benefit of the body, as each part does its work. There is one body with many parts, and such diversity serves the unified whole. But the most important consideration for the service of the body is love.

In the meantime, the church must remember who it is, having been set apart for Christ as his bride and living in the daylight rather than in darkness. Believers must put away all shameful acts and attitudes that are unfit for the people of Christ, as his Spirit works in and among them. While no believer will reach perfection in this lifetime, the church is called to be holy, while remembering that the grace of God is sufficient for all.

The church of God consists of believing Jews and gentiles, who are now unified in Christ Jesus. Nevertheless, Israel remains the recipient of the promises of God, and no one should forget Israel's privilege—salvation is first for the Jew and then for the gentile. God is completely sovereign over Israel's trajectory, even when it appears that the majority of Israel has rejected their Messiah. This partial hardening is so that the gentiles may come in, and it is not necessarily indefinite.

Believers are to strive for the unity of the Spirit because they are, in fact, already one. They share in the one body, the one Spirit, one hope, one Lord, one faith, one baptism, and one God and Father of all. But the oneness of the church is qualified by its diversity. Such diversity is undergirded by the measure of Christ's gift, producing some to be apostles, some prophets, some evangelists, some pastors and teachers. The people who occupy these roles for the church are Christ's gifts for its equipment and edification. But it is clear that the church grows through all its members, rather than by a "professional elite," for the real task of church leaders is to prepare the whole for its own works of service. The all-member service of the church is to enhance the unity in the faith, knowledge of Christ, and growth to maturity. Such maturity is to protect believers from false teaching as the church speaks the truth in love and grows further into Christ. From Christ, every part of the body works toward the growth of the whole. In order for the church to live out its maturity and growth, believers must replace their previous ungodly behaviors with those that are consistent with love and unity.

Christian Living

Paul's approach to ethics is always theological. That is, his instructions about how to live are grounded in theological truths about God, Christ, and what it means to be the people of God in Christ. His letters demonstrate this as their "practical" sections spell out the implications of their "theological" sections. A good example is the Letter to the Ephesians, in which the first three chapters contain Paul's main theological arguments and the second three chapters draw out their implications for living. This means that Paul cannot be described as a moralist. He does not prescribe moral actions just because they are the right things to do. He begins with the truth of who we are in Christ and draws that out to sketch a vision of the Christian life.

In order to live in a manner pleasing to God, believers are reminded of who they are in Christ, that their old selves have died with Christ and their new selves have been raised with him. We are taught to imitate our heavenly Father as his children. And we are to set our eyes on things above, where Christ is seated, rather than on things below. By keeping in step with the Spirit, believers will reap according to the Spirit. But if we sow according to the flesh, we will reap death and destruction.

Believers are to look to Christ, the consolation of his love, their fellowship with the Spirit, and the affection and mercy they have received to share the same love, being united in spirit with singular purpose. They are to resist acting out of selfish ambition or conceit and instead are to exercise humility in service of others, following the example of Christ. In light of his example, believers are to do everything without grumbling and arguing and are to be blameless, pure, and faultless, shining like stars in the world as they hold firm to the word of life.

Believers are to be characterized in general by rejoicing, graciousness, prayer, thanksgiving, and the lack of worry. They are to give their attention and focus to whatever is true, honorable, just, pure, lovely, commendable, excellent, and praiseworthy.

Paul says that believers should seek to lead a quiet life, to mind their own business, and to work so as not to be dependent on anyone. Believers are to do their own work to provide for themselves and not be a burden on others. And just as Jesus demonstrated extreme generosity in his loving self-sacrifice for the benefit of others, so Paul hopes that believers will have their hearts shaped by the same impulse. Financial giving is simply a practical outworking of a heart that has been shaped by the love of Jesus.

Life together will require humility, genuine love for one another, empathy, generosity, and harmony. Believers must not avenge themselves but rather are to conquer evil with good. Living well includes submission to the governing authorities, whose authority is granted by God. Believers should pay their taxes as good citizens. Living well requires love for one's neighbors, which fulfills the law. All of this is conducted in the knowledge that the time is short—the night is nearly over, and the day is near.

Life together requires wisdom in how to deal with debatable matters. Instead of looking down on those whose conscience prevents them from eating certain foods or who think that certain days are more important than others, believers should seek to build others up and promote peace. Believers are not to judge one another and must remember that all will stand before the judgment seat of God. Again, the principles are humility and love rather than being "correct" or insisting on one's own point of view to the detriment of others. Believers have an obligation to please their neighbors rather than themselves, as Christ did, and to live in harmony with one another so that God is glorified with one mind and voice. This means welcoming one another, just as Christ went to great lengths to welcome the gentiles into God's people.

Love is at the center of life together. Christian community, church, relationships with neighbors, and all the variegated dealings with others in various contexts are to be conducted in love. Love is the mark of Christian maturity and worship in response to the mercy and love of God.

Public domain / Wikimedia Commons

Luca Giordano, *The Fall of the Rebel Angels*, 1666

Spiritual Warfare

As savior, Christ has overpowered the authorities and forces of darkness that rule over this present age and influence those who do not know Christ. He has publicly put those powers to shame, having canceled their hold on humanity and having been seated above them in all authority. Though we do not yet see Christ's dominion over evil, sin, and death, his return will reveal his universal victory in glory.

Believers are therefore currently engaged in an ongoing battle with the spiritual forces of darkness—the unseen enemy. Yet, equipped and clothed with the armor and clothing of Christ, believers are able to make their stand against such evil powers.

Ministry

The task of church leadership is an ongoing struggle, and it is all too easy to lose direction. Paul's letters implicitly and explicitly acknowledge these difficulties. Paul draws on the glory of the new covenant to undergird his philosophy of ministry. Rejecting deception and distortion, he and his coworkers are open and honest. Though some have been blinded to the truth of the gospel, Paul and his partners preach Jesus Christ as Lord, since God has shone in their hearts the light of God's glory in the face of Christ. But this inner treasure is housed in "jars of clay," as Paul and his coworkers experience the frailty of their physical bodies through hardship and persecution. They carry in their bodies "the death of Jesus," enabling the life of Jesus to be revealed to others. The glory of the new covenant means that Paul and his coworkers do not lose heart, even though their physical experience is troubled and fading. They anticipate an eternal glory that far outweighs their passing challenges, with eyes fixed on eternal rather than temporary realities.

These eternal realities undergird Paul's ministry as he and his coworkers try to persuade others that Christ died for them so that they might live for him. No one is regarded from a worldly perspective, but those in Christ are nothing less than a new creation. Paul and his coworkers are Christ's ambassadors through whom God appeals to others to be reconciled to him through Christ. Paul is determined that the servants of God ought to commend themselves through enduring various kinds of sufferings and injustices, bearing the fruit of the Spirit, speaking the truth, rejoicing, and living in poverty while trusting in unseen eternal riches.

The glory of the new covenant profoundly shapes Paul's ministry so that it is grounded on eternal invisible realities rather than the tricks of passing human cleverness or strength. Girded by the power of God, his ministry does not rest on himself or his abilities but serves as a conduit for God's call to humanity to be reconciled to him through Christ. Paul is able to retain a posture of humility and weakness because he anticipates an eternal glory bestowed by God that is not dependent on Paul's own accomplishments and status in this world.

Rather than presenting himself as strong, impressive, or accomplished, Paul takes the opposite route. This approach achieves several strategic goals. First, it underscores the fact that God's grace reveals his power and our powerlessness. Second, it reminds his readers that the new covenant is eternal and glorious precisely because it does not depend on human and earthly means. Third, it challenges pride in worldly status and smug self-reliance. Fourth, it reveals that genuine apostolic ministry depends on the power of God and does not rest on outward displays of human impressiveness.

Rather than accepting a worldly assessment of their success, Paul and his coworkers view their hardships, beatings, imprisonments, hard work, and poverty as commending them as genuine servants of God. While they have nothing, they possess everything. They do not wield worldly weapons but engage divine power against the forces opposed to God. Rather than boast in worldly accomplishments, as the false apostles do, Paul points to his frequent imprisonments, floggings, beatings, stoning, shipwrecks, dangers, and hunger and thirst. If Paul must boast, he will boast in his weakness.

Human strength, power, accomplishments, and status are irrelevant for the success of new-covenant ministry. In fact, they cut across the power of God's grace, which is perfected in human weakness. Paul's ministry among the churches is a fitting actualization of God's grace working through weakness, as his mortal body, lack of worldly acknowledgment, and chronic suffering are utilized for the eternal glory of God.

Leadership responsibilities are frequently contrasted against the destructive missteps of false teachers. Instead of false teachers' preoccupation with meaningless, distracting, or just plain erroneous themes, church leaders are to hold on to what they've been taught, retaining the centrality of the Scriptures and the gospel message.

When Paul lays out his expectations for overseers and deacons, it is telling that nearly all their qualifications concern character, while the capacity to manage one's own household and to teach are the only mentioned abilities. For deacons, only household management is mentioned, implying that they are not required to teach. It is clear that church leadership is primarily concerned with *who* the leaders are, how they live, and how they set an example for others to follow.

In contrast are those who will depart from the faith, and it is the responsibility of leaders to point out such dangers to the brothers and sisters. They are to have nothing to do with misleading myths but are to train themselves in godliness, which holds promise for this life and the one to come. Leaders are to command and teach these things, setting an example for other believers in their speech, conduct, love, faith, and purity. They are to be devoted to the public reading of Scripture, exhortation, and teaching. They are to commit themselves to such things, making use of the gift within them, and making evident progress. They are to watch their life and teaching, which will be of benefit to themselves and others.

Church leaders are to flee the trappings of falsehood and instead pursue righteousness, godliness, faith, love, endurance, and gentleness. They are to fight the good fight, taking hold of eternal life. Finally, they are to guard what has been entrusted to them while they avoid false speech and knowledge. Church leaders are to present themselves to God as approved workers who correctly handle the word of truth and avoid empty speech and false teaching. They are to continue in what they have learned and believed, trusting in the God-inspired Scriptures, which are fit for teaching, rebuking, correcting, and training in righteousness so that God's people are fully equipped for every good deed. Church leaders are to preach the word; to be

Photo by Kevin Wailes / CC BY 2.0 / Wikimedia Commons

Stained glass, depicting Peter and Paul, in Church of St. Mary and St. Lambert, Stonham Aspal, UK

ready at all times to do so; and to correct, rebuke, and encourage their hearers with great patience. They must be prepared for a time when people will prefer false teaching and turn away from the truth. But leaders must be self-controlled, endure hardship, and fulfill their ministry.

False Teaching

Paul regards false teaching as an existential threat to the health of the first- and second-generation churches. He wants them to steer away from myths, endless genealogies, empty speculations, fruitless discussion, and misapplications of the law of Moses. These things impede the goals of Paul's instruction, which are love, purity of heart, good conscience, and sincerity of faith.

The Spirit predicted false teachers' departure from the faith as they allowed themselves to be led astray by deceitful spirits, demons, and hypocritical liars. Part of their message appears to involve a type of asceticism, in which the self-denial of good gifts from God is perceived as a desirable spiritual practice. This includes forbidding marriage and demanding abstinence from certain foods. But Paul regards such things as good gifts of God's creation, to be received with thanksgiving. In contrast to the false teachers, believers are to have nothing to do with pointless and silly myths.

False teachers manage to deceive gullible people who are easily led astray in their passions, seeking knowledge but not coming to a knowledge of the truth. In contrast, while impostors will become worse, deceiving and being deceived, church leaders are to continue in what they have learned and believed, holding fast to the sacred Scriptures, which are inspired by God and equip his people for every good work.

Christian Reading Questions

1. How would you summarize Paul's main concerns for how Christians ought to live?
2. Why is Jewish-gentile reconciliation so important to Paul? Is it still important today?

CHAPTER TWENTY

Reading Paul as Christian Scripture in the Twenty-First Century

We have taken a good look at Paul's writings, his history, and his mission and ministry. Of course, there is much more that could be discussed, and Pauline scholarship is brimming with fresh insights on a daily basis. But it is appropriate at this stage of the journey to reflect back and to look forward. In particular, it is important to consider what Paul might have to say to us today in the twenty-first century.

Obviously, the world has changed vastly since Paul's day. There is no Roman Empire. Institutionalized slavery is gone. People travel the world in airplanes. We can see and talk to one another on smartphones. The internet is the most comprehensive and accessible source of knowledge (as well as disinformation) the world has ever known. But the message Paul preached is still preached today, and more than a quarter of the world's population calls itself Christian in some sense. Paul would be totally bewildered by our world.

Perhaps Paul would be most surprised by the fact that—two thousand years later—Jesus has yet to return. And yet I expect that his response would be much the same as it was to the Thessalonians in the first century: we don't know when Jesus will come again, but it probably will surprise us. Maybe he would add that after two thousand years many would indeed be surprised by that event! But the followers of Jesus today must wait with patience and faithfulness just as they did in Paul's day. In that sense, little has changed.

Public domain / El Greco Museum / Wikimedia Commons

El Greco, *Apostle Saint Paul*, 1610–14

Paul would also be surprised to learn of today's scholarly fascination with him and his writings. Indeed, it would be hard to find an ancient figure—besides Jesus—who demands anywhere near as much scholarly attention as Paul. But, of course, Paul would want us to focus not so much on him but rather on his glorious central subject—Jesus Christ. Perhaps, as in any age, today's Christians are all too easily distracted from Jesus, and Paul would want us to "remember Jesus Christ, risen from the dead" (2 Tim. 2:8).

Paul might be less surprised by how much division, factionalism, and infighting exist within today's church, since there was already plenty of that within the churches of his day. But he would be saddened to learn that such things have persisted among the followers of Jesus during the past two thousand years. Paul would also not be surprised by how much and how often people have deviated from the gospel he preached, resulting in numerous alternate gospels that he would perceive as erroneous and dangerous.

At the end of the day, however, wondering what Paul would say to us today is less important than reading what he *did* say back then and thinking through how to apply it in our world. After all, Paul's writings are part of what we call Scripture, unlike our guesses about what he *might* say. So, what do we need to hear from Paul today? Here are a few thoughts.

Cosmic Christ

For many, their view of Jesus is simply too small. Some see him as a humble but revolutionary guru whose teachings remain important and influential: "Love your enemy," "Do unto others as you would have them do unto you," and so on. Some see Jesus as the instrument through whom God saves us: he died for our sins and rose again for our justification. Some even prefer to view him as Baby Jesus, meek and mild. But for Paul, any view of Jesus that does not see him as the ruler, sustainer, and center of the entire cosmos is too small a view.

Paul proclaims a cosmic Christ whose death not only was for our sins but also overpowered all the opposing forces of evil in the cosmos. His resurrection not only secured our justification but also put the nails in the coffin of Death itself. Jesus's death and resurrection established an entirely new realm in which believers may live in love, righteousness, and peace. And his death and resurrection contain in them the promise that the entire creation will one day be restored and renewed. Any view of Jesus's death and resurrection that does not appreciate their cosmic and universal significance for the entire created order has not yet fully apprehended Paul's message.

Too many believers today have faith in a domesticated Jesus, whose main purpose is to save us from our sins. A small Jesus leads to an overly individualized faith that ignores the social and cosmic implications of Jesus's ministry and fails to revere the cosmic Lord of the universe. Too many fail to see that the ultimate endpoint of all of God's work in history and in the world is to bring about the ultimate glorification of Jesus as the center of everything, everywhere, all at once.

Christ Crucified

Paul told the Corinthians that he preaches Christ crucified (1 Cor. 1:23). The cross of Jesus is obviously central to Paul's mission and ministry, and the atoning work of Christ remains an important theme in most churches today. However, in the original context it was not the atonement per se that was of particular interest to Paul. Rather, the cross of Christ undermined and overturned the worldly thinking of his day because that event—perceived as shameful and weak—was in fact the power of God for salvation. As such, Christ crucified makes foolish the world's wisdom as God's "weakness" is stronger than human strength.

Some churches and believers today may need to be reminded of the significance of the cross of Jesus—not simply for the forgiveness of their sins but as a critique of human wisdom and power. In recent years we have seen the rise of Christians engaged in the naked pursuit of political power for the sake of "Christian values." Many have embraced an approach to cultural influence in which the ends justify the means—even when the means have been sub-Christian.

For Paul, the way of Jesus is the way of self-sacrifice. It involves putting self-interest to death. It shuns worldly power that oppresses others or seeks its own benefit at their expense. The way of Christ crucified requires trust in God to deliver us rather than trust in ourselves or in our own power. Whenever the church or an individual believer sacrifices humility, kindness, or love for their enemy for the sake of political power, they have failed to

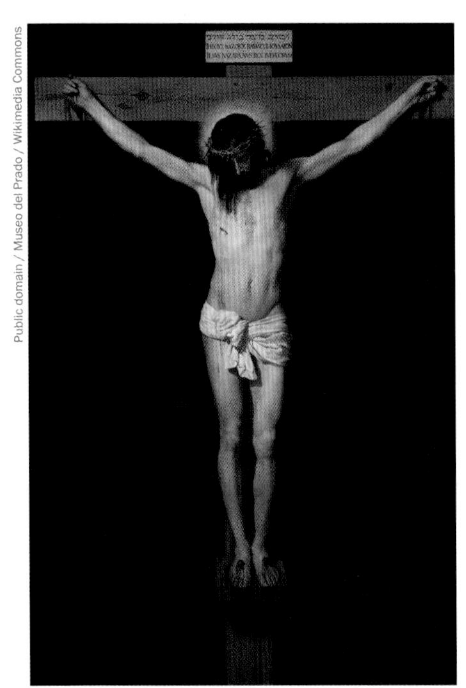

Diego Velázquez, *Christ Crucified*, 1632

heed Paul's central message of Christ crucified. They might preach Christ in their churches, but they undermine the message by their actions. It is little wonder that the surrounding society regards such people as hypocrites.

The Coming of Christ

One of Paul's central convictions was his belief that we are now in the last days and that Christ will one day return. This eschatological framework shaped his understanding of how to live now with hope for the future. But many of today's Christians—especially in the wealthy West—seem content to live for now with little thought of the coming of Christ. Perhaps, after two thousand years, believers think that it's probably unlikely to happen in our lifetime. Why should it? For two millennia Christians have waited, and that day has not come. Even if Jesus really does return, odds are that we will not be around for it. At least, that might be how some Christians think.

While understandable, a failure to take the return of Christ seriously is potentially devastating for believers. Once Christian faith is taken out of its eschatological context, it no longer works very well. Believers lose sight of the otherworldly themes of the Bible and find it harder to trust in God's redemption and salvation. If this world here and now is all we live for, it makes little sense to trust in otherworldly principles. It makes little sense to wait for God's resurrection of the dead or his judgment of evil. Without eschatology, Christians can become little more than decent citizens who really are no different from the world around them. Without the Jesus-shaped hope that Paul kept close to his heart, believers today will fail to follow the way of Jesus, with its sacrificial self-lowering in trust that God will raise up those who humble themselves.

Union with Christ

At some point the Western church lost sight of Paul's precious theology of union with Christ. Gladly, steps have been taken in recent years to recover its importance for the church and for Christian living. One of the reasons it is important to grasp the nature of our union with Christ is to correct an all-too-common transactional understanding of our relationship with Jesus. Without an understanding of union with Christ, believers can reduce Jesus to God's mechanism for our salvation: he became a man, lived, died, and was resurrected so that believers can be redeemed and live with God.

Paul was not so reductionistic. He believed that through faith believers are connected to Jesus in a profound, personal, and permanent way. Believers are in him and he is in us by his Spirit. Believers participate in the major events of Christ's narrative. Believers become members of his body, which has endless implications for our relationships with others and even what we do with our bodies. Union with Christ was of vital importance to Paul and ought to be so for believers today.

Christ Coming in Glory, illustration from William A. Spicer, *Our Day in the Light of Prophecy and Providence*, 1921

Christian Love

Paul understood Christ to be proof of God's profound love for his enemies: while we were still sinners, Christ died for us (Rom. 5:8). In keeping with the teaching of Jesus to love our enemies, Paul endorses love that reflects the love of God for all people. Genuine love for others—especially for those we perceive as the enemy, or who do not show love to us—remains a challenging call for all believers.

While such love is difficult and tests how much our hearts have been transformed by Christ, a failure to love is perhaps the greatest indictment that could stand against the followers of Jesus. Without love, believers are just a noisy gong or a clanging cymbal (1 Cor. 13:1). They might be full of words—including preaching and evangelism—but such words are meaningless without love. More than that, they are annoying and disturbing.

Christians must learn again the importance of genuine love. And when we fail to live up to it, we must look again to Jesus and relearn what it's all about. Loveless Christians are the worst advertisement for Jesus in our world, which was something that Paul understood deeply. Only by loving others could his message become intelligible and compelling. But without love, the Christian message is neither compelling nor attractive.

Pier Francesco Sacchi, *Saint Paul Writing*, ca. 1520

Conclusion

Paul remains a radical figure who is as provocative and controversial today as he was two thousand years ago. Love him or hate him, Paul has influenced our world more than we could imagine. He has shaped Christian teaching for millennia and offers an intellectual challenge to contemporary skepticism and materialism. This book has explored Paul's key themes and arguments, his intellectual and spiritual heritages, and his vast contributions to the New Testament and to Christian theology, mission, and ministry.

Of the highly influential twentieth-century theologian Karl Barth, it has been said that he was obsessed with talking about Jesus, while Barth's fans are obsessed with talking about Barth. The same can be said about Paul. Incredible, inspiring, and influential Paul may be, but the best way to appreciate and honor him and his work is to look to the one to whom Paul devoted his life—the Lord Jesus Christ, risen from the dead.

Notes

Chapter 1 Reading Paul as Christian Scripture

1. Patrick Gray, *Paul as a Problem in History and Culture: The Apostle and His Critics through the Centuries* (Grand Rapids: Baker Academic, 2016).
2. J. K. Elliott, ed., *The Apocryphal New Testament: A Collection of Apocryphal Christian Literature in an English Translation* (Oxford: Oxford University Press, 2005), 372–74.
3. E. P. Sanders, *Paul and Palestinian Judaism: A Comparison of Patterns of Religion* (Philadelphia: Fortress, 1977).
4. Albert Schweitzer, *The Mysticism of Paul the Apostle*, trans. William Montgomery (London: A&C Black, 1931).
5. Gray, *Paul as a Problem*, 5–6.

Chapter 4 Paul the Jew and the Risen Jesus

1. Krister Stendahl, *Paul among Jews and Gentiles* (Philadelphia: Fortress, 1976).

Chapter 8 Philippians

1. John Chrysostom, *Interpretatio omnium epistolarum Paulinarum per homilias facta*, ed. Frederick Field (Oxford: J. H. Parker; London: F&J Rivington, 1849–61), 5:74–77; translation from Mark J. Edwards, ed., *Galatians, Ephesians, Philippians*, Ancient Commentary on Christian Scripture 8 (Downers Grove, IL: InterVarsity, 1999), 247–48.

Chapter 9 1 and 2 Thessalonians

1. Margaret Mackay, "Asleep in Jesus! Blessed Sleep" (1832), in W. G. Polack, *The Handbook to the Lutheran Hymnal*, 2nd ed. (St. Louis: Concordia, 1942), 416.

Chapter 10 1 Corinthians

1. John Calvin, *Institutes of the Christian Religion: 1541 French Edition*, trans. Elsie Anne McKee (Grand Rapids: Eerdmans, 2009), 356.

Chapter 11 2 Corinthians

1. James John Lias, *The Second Epistle to the Corinthians*, The Cambridge Bible for Schools (Cambridge: Cambridge University Press, 1879), 8.

Chapter 12 Introduction to Paul's Third Mission

1. Gary G. Hoag, *Wealth in Ancient Ephesus and the First Letter to Timothy: Fresh Insights from "Ephesiaca" by Xenophon of Ephesus* (Winona Lake, IN: Eisenbrauns, 2015), 228.

2. Linford Stutzman, *Sailing through Acts: Across the Mediterranean in the Wake of St Paul* (Oxford: Monarch Books, 2007), 14–15.

Chapter 14 Ephesians

1. Raymond E. Brown, *An Introduction to the New Testament*, Anchor Bible Reference Library (New York: Doubleday, 1997), 620.

Chapter 16 Romans

1. The majority of commentators see the first section of Romans as chaps. 1–4 and the second as chaps. 5–8. Chapter 5 bridges the first and second sections of the letter (and therefore can be understood as belonging to either), and I prefer to take it with the first section.

Chapter 18 Paul's Theology (1)

1. Matthew W. Bates, *Gospel Allegiance: What Faith in Jesus Misses for Salvation in Christ* (Grand Rapids: Brazos, 2019), 86–87.

Index